Talavera

Wellington's First Victory in Spain

Talavera

Wellington's First Victory in Spain

Andrew W. Field

Pen & Sword
MILITARY

In memory of a loving mother

First published in Great Britain in 2006 by
Pen & Sword Military
an imprint of
Pen & Sword Books Ltd
47 Church Street
Barnsley
South Yorkshire
S70 2AS

ISBN 1-84415-268-5

A CIP catalogue record for this book is
available from the British Library

Typeset in 11/13pt Plantin by Mac Style, Nafferton, E. Yorkshire
Printed and bound in England by CPI UK

Pen & Sword Books Ltd incorporates the Imprints of Pen & Sword Aviation,
Pen & Sword Maritime, Pen & Sword Military, Wharncliffe Local History, Pen
& Sword Select, Pen and Sword Military Classics and Leo Cooper.

For a complete list of Pen & Sword titles, please contact
Pen & Sword Books Limited
47 Church Street, Barnsley, South Yorkshire, S70 2AS, England
E-mail: enquiries@pen-and-sword.co.uk
Website: www.pen-and-sword.co.uk

Contents

List of Maps

Preface

Ironically, it was while touring battlefields of the Spanish Civil War that I first visited Talavera. As the group were not too far from that town I stole away to visit a battlefield where two of the predecessors of my own regiment, the Worcestershire and Sherwood Foresters Regiment (29th/45th Foot), had fought nearly 200 years before. I had little knowledge of the battle before this visit but, inspired by how little the area has changed, I determined to find out more. I was surprised to find that it was the only major battle of the Peninsular War that didn't appear to have a single volume dedicated to it.

When I began this book my aim was not to write the definitive study of the battle, rather a comprehensive account that would serve as useful background for a satisfying visit to the battlefield. My researches, however, revealed more and more detail that I felt obliged to include, and the account is probably the most detailed and accurate that is currently available. While I have made every effort to follow the true course of the battle I have deliberately left out speculation and rumour, and have tried to examine the evidence available on the more controversial or contentious events.

I have used the excellent volumes of Sir Charles Oman's *A History of the Peninsular War* as the bedrock of my narrative. His impressive account, written about 100 years ago, is acknowledged as the best researched, and consequently the most accurate, of the multi-volume histories. While Colonel Napier's *History of the War in the Peninsula* is an easier and rather more exciting read, it has a strong jingoistic theme, and his account of Talavera is rather superficial.

Since Oman's work on the Talavera campaign was written, a myriad of memoirs and first-hand accounts have been published that were not available to him. I have incorporated these into my own narrative and used them where safe to amend Oman's own account. Fortescue's *History of the British Army* is a mine of interesting detail, but regrettably he rarely gives the source of his information and it is impossible to be sure if some of it is merely speculation. Needless to say, Wellington's dispatches form a vital and fascinating source of dependable information and are vital to an understanding of the campaign in the wider political, as well as military, context.

Oman became famous for his essay on the column *v.* line tactical debate, and his views were perpetuated for many years. While his arguments have recently been accepted as flawed, they only reflected his own lack of military experience and the conceited British view of their own military superiority that was typical of the time in which he wrote. However, as some knowledge of the tactical systems used by each side is fundamental to the understanding of how a battle was fought, I have rather indulged my own interest in this topic. My discussion on tactics is based purely on my own interpretation of extensive research and study and may prove equally contentious to some, but I trust it will enhance the reader's understanding of how and why each side fought the way it did.

In contrast to the many British memoirs there are few French first-hand accounts of the battle from more junior ranks. Girod de l'Ain offers perhaps the most detailed and balanced, and his account of the night attack is fascinating and vivid. Otherwise we must depend on the accounts of King Joseph and Marshal Jourdan, his chief of staff. Unfortunately these reflect their need to justify their failure to Napoleon rather than to present an accurate and balanced account of the battle. Contemporary and later French historians, while critical of the French performance, also spend rather too much space finding excuses for the defeat or painting it as a victory.

Spanish accounts of the campaign are hard to come by and as I have difficulty in pronouncing the Spanish word for 'beer' I have not been in a position to pursue one with any confidence! My only excuse was that while they had a major impact on the campaign, they took little part in the fighting at Talavera, and that is where the emphasis of this book lies.

It would be remiss of me not to offer a word of thanks to some of the many people who have helped and encouraged me in the preparation of this book. In particular I would like to thank Zöe Marsh and Debra Gill of the Sennelager library for their unstinting enthusiasm and efficiency in feeding my insatiable quest for various books and sources, and the staff of the Prince Consort's Library in Aldershot. Jacqui Minchinton put in many hours in the archives at the museum of the Northamptonshire Regiment, and Corporal Gorman at the Regimental Headquarters of the Scots Guards provided the key to tracking down the picture of the 1/3rd Guards at the battle. Thanks are due also to Griff Rhys-Evans, my Spanish speaker who tried hard to supply more detail on the Spanish contribution to the battle, and last but not least to my wife, Paula, for her patient encouragement and critical reading.

Introduction

In October 1807, aided and abetted by their erstwhile Spanish allies, the French invaded Portugal. Militarily ill-prepared to meet the conquerors of most of Europe, this small country offered no resistance, and its royal family fled to Brazil in British warships. It was Portugal's continuing friendship with Great Britain that had led to its misfortune; its refusal to support Napoleon's Continental System to exclude British trade with Europe had been all the reason the Emperor of France needed to extend his hegemony still further.

Spain's connivance in its neighbour's downfall was not enough to save it from a similar fate. Early in 1808 Napoleon invaded Spain with the support of its heir apparent, Ferdinand. However, tricked into entering France soon afterwards, he was taken prisoner and exiled to Valençay. Napoleon declared his brother Joseph as king in Ferdinand's place but the Spanish people rose in spontaneous revolt. A revolutionary junta based in Seville approached Britain for money and arms. In July of that year Lieutenant General Sir Arthur Wellesley sailed from Cork with an advance guard of 14,000 British troops who were to be reinforced with a further 16,000.

At this early point in the war the Spanish were desperate for material aid but were not yet ready to have another foreign army, albeit a friendly one, on their soil. Refused permission to land in Spain, the British advance party finally landed at Oporto, the second city of Portugal. Once ashore, Wellesley found that not only had the Spanish armies suffered successive defeats at the hands of the French, but also that he had already been superseded in command.

Spanish morale was given a lift by the capitulation of a French force at Bailén in July 1808, but Wellesley's immediate problem, pending the arrival of his successor, was the remaining French forces in Portugal. Although the main body of his small army had still not arrived, and facing odds of two to one, Wellesley marched south towards Lisbon. A small French force sent to delay him was defeated, but not decisively, at Roliça, and Wellesley was reinforced by the arrival of more British troops under the command of Lieutenant General Sir Harry Burrard, his senior. However, before General Burrard could take

Los dos mayos. The Spanish uprising against the occupation of Madrid caught the French forces unprepared, and they suffered considerable loss of life before brutally restoring order.

command, Junot, commanding the French army in Portugal, had advanced from Lisbon and faced Wellesley at Vimeiro. Wellesley's victory was decisive, and was the first step in establishing his own reputation of invincibility and re-establishing the British army's own reputation after a decidedly mixed performance during the Revolutionary Wars.

The French proposed an immediate armistice after their defeat and a formal convention for their withdrawal from Portugal. Because of the loss of his command, Wellesley put his signature with reluctance to what became known as the Convention of Cintra. After the initial celebration of victory in England there was a quick change towards public indignation as the terms of the convention became known. The thought of British ships evacuating the defeated French army back to France, along with all the plunder they had amassed in Portugal, was particularly resented. However, the subsequent court of inquiry exonerated Wellesley of any blame.

Back in Portugal, a general of growing reputation, Sir John Moore, had taken command of the British army. The French humiliation at Bailén and King Joseph's subsequent flight from Madrid provoked Napoleon's own appearance in the Peninsula with a veteran army of 120,000 men. Moore was clearly not able to face this army alone, but to relieve the pressure on his

A General Map of the Peninsula.

The final, futile attempt to stop Napoleon's advance on Madrid in 1808 was made just north of the capital at the Samosierra pass. After a stubborn initial resistance, the hotchpotch Spanish force was scattered by a charge of the Polish Chevaux-Légers. In their flight, they still found time to murder their commander for his failure to lead them to victory.

Spanish allies he reluctantly advanced to threaten Napoleon's communications with France. This inevitably drew the French Emperor's overwhelming strength against his own small army. Greatly outnumbered, he was forced into a precipitate retreat in desperate conditions in order to be evacuated by the Royal Navy from Corunna. With the danger posed by the British army now almost extinguished and in the face of an increasing threat from Austria in central Europe, Napoleon now handed over his army to Marshal Soult and headed back to France. As the British army reached the coast it became obvious to Moore that he could not evacuate his exhausted men safely without first delivering a check to the French. At the subsequent battle at Corunna in Galicia, Moore was victorious, but this promising general paid with his life.

After the evacuation of Moore's army back to Britain, only a token British force remained in the Portuguese capital, and although the Spanish armies suffered further reverses their resistance remained unbroken.

Sir John Moore's ill-fated expedition to the Peninsula resulted in a rather ignominious retreat to Corunna and his own death at the battle there. It is interesting to speculate as to whether he would have commanded the 1809 expedition instead of Wellesley if he had survived.

Chapter One

Wellesley Returns to the Peninsula

The Strategic Situation

On 6 April 1809 Wellesley was named commander-in-chief of the British forces in the Peninsula, and sailed for Lisbon from Portsmouth on the frigate *Surveillante* on the 14th. The situation to which he returned was far from promising. Since Napoleon's departure early in January 1809, the Spanish armies had suffered the fall of Zaragoza (20 February) and defeat in battle at Valls (25 February), Ciudad Real (27 March) and Medellin (28 March). In Portugal, things were little better: despite the best efforts of the Portuguese regency to reorganize and train its army when Soult invaded from Galicia in early March, the army was spread across the country in individual units, recruiting and training. Consequently it was in no position to offer serious, coordinated resistance to the invasion. The result was never in doubt, and Soult successfully stormed the weakly, if enthusiastically, defended city of Oporto on 29 March. The city was thoroughly sacked by the French, and a huge store of British arms and other military equipment was captured.

Although Wellesley had stated that the Portuguese army (calculated at about 16,000 men) and the 30,000 British troops he had been promised were sufficient for the defence of Portugal, only offensive action into Spain would expel the French from the Peninsula and offer succour to the Spanish. But at this time there were no fewer than 275,000 French troops in Spain and Portugal. Of these, nearly 70,000 were in hospital and 35,000 were tied to protecting the lines of communication back to France. This left 175,000 effective French troops in the various *corps d'armée*.

Victor's I Corps (about 22,000 men) was in the Tagus valley around Mérida, holding down Cuesta's Army of Extremadura and threatening an advance into southern Portugal. Soult's II Corps (about 20,000 men) was in Portugal holding Oporto, and Suchet's III Corps (about 15,000 men) was around Zaragoza, that city having finally fallen to the French, after a heroic defence, in February. Sébastiani and his IV Corps (about 20,000 men) were facing

The heroic, but ultimately unsuccessful, defence of Zaragoza came to define the stubborn Spanish resistance to the French occupation and showed that whatever they might lack in military art they more than made up for in courage and tenacity.

Venegas's Army of La Mancha to the south of Madrid in the area of Ciudad Real, having convincingly defeated the Spanish general there in March. Mortier's V Corps (about 15,000 men) was to the north at Burgos, Ney's VI Corps (about 17,000) in Lugo, fighting the Galician guerrillas, and St Cyr with the VII Corps (14,000) around Gerona and Barcelona fighting the Catalonian *Somatenes* (the name for the local guerrillas). There were other, smaller forces under Bonnet (5,000) at Santander and 7,000 men under Kellerman moving to the Asturias to be in a position to support Ney. Finally, Joseph was in Madrid with his reserve of 12,000.

Facing this seemingly gigantic force were the shattered remains of the Spanish armies that had confronted Napoleon's invasion the previous year. Cuesta's Army of Extremadura (about 23,000 men) had been quickly reconstituted after his defeat at Medellin, and lay at Monasterio. Venegas and the Army of La Mancha (about 20,000) were licking their wounds south of Ciudad Real facing Sébastiani. Blake's Army of the Right consisted of only 9,000 men in Aragon, while La Romana, with only 8,000, submerged themselves in the guerrilla war with Ney in Galicia while trying to recuperate from their exertions in December the previous year. The Asturian Army of

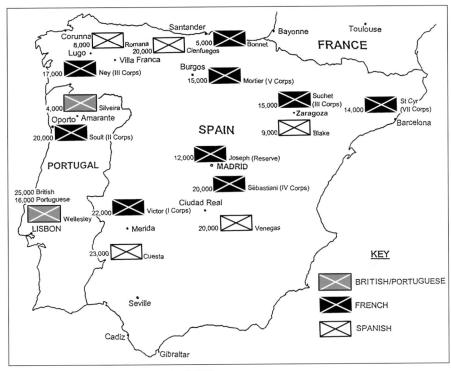

The Situation of the Main Armies, April 1809.

20,000, although more formidable than many of the other Spanish armies, was tied to its own region by the decision of its junta.

The odds seemed to be overwhelming, but Wellesley believed that the French would be unable to concentrate more than 100,000 men for an invasion of Portugal. Although they had considerably more troops than that, he correctly assumed that they would never be able to form an army of that size without having to give up to the guerrillas the areas from which they had been withdrawn, and because of the difficulties of feeding so many men from the scarce resources of the country across which they would be operating. It was said that in Spain a small army would be beaten and a large army would starve. The French faced the option of holding much of Spain weakly or concentrating to fight the British and having to give up large parts of the country for which they would have to fight hard to regain. In this relative security Wellesley now planned the coming campaign.

Wellesley's Plan
Wellesley's first priority was to secure Portugal from the immediate threat from the 54,000 French troops of marshals Soult (II Corps) and Victor (I Corps). The corps of these two marshals were not concentrated and not expecting an attack: Soult appeared unwilling to move from his base in the key Portuguese

city of Oporto, while Victor lay to the south around Mérida on the Guadiana river – still in Spain but close to the Portuguese border. These two corps were therefore widely spread, and Wellesley found himself occupying a central position from which he could strike at either without the other being able to interfere. He planned to strike at one and then the other in an effort to beat them with sequential offensives in each of which he would enjoy superior numbers.

Wellesley's preferred option was to strike at Victor first as this would allow him to act in concert with the Spanish Army of Extremadura: this force, commanded by General Cuesta, was little over 20,000 strong, even after its recent defeat by Victor at Medellin. However, it would take time to coordinate his movements with the Spanish, and as Soult already occupied the second city of Portugal and was a greater threat to the Portuguese capital, Wellesley was driven by political imperatives to move against him first. As the weaker of the two French forces Soult's was also the more vulnerable. Consequently Wellesley left a strong force to protect Lisbon from Victor and, securing his flank with a force of Portuguese troops commanded by the British general Beresford, marched north against Soult.

Because of the difficulty of obtaining information from a hostile local population and the fact that he was not expecting an attack, Soult was unaware of Wellesley's offensive until the British general was already close to Oporto. On learning of the British advance, the French commander was not unduly

The crossing of the Douro and the ejection of Soult's corps from Oporto prior to the Talavera campaign was a daring and spectacularly successful operation for which Wellesley has never been given due credit.

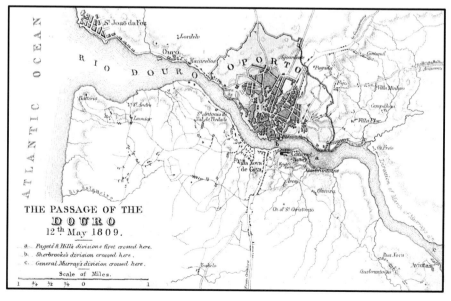

worried as the formidable River Douro ran between them, all the bridges had been destroyed and all boats collected on the French side. However, on 12 May, by a daring and risky crossing, using only a few small boats that had been hidden from the French, Wellesley surprised Soult and threw his troops out of the city in disarray. The French conducted a hasty and disorganized retreat towards Galicia in the north, suffering over 4,000 casualties on top of those lost in the fighting at Oporto. They also lost all their baggage and artillery that could not negotiate the dismal tracks that offered their only passage over the mountains. Once Wellesley was content that Soult posed no further threat, he turned his army around and directed it on Abrantes.

While Wellesley was humiliating Soult, Victor had remained rather passively near the Portuguese border in Extremadura. In ignorance of what Soult was up to and lacking information on where the British army was, he was reluctant to commit himself to an advance into Portugal. Other than skirmishing with Portuguese forces under British command on the border, he spent most of his energy in trying to supply his corps. He complained to Joseph that, 'The troops are on half rations of bread: they can get little meat – often nothing at all. The results of starvation are making themselves felt in the most deplorable way ... The whole population of this region has retired within Cuesta's lines, after destroying the ovens and mills, and removing every scrap of food ... We are menaced by absolute famine.'[1]

French soldiers loading a supply caisson: 'We are menaced by absolute famine.' Both sides suffered greatly from the lack of supplies available from the local area due to the constant passage of armies. Whilst Wellesley insisted on his commissaries paying for everything, the French were famous for 'living off the land'. This was supposed to mean that the commissariat was responsible for providing the basics of bread (shown here) and meat, and the soldiers were to supplement this basic ration using their pay. However, they were famous for their marauding.

With his corps wasting away and concerned by the presence of Cuesta's army, Victor pressed Joseph to allow him to withdraw to a safer area where he would be able to feed his men. Joseph finally acquiesced, and I Corps left Mérida on 14 June and eventually took up a position along the Tagus covering the crossings from Almaraz to Talavera.

Wellesley Moves against Victor

Wellesley had been planning his first campaign into Spain for some time, and had corresponded with the Spanish general Cuesta proposing an option of two plans. Cuesta proposed three different ones in reply. Getting an agreement proved rather easier said than done, and Wellesley began to experience the frustrations and difficulties that were to mark the relationship between the two commanders: 'The obstinacy of this gentleman is throwing out of our hands the finest game that any armies ever had.'[2] However, owing to the need to cooperate with his ally, a plan was finally agreed. This foresaw a concentration of the two armies and a joint advance against Victor, who would be considerably outnumbered. Concurrently, an advance by the Spanish Army of La Mancha under General Venegas would fix the French IV Corps (General Sébastiani) to the south-east of Madrid and would stop them from moving to the support of Victor.

Wellesley's force had grown to 25,000 British and German troops, with another 8,000 en route. Cuesta now commanded 30,000 Spaniards, although their quality was suspect and many of them had already suffered a convincing defeat at Victor's hands at the Battle of Medellin. However, the most crucial part of Wellesley's plan was the Spanish promise to provide the British with the necessary supplies that were always so difficult to obtain in Spain, and a lack of which was already forcing Victor to move closer to Madrid.

The campaign that was to end at Talavera began on 27 June 1809 when Wellesley left Abrantes having received permission to cross into Spain on only the 11th. He crossed the border on 2 July at Zarza la Mayor in order to join Cuesta's army at Oropesa as arranged.

Chapter Two

The Armies

The British Army

The British army that the future Duke of Wellington led at Talavera still had much tough fighting to do before it was to become the almost invincible force into which he was to forge it. Its most famous Peninsular victories at Salamanca and Vitoria were still some years away, and the tactics that were to defeat some of Napoleon's most famous marshals were still to be fully refined.

The British army had not covered itself in glory against the French in the campaigns in the Netherlands between 1793 and 1799, and, despite performing creditably in Egypt in 1801, its performance during the Revolutionary Wars could be described as inconsistent at best. The situation improved only after the short Peace of Amiens of 1802. With war against France once more declared, the militia was re-embodied and the strength of the regular army was increased. Of particular significance was the emphasis that was put on training, and by the time it was called on to fight in 1805 the line regiments were reasonably strong and ready for action, and the militia was drilled and well disciplined.

British defence policy at this time was based on a need to defend its growing worldwide empire. The government felt a strong navy and a small, professional army best served this requirement, and it was always unlikely that Britain would be prepared to deploy the army into the cauldron of central Europe. Therefore, before finally committing itself to maintaining a sizeable deployment in the Iberian Peninsula, the army cut its teeth on a series of short duration expeditions to Italy, Egypt, Buenos Aires and Denmark. Although the second and third of these were something of a fiasco and the latter a rather one-sided affair against ill-trained militia, the expedition to Naples on the Italian mainland proved more significant. At the Battle of Maida in 1806 a British force of just over 5,000 men, commanded by General Sir John Stuart, faced a similar force of Frenchmen in a fair, stand-up fight. The result was a hard-fought but complete victory for the British and was to mark the ascendancy of British arms over the French.

When the French invaded Portugal, Britain's oldest ally, in 1807, and then followed this by overthrowing the Spanish Bourbons the following year, Britain was suitably outraged. Following an approach for support by these two countries it was decided to send a small army to the Peninsula, even though Britain was still technically at war with the Spanish, who had allied themselves to France in 1804. Although this was rather more than a mere technicality, it was put aside until peace was officially declared on 5 July 1808. An initial force of 9,000 men was sent and a decision was made to eventually increase this to 30,000. Not all these men had arrived when Wellesley took the offensive and gained his first victories over the French at Roliça and Vimeiro. By the time of Talavera in mid-1809, Wellesley's British contingent had reached a strength of still only 25,000 men, although further reinforcements were due to arrive.

The high reputation of the British army has always been founded on the quality of its infantry: stubborn, determined, dependable, unshakable and disciplined. This, however, should not necessarily imply criticism of the cavalry and artillery, but reflects the fact that more often than not the British army had a much lower proportion of these two other arms to its infantry than its opponents. This was true throughout the Napoleonic Wars and was certainly true at Talavera, where the British were significantly outnumbered in both artillery and cavalry in their sector of the field. It was only much later in the Peninsula that the gap narrowed as Napoleon withdrew large numbers of both of these to reinforce his armies in central Europe in 1813 and 1814 and the British reinforced their own army with these arms.

By the time of Talavera, Wellesley's infantry were beginning to gather the experience of campaigning and battle that would turn them into veteran troops. However, they were far from the finished article: looking back on the army of that time, Lord Munster was to write, 'we were by no means such good soldiers in those days as succeeding campaigns made us'.[1] Wellesley had twenty-two British battalions at Talavera. Of these, twelve were first battalions, eight were second battalions and two were battalions of detachments.

At this time each British regiment consisted of two battalions. The first was the 'war' battalion that consisted of ten companies. One of these companies was designated as the Grenadier Company and was made up of the biggest and most experienced men, while another was designated as the Light Company that provided the battalion's skirmishers. The other eight were known as the Centre Companies (after the fact that the Grenadier Company took the position of honour on the right, and the Light Company on the left of the battalion when formed in line) and contained the balance of the men. Companies generally consisted of about 100 men, but as each battalion depended on the success of its recruiters this was rarely achieved in peacetime, and impossible to maintain in war. The best source of recruits was the established militia battalions. These were fully activated during times of war for the protection of the homeland and were not liable to overseas service.

However, after a year of service a member of the militia could volunteer for the regular army and, surprisingly perhaps, many chose to do so. Despite having a relatively poor reputation with the 'regulars' they proved superior to young recruits who had been railroaded into the army or those who had joined for less creditable reasons.

The second battalion was supposed to be based at the regimental depot in Britain and was responsible for the recruitment and training of replacements for the first battalion. However, the pressing need for building up the strength of the army meant a number of second battalions were pressed into service abroad. These often consisted of recruits who had not completed their training and hastily recruited militiamen, often commanded by second-class officers and NCOs. For example, in 1807 the 2/24th received no fewer than 477 men from the militia while directly recruiting only 90.[2] Second battalions also tended to be weaker in strength, as the fitter and better-trained manpower was regularly sent to bring their first battalion up to strength. Returning to the 2/24th, in the same year that they received such an influx of militiamen they sent 200 men to the 1/24th that was serving in the Cape.[3] Some of these battalions struggled during the early part of their service, as we shall see at Talavera, but after a little experience became every bit as good as the first battalions. Later in the war, as more first battalions became available, Wellesley was reluctant to send these battalions back to England, as he preferred to keep the experience they had gained with the army, rather than replace them with an inexperienced first battalion. As a battalion's strength dwindled because of casualties and sickness, first and second battalions were amalgamated, or all the privates were sent to the first battalion while the cadre of officers and NCOs of the second battalion returned to Britain to recruit.

The real backbone of the army, then, was the twelve first battalions. However, none of these had served with Sir John Moore, as the sad remains of his army were still recruiting and training in England. Five of his battalions (29th, 1/40th, 1/45th, 5/60th and 97th) and some of the detachments had fought at Roliça and Vimeiro, where they had developed a healthy respect for their French opponents but had also started to establish a moral ascendancy over them that they would retain throughout the war. Even if they had deployed to the Peninsula at full strength, none of them were near that strength now because of sickness, straggling and casualties. The strongest battalion at Talavera was the 1st Battalion, 3rd Guards, who had just over 1,000 men present. But the Guards battalions had a stronger establishment than the regiments of the line, the strongest of which was the 1/48th (later the Northamptonshire Regiment), who mustered just over 800. However, they were only this strong because they did not join the army (along with the 1/61st) until just before Talavera, and had not yet lost significant numbers of men to sickness and straggling. The rest of the battalions numbered between 500 and 787, with an average of about 640.

Two 'battalions of detachments' also fought at Talavera. These consisted of recovered invalids, detached platoons and recruits of battalions in Moore's army that had been unable to join their parent regiments during the retreat to Corunna and had been formed into these ad hoc units. The 1st Battalion of Detachments had companies from the 92nd, 42nd, 79th and 95th Rifles, and the 2nd Battalion had companies from the 2nd, 2/43rd, 52nd, 82nd and 95th Rifles, who were the only survivors of Moore's army that were to serve at Talavera. Both were commanded by lieutenant colonels from the 3rd Foot. Once again, Wellesley was reluctant to send these back to form cadres for new battalions, as it meant losing the experience that they had built up. However, in these early days they did not exhibit the cohesion and discipline of regular battalions. Lord Londonderry, Wellesley's adjutant general, wrote: 'I wish these detachment battalions were replaced. I am sure they are the cause of great disorder – no *esprit de corps* for their interior economy among them, though they will fight. They are careless of all else, and their officers do not look to their temporary field officers and superiors under whom they are placed, as in an established regiment. I see much of their indiscipline.'[4] These battalions were due to be replaced when reinforcements arrived from England, but this did not happen before Talavera was fought.

As British armies were notoriously small, they almost always recruited

A soldier of the 29th Foot (later the Worcestershire Regiment) as he would have appeared at the battle. His 'red rag' has yellow facings and he wears the grey coveralls that replaced the breeches and gaiters for campaign wear. The condition of his uniform and equipment suggest he is a recent arrival in Spain.

auxiliaries from other countries to boost their numbers. Foremost among these in 1809 were the King's German Legion (usually abbreviated to KGL). Recruited from the Hanoverian army that fled its homeland for England after its invasion by France in 1803, it was originally intended to form a body of 5,000 men. By 1806, however, the recruiting was so successful that they were able to man two light battalions, seven line battalions, two heavy and three light dragoon (hussar) regiments, two horse artillery troops and four foot artillery companies. These units were organized and uniformed like their British counterparts.

When recruiting finished, the strength of the KGL was set at 14,000 men. In 1808 a strong force of the Legion was sent to Spain. Some of these men fought with Sir John Moore and were evacuated back to Britain; the remainder who stayed in Portugal formed a permanent part of Wellesley's army and fought their first major battle at Talavera in von Löw's and Langwerth von Simmern's brigades. Although prone to desertion and showing some inexperience at that battle, they were soon considered every bit as good as their British counterparts; indeed their cavalry was generally considered superior.

The troops of the King's German Legion were not the only Germans in Wellesley's army. Both the 97th Foot and 5/60th Rifles were almost exclusively German, and so both had problems recruiting once the KGL started expanding. The 5/60th had hoped to absorb '200 fine Swiss recruits who had served as Voltigeurs [*sic*] in the French Army'[5] who had been captured the year before, but they were sent back to Britain to be incorporated into other battalions of the regiment. The commanding officer then proposed to recruit among other Germans who had deserted from the French but was also denied this option, as it was believed that they might return to their old comrades while on outpost duty. The 5/60th provided the bulk of Wellesley's rifle troops, although two companies of the 95th Rifles served in the battalions of detachments. During the Talavera campaign the 5/60th were ten companies strong and part of Donkin's brigade; however, five of the companies were attached to other brigades to supplement their own light infantry companies.

Until its arrival in Abrantes, the army was so small that it was only broken down into brigades, and as there were so few of these there was no reason for another level of command between the brigade commanders and the army commander. However, when Wellesley received reinforcements at Abrantes, after his successful campaign against Soult, he formally organized his growing army into divisions for the first time. To do this just before moving against Victor can be interpreted as a risky move, as he had neither experienced divisional commanders nor staff. However, given his autocratic command style it will become clear that he had no intention of encouraging his new divisional commanders to use their initiative. This reorganization meant he now had to correspond with only five divisional commanders instead of thirteen brigade commanders. It was not until 1815 that he organized his divisions into corps in the French style.

Wellesley commanded one cavalry and four infantry divisions at Talavera. Sherbrooke's 1st Infantry Division contained four brigades each of two battalions, while Hill's 2nd, Mackenzie's 3rd and A. Campbell's 4th had only two brigades, though all but one of these had three battalions. Sherbrooke's division was thus considerably stronger than the others. The Cavalry Division consisted of three brigades: one of two heavy regiments and the other two of two light cavalry regiments.

Cavalry rarely had a truly decisive effect on the battlefields of Spain. That is not to say that there were no successful cavalry actions, nor that they did not render important services in reconnaissance and actions in advance or rear guards. The major problem was that the climate and forage did not seem to suit the British, nor indeed the French, horses. It was not long before a large number of horses were falling sick: in May 1809 Captain Fenton of the 4th Dragoons wrote: 'We have more than eighty horses unfit for service, and should we march immediately that number will be doubled'.[6] Just before Talavera he wrote again: 'I have had to go out to procure forage for the horses, which in this part of the country is difficult to get. The poor horses frequently go without for a day.'[7] It was because of this problem of looking after their horses, as well as the unsuitability of much of the terrain for mounted action, that the British did not deploy large numbers of their own cavalry to the Peninsula.

Wellesley's cavalry at Talavera consisted of two regiments of heavy cavalry, the 3rd Dragoon Guards and the 4th Dragoons, and four regiments of light dragoons, the 14th, 16th, 23rd and 1st KGL. Two of the regiments had already seen some action: the 16th Light Dragoons and a squadron of the 14th had conducted successful charges during the advance on Oporto. In contrast, the 23rd Light Dragoons had arrived in Lisbon on only 23 June, so both its horses and riders had not had an opportunity to acclimatize and settle into the campaign before they were to be thrown into action.

There was no difference between Dragoons and Dragoon Guards except in their names, although doubtlessly the Dragoon Guards believed they were a better type of dragoon. The establishment of both heavy and light cavalry regiments was four squadrons with a total of just over 900 men, including the headquarters. However, the fourth squadron was usually left in Britain to recruit and to send replacements to the regiment in the field. With units deploying for operations without their full establishment and in light of the inevitable losses of men on campaign, it is no surprise to find the two heavy regiments present at Talavera at strengths of 525 (3rd) and 545 (4th) and the light dragoons at between 450 and 525.

Tactically it seemed that it was only the glamour of the all-out charge that appealed to the British cavalry, and this seemed to dominate their training to the exclusion of all else. Given that the main role of light cavalry was reconnaissance and outpost duty, this may seem rather curious. However, the British cavalry regulations concentrated wholly on the charge and did not cover these other vital roles of light cavalry, so it is no surprise that even this branch of the cavalry arm saw the charge as their *raison d'être*. Indeed the regulations did not even differentiate between light and heavy cavalry or their respective duties.[8] It is surprising therefore that the light cavalry regiments that had been a part of Moore's army in 1808 had done an outstanding job with the rearguard during the retreat to Corunna, but these had been evacuated back to Britain with the rest of that army and were not available to Wellesley. It appears that his own British light cavalry had to learn these less exciting but vital duties as they went along, as Captain Tomkinson of the 16th Light Dragoons observed: 'To attempt giving men or officers any idea in England of outpost duty was considered absurd, and when they came abroad, they had all this to learn.'[9] It is no surprise that the Hussars of the King's German Legion were considered their superiors.

A cavalry drill school was set up at Woodbridge near Ipswich after the Peace of Amiens, and all cavalry regiments were rotated through it. However, it seems clear that although they became very proficient at the charge it was not practised with sufficient attention to its control and the rally. Tomkinson again: 'In England I never saw nor heard of cavalry taught to charge, disperse and form, which, if I only taught a regiment one thing, I think it should be that.'[10] Hence the cavalry soon acquired a reputation for spectacularly successful charges, which then degenerated into an uncontrolled pursuit that was often counter-charged and routed by French reserves.

Although at the time of Talavera this reputation was not fully established, the cavalry's performance at this battle was to make its own contribution to this tendency. In 1808 the 20th Light Dragoons had first given Wellesley a glimpse of what was to come. At the Battle of Vimeiro this regiment, rather less than 400 strong, conducted a most successful charge that dispersed the opposing French cavalry. However, instead of immediately reforming, the men charged on into the French infantry and found themselves cut off from their own lines and penned in by enclosures. They were saved only by an infantry advance after losing 55 men. Despite the undoubtedly fine work the cavalry did during its time in Spain, this and the few other occasions when it exhibited a lack of control permanently tarnished its reputation in the eyes of Wellesley. Rather like the Spanish army it was never able to shake off the poor first impressions that he had of it. He was later to complain of:

> the trick our officers of cavalry have acquired of galloping at everything, and their galloping back as fast as they gallop on the enemy. They never consider the situation, never think of manoeuvring before an enemy – so little that one would think they cannot manoeuvre, excepting on Wimbledon Common; and when they use their arm as it ought to be used, viz, offensively, they never keep nor provide for a reserve.[11]

Wellington was to offer a slightly more considered opinion in a conversation with Lord Stanhope in 1839: 'With one squadron of English cavalry I could beat two French; with two, I believe I could beat three; but if it came to larger numbers, I believe that a smaller body of French cavalry would beat me with a larger of English.'[12] He later went on to explain why this was: 'The French cavalry is more manageable and useful than the English, because it is always kept in hand, and may be stopped at the word of command.'[13]

The British army never put the same emphasis on the need for a strong force of artillery as the French did. Officially the British artillery was not part of the army as it came under the responsibility of the master general of the ordnance, and as a technical arm its officers were promoted by seniority rather than purchase. The gunners were well trained and took pride in defending their guns to the last rather than have them fall into the hands of the enemy. An excellent new 9-pound bronze gun had just come into service, but neither it nor any batteries of the new horse artillery had arrived in time for Talavera. Consequently only thirty guns, eighteen British and twelve of the KGL, served the army at that battle. Each battery consisted of six pieces, five guns and a howitzer, and was named after its battery commander, who was a captain. The three British batteries were thus known as Baynes's ('light' 6-pounders), Sillery's ('light' 6-pounders) and Lawson's (3-pounders). However, Sillery was sick and his battery was commanded by his 'second captain', Lane, and Baynes was wounded on the 27th, the day before the main battle, and was replaced in command by Captain Eliott, who was present but without a command.[14]

Although some artillery remained in Portugal after the British army's evacuation from Corunna, three further batteries arrived at Lisbon on 6 March. Rather surprisingly they deployed to the Peninsula without any horses, on the expectation of acquiring them on arrival. The same thing had happened when Wellesley had first arrived in Portugal in 1808 and had been forced to leave a battery behind in Lisbon because there were insufficient horses to pull its guns. While this may seem surprising, the number of horses required for six guns was considerable. The commander of the artillery in Portugal calculated that, 'Every artillery carriage in this country, and Spain, will require to be drawn by six horses; the long 6 pounder guns by eight; and the 12 pounders by 10.'[15] He goes on to say that with the standard load of ammunition held in caissons and spare horses the total required by even a light battery was 110, with the 'long' 6-pounder requiring 123 and a 12-pounder battery no fewer than 165. It can be seen that a battery of six guns actually required more horses than an average squadron of cavalry, and this did not take into account any reserve ammunition caissons and other baggage carts. But draught animals were not the only problem. The limbers and caissons were clearly not designed for the poor condition of the roads or the mountains of the Peninsula and deteriorated quickly.

Because of the large number of horses required to pull a 12-pounder battery over bad roads, the commander of artillery recommended that the heaviest guns should be 9-pounders. One battery at Talavera was equipped with only

3-pounder guns that fired a comparatively small ball, but they were considered useful for supporting light troops. Indeed, early in the campaign they were attached to the cavalry in the absence of any horse artillery.

As the time to march on Oporto approached there were still insufficient horses to pull the artillery batteries, and desperate letters were dispatched to England to send horses out. An officer was even sent to Tangier to try to buy horses, but to no avail. Eventually the army was forced, like the French, to rely on mules for the majority of its draught animals.

Wellesley was not one to concentrate his guns in the French manner, but spread them reasonably evenly along his line. He was more interested in using his artillery to cause casualties to the vulnerable French columns where a single round shot could take down an entire file, rather than to engage in counter-battery fire. It was also good for the infantry's morale to have artillery nearby. During the battle, the British artillery struggled to counter the vast superiority in the numbers of guns enjoyed by the French, but only had one gun dismounted. However, their inferiority in artillery is highlighted by the fact that in the afternoon two Spanish batteries reinforced them, and it was noted that these, although old and with inferior sights, substantially increased British firepower.

At the beginning of July 1809 there were, on paper at least, 33,000 British soldiers in Portugal. However, of this total no fewer than 4,500 men were sick, some were left behind for the defence of Portugal, and with other necessary detachments no more than 22,000 marched into Spain and only 20,600 fought at Talavera.

Wellesley was lucky to have inherited a well-trained and well-motivated army, if one still lacking somewhat in the experience of battle and the rigours of campaign. However, it was his leadership, discipline and tactical system that were to combine to create the almost unstoppable fighting machine that was to throw the French out of Spain and contribute in no small measure to the eventual overthrow of Napoleon.

The Spanish Army

While the popular uprising that met France's invasion of Spain was ruthlessly suppressed in Madrid, the French did not have sufficient troops to pacify the whole country. So when Spain's central government collapsed, many regional Juntas were formed in those areas free of French occupation. After the French had been evicted from Madrid in 1808, a Central or 'Supreme' Junta was formed as a new central government to coordinate the fight against the French. Initially it enjoyed the confidence and support of the provincial juntas, but when Napoleon reoccupied the Spanish capital it was forced to flee to Seville, from where it failed to fully exert its previous authority over the others. Each junta raised an army to fight the French but, without undisputed central control, the lack of coordination and regional jealousies led to regular defeat.

However, the ad hoc Spanish armies, when defeated or driven into a corner, did not capitulate, but dispersed and fled in small parties into the hills. Although many did not rejoin the colours, many others quickly and enthusiastically rallied around the hard core of regulars, and conscripts or volunteers quickly replaced those who did not. Thus the Spanish armies were rarely destroyed and it was this determination not to accept defeat that convinced the British government to act in their support.

The Spanish armies finished the wars with an abysmal reputation that in the early years at least was generally well earned. In most major battles in which they fought on their own against the French they were comprehensively defeated. Furthermore, their generally poor performance when they fought alongside the British quickly generated a lack of confidence in them at every level of the British army, from the commander-in-chief to the meanest soldier. However, to be fair to the Spanish soldiers of this time it should be pointed out that their improvement was steady, and by the end of the wars they were frequently complimented by the then Duke of Wellington and even recruited into British regiments. Unfortunately they have never been able to completely shake off the reputation they had acquired earlier in the wars.

The regular Spanish army had been consistently neglected in the years before 1807 and it is no surprise that it was unable to put up a very creditable resistance to the French invasion. Indeed, in its temporary alliance with the French against Portugal, Napoleon had been able to siphon off the best Spanish troops for use in his own army on the Baltic coast of Germany. Although the British navy repatriated some of these, many others perished in Russia in 1812 still serving the French. Those that made it back to Spain were able to form a small but important nucleus around which to build new armies. When these armies were defeated or dispersed by the French it was inevitably this nucleus of regulars that rallied and, reinforced by a new batch of volunteers and conscripts, took the field again.

Most of the conscripts, though enthusiastic, had no military experience, and the imperatives of the strategic situation meant that there was little or no time for training before these barely equipped young men had to be sent into battle. Apart from those units that were at the French defeat at Bailén, all the Spanish armies had an almost unbroken record of defeat. Despite the advantages of campaigning in their own country they often suffered as badly from a lack of supplies as both their allies and enemies, and the incompetence and political intrigues among their leaders were unlikely to improve their lot or their confidence. In the early days of the conflict, flushed with the enthusiasm of a popular war, the untrained masses forced their generals to fight battles that they were totally unprepared for and consequently were catastrophically beaten. It was then not unusual for the army to execute the same general for treason, a regular cry after an army was routed. The Spanish general San Juan was given the impossible task of defending the Somosierra pass with insufficient numbers against Napoleon himself in 1808; after his inevitable defeat he was subsequently shot and then hanged by his own army, which suspected him of being about to surrender to the French.

The Army of Extremadura that fought at Talavera was made up of troops from four sources. The first was the sad remains of the army that had been thoroughly beaten at Gamonal in November of the previous year. Secondly there were the remains of the small army of San Juan that had vainly attempted to stop Napoleon's march on Madrid at Somosierra. Thirdly there were hastily raised and poorly trained and equipped levies, and finally four regular dismounted cavalry regiments that had been sent to the area to procure horses and equipment.

Lord Londonderry, Wellesley's adjutant general, gives us the following description of the army when he accompanied the British commander to a review just two weeks before the battle:

> They were all, without exception, remarkably fine men ... it would not have been easy to find a stouter or more hardy looking body of soldiers in any European service ... There were battalions whose arms, accoutrements, and even clothing might be pronounced respectable: but in general they were deficient, particularly in shoes. It was easy to perceive, from the attitude in which they stood, and the manner in which they handled their arms, that little or no discipline prevailed among them: they could not but be regarded as raw levies. Speaking of them in the aggregate they were little better than bold peasantry, armed partially like soldiers, but completely unacquainted with a soldier's duty. This remark applied as much to the cavalry as to the infantry. Many of the horses were good, but the riders manifestly knew nothing of movement or of discipline: and they were on this account, as also on that of miserable equipment, quite unfit for service.[16]

Wellesley's first impressions were good: 'The troops were ill-clothed but well-armed, and the officers appeared to take some pains with their discipline. Some of the corps of infantry were certainly good, and the horses of the cavalry were in good condition.'[17] However, after their generally poor performance in the Talavera campaign, Wellesley was rather more scathing about them:

> The Spanish cavalry are, I believe, nearly without discipline ... I have never heard anyone pretend that in one instance they have behaved as soldiers ought to do in the presence of the enemy. They make no scruple of running off ... The Spanish artillery are ... entirely unexceptionable ... In respect ... to the infantry, it is

lamentable to see how bad that of the Spaniards is, and how unequal
to a contest with the French.[18]

While the raw material seemed to be fine, there was a clear lack of training,
discipline, equipment and leadership.

The fact that there was little or no time for training was crucial. The advance
of the French armies throughout the country meant the Spanish conscripts
had to be thrown straight into battle without the opportunity to impose
discipline, gain confidence in themselves or to practice their drill. These
requirements are closely related as they encourage a soldier to do his duty in
circumstances in which all his natural instincts tell him to run away. Drill was
an immensely important aspect of the Napoleonic battlefield; without it, troops
were incapable of moving in formation, and it is therefore significant that
Wellesley wrote: 'owing to their miserable state of discipline and their want of
officers properly qualified, these troops are entirely incapable of performing
any manoeuvre however simple. They would get into irretrievable confusion,
and the result would probably be the loss of everything.'[19] Proficiency at drill
gave an army the confidence and tactical flexibility that distinguished good
troops and allowed them to manoeuvre quickly, a telling advantage during a
battle. It was only later in the wars, when Wellington was given direct
command of Spanish troops and as the efforts of the British army eased the
pressure on at least some of the Spanish armies, that they were able to go some
way to overcoming this deficiency. This breathing space allowed the Spanish
the time to train and discipline their troops and give them a little more
experience and confidence.

Wellesley was well known for endeavouring to maintain strict discipline
within the British army, and supported corporal punishment and even the
death penalty. He clearly felt that strict discipline was what the Spanish army
really required. However, it must be remembered that strict discipline, while it
might suit a small volunteer army that recruited from the 'scum of the earth',
was not likely to be as effective with Spanish conscripts and enthusiastic
volunteers motivated by a strong sense of patriotism, and could well have been
counter-productive. Both the French and the reformed Prussian army
recognized this when they banned corporal punishment in their armies.

The need to raise a large army quickly inevitably strained the finances and
manufacturing capabilities of the juntas. Their men were therefore necessarily
badly uniformed and ill-equipped. Britain made considerable contributions of
uniforms, equipment, muskets and even artillery. Between 1808 and 1809 it
sent 155 artillery pieces, 200,000 muskets, 39,000 sets of accoutrements, 61,000
swords, 79,000 pikes, 40,000 tents, 50,000 canteens, 54,000 knapsacks, 92,000
uniforms, shoes and hats, along with almost £1.5 million in cash and bills of
exchange, and this level of aid continued throughout the wars.[20] The problem
was that each region had to have its share, and the regular disintegration of the

various Spanish armies, and the high levels of desertion, meant that supply could never keep up with demand as new armies were raised. Wellesley wrote: 'This practice of running away, and throwing off arms, accoutrements, and clothing is fatal to everything, excepting a reassembly of the men in a state of nature, who as regularly perform the same manoeuvre the next time an occasion offers.'[21] After Talavera, Wellesley complained that the Spanish were collecting up all the British equipment from the battlefield and carrying it off for their own use instead of returning it to their allies.

Commandant Colin, a respected French military theorist, wrote: 'There are no troops so bad that good generals cannot fire them. Perhaps the value of the leader outvalues all others.'[22] On the basis of this hypothesis, the lack of a reliable officer corps was certainly the worst deficiency in the Spanish armies. A British officer described their officers as 'the most contemptible creatures that I ever beheld … utterly unfit and unable to command their men'.[23] Those few officers who were commissioned through the ranks had no chance of rising beyond captain, and the remainder were drawn exclusively from the aristocracy with few, if any, qualities that suited them for command.

Unfortunately the Spanish were no better served by their senior officers, most of whom seemed to have a mania for fighting pitched battles against a technically superior enemy with armies that were virtually untrained. After Wellesley's review of Cuesta's army described above, Lord Londonderry also wrote: 'The generals appeared to have been selected by one rule alone – that of seniority. They were almost all old men, and, except for O'Donoju and Zayas, evidently incapable of bearing the fatigues or surmounting the difficulties of campaign.'[24] There was much competition and jealousy between the generals appointed by the different juntas, and it never seemed possible to coordinate their movements for the common good. While unity of command might be a principle of war, the Central Junta made no attempt to appoint a supreme commander and seemed to encourage the generals to scheme against each other. Wellesley was quick to learn of the unreliability, deceitfulness and incompetence of General Cuesta, with whom he was forced to cooperate during his advance into Spain.

The French view of the Spanish army is interesting. While Napoleon fully expected his troops to be able to defeat twice their own numbers of Spaniards, the French troops respected their tenacity and ferocity when fighting in sieges or behind fortifications. De Rocca, a French hussar officer, also respected their motivation and dedication:

> The pride of the Spaniards is such, that they would never attribute their misfortunes to their want of experience, or to the military superiority of their enemies: the moment they were beaten, they accused their chiefs of treason. The ardent desire they had for conquest, made them support, with admirable patience, privations

to which all the power of the severest discipline could never have subjected the best regular troops.[25]

As a junior French officer, de Rocca also seems to have had an understanding of the situation that even Napoleon missed: 'No Spaniard would believe in the disasters of Spain, or own that she could be conquered: these sentiments, inherent in every mind, rendered the nation invincible, notwithstanding the frequent defeats, and the individual losses of its armies.'[26]

As early as 1809 it was hardly fair for Wellesley to expect the same high standard of training from the newly raised Spanish armies that his own troops had achieved. Later in his life Wellington gave perhaps a more balanced view on his Spanish allies: 'The Spanish make excellent soldiers. What spoils them is that they have no confidence in their officers – this would ruin any soldiers.'[27]

Cuesta's army at Talavera was about 33,000 strong (see Annex C) and its strength and weaknesses reflected those of all the Spanish armies. It was a hotchpotch of conscripts and volunteers, with only a sprinkling of regulars, mostly formed into new regiments that lacked, through no fault of their own, the training, discipline or cohesion that would make them truly effective on the battlefield. While the rather arrogant and jingoistic views of many of their British contemporaries may have been accurate if comparing like with like, given the particular difficulties the Spanish authorities faced in trying to rid their country of the invader, it was inevitable that the performance of the Spanish armies left something to be desired. Their conscripts had only their nationalist enthusiasm and personal courage to qualify them as soldiers. In their battles with the French they often fought with courage and tenacity, but were usually outmanoeuvred and outgunned; what often started as stiff resistance deteriorated into panic and rout as units lost cohesion, broke ranks and fled. Oman sums it up nicely in his history of the war: 'They [the juntas and generals] would not see that courage and raw multitudes are almost helpless when opposed by equal courage combined with skill, long experience of war, superior tactics, and intelligent leading.'[28]

The Guerrillas

Though they were not part of the Spanish army we must not leave the Spanish forces without a quick word on the guerrillas. Of course they took no part in the fighting at Talavera but they still had an impact on the campaign. Their activities made communications between the various French armies very difficult and this was to make effective synchronization between the armies of King Joseph and Soult almost impossible. Furthermore, couriers sent between the two were often captured, and the information that they carried inevitably proved useful to Cuesta and Wellesley.

Having a British army operating in Spain took tremendous pressure off both the Spanish armies and the guerrillas. The French inevitably saw defeating the

French soldiers come across the bodies of their comrades hanged by Spanish guerrillas. The guerrillas played a vital role in the gathering of intelligence, the harassment of the French lines of communication and the lowering of morale in the French army.

British as their main effort, and this was well illustrated when, in 1808, Napoleon himself turned quickly and decisively on Moore when he finally got conclusive information on where the latter was. In 1809 the French maintained more than seven corps in the Peninsula, and until Wellesley's army marched into Spain they were spread throughout the country, either maintaining control over the territory they occupied or facing the weak Spanish armies that were still in existence. The attempt to destroy Wellesley and Cuesta forced Joseph to concentrate the best part of five of them as well as his central reserve. This inevitably took the pressure off the other Spanish armies, allowing them to recruit and train, and allowed the guerrillas to re-exert their control over the areas the French had been forced to evacuate in order to concentrate their forces.

Once the threat from the British had been removed, the French were then forced into a long and bloody battle to reassert their control over the provinces they had been recently forced to abandon. A Polish officer of the Vistula Legion summed up the impact of the guerrillas rather neatly:

> It was a real see-saw battle between the partisans and ourselves: they were everywhere we were not, they disappeared upon our approach, escaped our clutches and re-appeared behind us. As most of the people of the region were on their side, they inevitably had all the advantages. We had to be vigilant at all hours of the day or night so as not to be taken by surprise and risk a loss of life or honour.[29]

Even when they reoccupied an area, 'Our reign over the region stretched for just a musket-shot beyond the walls.'[30] So despite the fact that they did not appear on the battlefield, the guerrillas were still to have a significant impact on the campaign. While Wellesley and Cuesta received regular and accurate information on their adversaries, the French were forced to try to coordinate their movements with little or no intelligence on the positions of their enemies, and to operate in the fog of war where they could be sure of only what the situation was in those areas over which they had control and observation, a significant disadvantage in war.

The French Army

By 1809 French armies had been the scourge of Europe for the best part of twenty years. But it was only the appearance of Napoleon Bonaparte that finally moulded them into a military machine that for several years appeared invincible. The Grande Armée destroyed the military ambitions of Austria, Prussia and then Russia in a series of stunning victories at Austerlitz (against Austria and Russia in 1805), Jena/Auerstadt (against Prussia in 1806) and Friedland (against Russia in 1807). By 1807 the whole of central Europe lay subservient to the French and only the British appeared to threaten Napoleon's dominance over the whole continent. Unable to challenge British naval superiority, the French Emperor hoped to bring his final adversary to heel by imposing a total boycott on British exports on his vassals and allies, which was known as the Continental System. Portugal's rejection of this trade embargo and Spain's half-hearted participation laid the foundations for Napoleon's further imperialist ambitions in the Iberian Peninsula.

After his successes against the Russians in 1807, the majority of the Grande Armée was in garrison in Germany. Napoleon had no intention of using these battle-hardened veterans for his adventures in Portugal and Spain, and raised new regiments full of young and poorly trained conscripts for what was supposed to be a sideshow. Indeed, although many Spaniards laughed at the awkward young soldiers who marched into their country, the lack of any resistance in Portugal and the neglected state of the Spanish army meant that their fighting powers were not tested. Only later, as Spanish resistance began to be properly organized and a British army landed in Portugal, did Napoleon feel it necessary to march into Spain at the head of his most experienced troops.

When the French Emperor left Spain to confront Austria in the first days of 1809, he left most of his veteran formations behind under the command of Marshal Soult to dispose of Moore's small British army. The vast majority of the French troops that fought at Talavera had marched into Spain with Napoleon and represented his most experienced regiments. Of the seventeen French regiments at Talavera, all of them had fought in at least one of the major battles of Austerlitz, Jena and Friedland, and five of them had fought at all three. Six had also fought at Ulm and another five at the bloodletting at

Eylau. Inevitably, of course, the regiments had suffered heavy casualties in these battles, and therefore received many young and newly trained replacements; but the ratio of veterans was still high enough to ensure that these had been absorbed without a significant loss in effectiveness. By Talavera even these latest recruits had already experienced ten months of campaigning in Spain and had taken part in a number of successful actions against the Spanish. Two battalions, one of the 32ème and one of the 58ème, had fought against the British at Vimeiro before rejoining their parent regiments on their arrival in Spain.

Like most other countries, the French infantry was divided into line infantry (*ligne*) and light infantry (*légère*). Each wore its own distinctive uniform and superficially at least had very different responsibilities. Each French division generally had one regiment of *légère* in its order of battle, and at Talavera only Sébastiani's division did not have one. This was primarily to provide the swarm of skirmishers for which French attacks had become renowned. However, they were also trained to fight in close order in the same way as the *ligne*. When deployed in close order they were often used as the lead assault troops where the extra *esprit de corps* that comes with a specialized role was seen as fitting them well for this position of honour. Unglamorous as the *ligne* infantry were, it was they who accounted for the highest proportion of the army and they who did most of the hard fighting and dying.

Early in 1808 Napoleon reorganized his infantry. Each infantry regiment was to be increased from four battalions to five. One of these was to be the depot battalion that was responsible for training recruits and local security duties in much the same way that British second battalions were. The other four battalions were termed as 'war' battalions and ideally would serve together, possibly forming one of the brigades in a division. In fact this rarely happened, and as the wars dragged on it became more and more unusual to find all the

A campaign-hardened French light infantryman. In the fierce heat of a Spanish summer, the French often discarded their thick habit veste and simply wore the long-sleeved waistcoat as shown here. This was blue for the light infantry and white for the line. This soldier has also covered his shako to protect it from the sun and dust, and replaced his issue trousers with a more comfortable, locally manufactured pattern.

battalions of a regiment serving together. At Talavera most regiments were represented by only three of their four battalions, as their recently raised fourth battalions were kept back in France to form the new army Napoleon was putting together for the coming confrontation with Austria. Thus the fourth battalions of thirteen of the seventeen regiments that fought at Talavera accompanied Napoleon into Austria.

By increasing the number of battalions in a regiment in this way, Napoleon was able to expand his army without raising new regiments, which was expensive, and the existing battalions would find the officers and NCOs for the new unit. The reorganization also reduced the number of companies in a battalion but increased the strength of each. This way he was able to maintain the strength of the battalion but require less officers and NCOs that could then be used as the cadre for the new fourth battalions. The flaw in this plan was that the ratio of officers and NCOs to men was reduced, therefore weakening command and control.

The new establishment of the battalions now gave them six, as opposed to the previous nine, companies. As in British units, one of these, containing the biggest and most experienced men, was designated as grenadiers, and another, with the smaller, more athletic men, was designated as light infantry. The former was used to spearhead attacks or provide a solid and dependable reserve, while the latter provided the battalion's skirmisher screen. Unlike the British, who were prone to drawing all the light infantry companies into an ad hoc light battalion, the French, with a higher number of light infantry units, more often concentrated their grenadier companies into a temporary grenadier battalion. This was at the discretion of the divisional commander, but it was not unusual for a corps commander to form several of these battalions to provide an elite corps reserve. At Talavera it is certain that at least Villatte's division formed such a battalion. Most of the French infantry brigades at Talavera consisted of two regiments giving six battalions. This made them considerably stronger than the two or three battalion brigades of Wellesley's army.

At this stage in the wars, Napoleon and his commanders enjoyed one clear advantage over their British counterparts. Wellesley commanded a relatively small army but was acutely aware that it was the only British field army and its loss would be catastrophic. In contrast, Napoleon was at the height of his power, and his repeated requests for more conscripts went unchallenged. Since the introduction of the *levée en masse* the French armies had an enormous source of manpower that could repair the heaviest losses. This allowed their commanders to act with a cavalier attitude to the consequences of such losses if they bought success. Their frequent battlefield use of the bludgeon, rather than the rapier, was often evident in their tactics.

Like the British, the French also used allies to supplement their manpower. Some of these were enthusiastic supporters of Napoleon, while many others showed more reluctance. Joseph's army at Talavera included Poles and Dutch, as well as contingents from the German states of Westphalia, Nassau, Hesse-Darmstadt, Frankfurt and Baden. The Poles were the most constant of French allies, and their troops were considered every bit as good as the French. The Dutch were still a separate kingdom under Napoleon's brother Louis, but a year after Talavera the country and its army were both absorbed into France. The Dutch soldiers were considered 'slow and unwilling'[31] by their French comrades. The other allies were fresh from expanding their territory and influence as a result of Napoleon's patronage, and not until later in the wars did their enthusiasm for the Emperor begin to wane. These early contingents were of excellent quality, and the regiments from Hesse-Darmstadt and Baden particularly distinguished themselves during their early service in Spain. The Westphalian cavalry was considered among the best in Europe, but all the German contingents felt an increasing disillusionment with their French allies, who tended to treat them as second-class citizens.

The mountainous country of Spain was not ideal for the employment of battlefield cavalry, although the need for light cavalry for reconnaissance and security duties was no less important here than anywhere else. Each corps had its own light cavalry brigade for these types of duties, though they were often

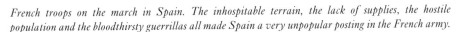

French troops on the march in Spain. The inhospitable terrain, the lack of supplies, the hostile population and the bloodthirsty guerrillas all made Spain a very unpopular posting in the French army.

called on to fight on the battlefield like their heavier cousins. Although a considerable amount of cavalry was present at Talavera, the battle was almost exclusively an infantry affair and what little cavalry action there was, was conducted by light cavalry.

Napoleon employed a far higher proportion of cavalry to infantry compared to either the British or Spanish. However, given the difficulties of the terrain and climate, and those of finding sufficient fodder, he was not prepared to send the cream of his heavy cavalry, his cuirassiers. Consequently, at Talavera we see dragoons making up the majority of the French cavalry formations. Napoleon had not been impressed with their performance in 1805 to 1807 and had therefore sent most of them to Spain. Although frequently bettered by the British cavalry, the considerable experience they built up in five years campaigning in the Peninsula turned them into veteran troops who made a considerable impact when drawn back to rebuild Napoleon's cavalry after its destruction in Russia in 1812.

The French army was always strong in artillery, mainly because this arm had been least affected by the changes brought to the army by the Revolution. Of course its case was helped by the fact that Napoleon himself was a 'gunner' and is often quoted as saying, 'Great battles are won by artillery.' The French artillery maintained a high reputation throughout the Napoleonic Wars and benefited from the relatively recent issue of well-designed, high-quality equipment. Each French division had a battery as an integral part of its organization and these could be supplemented at the critical point by a reserve held at corps level. This was generally true for both infantry and cavalry divisions.

Unlike the British total of six pieces, each French foot battery consisted of eight: six guns and two howitzers. But not only were there more guns in a French battery than a British one, but at this time they also tended to be of greater calibre and with a greater range. At Talavera, though the Anglo-Spanish army had a similar number of guns to the French, by merely screening the Spanish troops with some cavalry Joseph was able to concentrate all his artillery against the British. In this way Wellesley found himself outnumbered two to one by the French artillery, and, well aware of its power, he formed the tactic of leaving as many of his troops as possible on a reverse slope where they were sheltered from its fire. Where this was not possible he insisted that troops should lie down. As if he needed reminding, the performance of the French artillery at Talavera served to reinforce this lesson.

In contrast to the small expeditionary operations of the British army, the French had long experience of large-scale, high-intensity operations against other powerful military powers. It would have proved impossible to command and control their comparatively huge armies if they had been merely broken down into brigades or even divisions in the British fashion. The French armies were thus broken down into corps, or *corps d'armée*. These were generally composed of two, three or four divisions and could number up to 30,000 men. They were inevitably combined arms formations including infantry, cavalry and artillery that were capable of fighting independently, even against superior numbers, until other corps could come to their assistance. At Talavera, Joseph's army consisted of two such corps, two independent cavalry divisions and a reserve. Victor's I Corps consisted of three infantry divisions and a brigade of cavalry, as well as six batteries of artillery. Each division and probably the cavalry brigade would have had a battery attached, with the balance forming the corps reserve. Sébastiani's IV Corps also had three infantry divisions, although one was much depleted by the need to provide a force to cover Madrid before Venegas. The IV Corps had a full division of cavalry attached, as well as five batteries of artillery (see Annex D).

Perhaps it is fitting to finish with an objective view of the French army. However confident he always seems to have been of beating the French, Wellington clearly respected them, recalling, 'They were excellent troops; I never on any occasion knew them to behave otherwise than well. Their officers too were as good as possible.'[32] There can be no doubt that the French army at Talavera was, on paper at least, the most formidable on the field. Strongest in manpower, composed largely of battle-hardened veterans and buoyed by an unbroken record of success against the best that Prussia, Russia, Austria and Spain could put into the field, they must have approached the battlefield with every expectation of victory.

Chapter Three

The Commanders

Lieutenant General Sir Arthur Wellesley

Like the army he commanded, Wellesley had made an impressive start to his career in the Peninsula, but he was still to finally establish his reputation as a great captain. Although he was clearly a competent and ambitious junior officer, his early promotion was by purchase and facilitated by his family's relative wealth rather than his own performance. Having obtained an initial commission into the 73rd Foot when he was seventeen, thanks to the influence of his brother, he then went on to serve in the 76th and 41st Foot and then the 12th Light Dragoons before purchasing a captaincy in the 58th Foot. He then served for six years as aide-de-camp to the Marquess of Buckingham, who was the lord lieutenant of Ireland, during which Wellesley also became a member of the Irish parliament. When war broke out with France he was a captain in the 18th Light Dragoons, but quickly bought himself a majority in the 33rd Foot, which he commanded with some distinction as a lieutenant colonel in the Netherlands (in 1794), aged only twenty-five.[1]

As purchase was the usual method of advancement in the army of those days and moving regiments to avoid unpopular postings was quite common, we must not be too critical of these regimental wanderings. In 1796 Wellesley took the 33rd to India, a move that had spelt doom for many a military career. However, here he flourished, and he was promoted to major general in 1802. His successes were crowned at the Battle of Assaye, where he defeated an army much bigger than his own in a ferocious battle in which he had two horses killed under him. Returning to England in 1805 with a considerable reputation and financially secure, he entered politics and soon came to the attention of Castlereagh, the British secretary of state for war. William Pitt, at that point the British prime minister, described him as:

> quite unlike all other military men with whom I have conversed. He never makes a difficulty or hides his ignorance in vague generalities. If I put a question to him he answers it distinctly; if I want an

explanation, he gives it clearly; if I desire an opinion, I get from him one supported by reasons that are always sound. He is a very remarkable man.[2]

After further enhancing his reputation during the expedition against Denmark in 1807, Wellesley's opportunity finally arrived with the French invasion of Portugal and Spain. Promoted to the rank of lieutenant general in April 1807 he found himself in only temporary command of the first expedition that departed from Cork for the Peninsula in July 1808. Short of men and awaiting lieutenant generals Dalrymple and Burrard to succeed Wellesley in command, the small army landed at Mondego Bay. In these circumstances perhaps most officers would have been content with consolidating their position and awaiting the arrival of the senior commander. Wellesley, however, wasted no time in advancing with his 14,000 men towards Lisbon and beating first the French advance guard at Roliça, and then Junot's main force at Vimeiro. Having subsequently handed over command he survived the public outcry over the Cintra convention, and in April 1809 was appointed to command a second expedition to Portugal that was to lead to the Battle of Talavera.

As we shall see, even before his arrival in Portugal, Wellesley had developed in his mind a tactical system to defeat the French in battle. The refinement of this system resulted in an unbroken string of successes that would eventually see the French run out of Spain. However, Wellesley's generalship is not without its critics, and he has been accused of being a predominantly 'infantry' general who rarely seemed to exploit his victories with a relentless pursuit in a manner for which Napoleon became famous: the pursuit *à l'outrance*. As this was essentially a cavalry responsibility, it is quite possible that Wellesley's distrust of his mounted arm was the main reason for this.

Although best known for his exploits on the battlefield, Wellesley was as able a strategist as he was tactician. His greatest achievements were undoubtedly strategic and have not necessarily been given the credit they deserve. Before the campaign began, he displayed his strategic acumen by writing his 'Memorandum on the Defence of Portugal'[3] in which he predicted, with stunning accuracy, the way the campaign in the Peninsula would unfold. He displayed an uncanny ability to anticipate the problems the French would face and the movements they would make, and foresaw that the Spanish would not be able to liberate their country on their own. Perhaps his greatest achievement was his ability to grasp the political, geographical and moral factors of every situation he faced. He understood that his army could not easily be replaced and that he could not take risks that might result in its destruction.

Wellesley was forty years old in 1809 and considered physically fit. He certainly took on a mammoth workload, especially early in the war when he did not consider his subordinates sufficiently experienced to do it for themselves. His unswerving belief in his own abilities meant that he rarely asked for the

By the time of Talavera, Sir Arthur Wellesley was still to earn his reputation as a general who had the full measure of the French.

advice or opinions of others and never allowed discussion as long as he held supreme authority in the field. He could therefore be a thankless taskmaster, pitiless in resenting a mistake or an apparent disobedience of orders. This unwillingness to concede any latitude in the interpretation of his instructions to his subordinates meant that, rather like Napoleon, he trained admirable divisional generals but not commanders with the initiative to be able to take an independent command.

Perhaps Wellesley's biggest fault was his man management. He was clearly a very arrogant man with a supreme confidence in his own ability and judgement that was no doubt the product of his aristocratic upbringing. He was feared, respected and followed unquestioningly, but never idolized in a way that so many great captains of history were by their soldiers. All his subordinates seemed to feel that while he looked on them as the perfect tool with which to carry out his plans, and therefore found it necessary to ensure that they were fed and equipped, he took no interest in their welfare. His many disparaging remarks about his soldiers are well recorded, and he had the greatest contempt for any idea of appealing to the men's better feelings or trying to motivate them by sentiment. His ideas of discipline are described by Oman as 'worthy of one of the drill sergeants of Frederick the Great',[4] and he is quoted as saying, 'I have no idea of any great effect being produced on British soldiers by anything but the fear of immediate corporal punishment.'[5] But he was quite wrong in this belief, and this is borne out in the many memoirs of both officers and other ranks.

Well known for his simple but rather unmilitary attire, Wellesley regularly spent his days in civilian clothes. This lack of interest in his military dress was reflected in his attitude to the dress of his army:

> Provided we brought our men into the field well appointed, and with 60 good rounds in their pouches, he never looked to see whether our trousers were black or blue or grey. Scarcely any two officers dressed alike. Some wore grey braided coats, others brown, some liked blue: many through choice or necessity stuck to the 'old red rag'. We were never tormented with that greatest of bores on active service, uniformity of dress.[6]

Although he was a great intellect, strategist and tactician, Wellesley had few redeeming personal qualities that were likely to generate any kind of affection for him. 'Unsparing of himself, careless of praise or blame and honest in word and deed,'[7] he treated others as if they shared these attributes and seemed to think less of them if they did not. While there was much to admire and respect in Wellesley there was little to endear him to his men.

Don Gregorio Garcia de la Cuesta

The commander-in-chief of the Extremaduran Army was Captain General Cuesta. Cuesta's age at Talavera is variously given as between sixty-four and sixty-nine, but whatever his exact age he was clearly an 'old man' by the standards of the day. He was a career officer who had joined the army against his father's wishes, and enjoyed a distinguished career as a junior officer. His service included action against the British during the early part of the Siege of Gibraltar, and later on in skirmishes against the French during the

Revolutionary Wars. As promotion in the Spanish army was dictated more by seniority than competence, it was natural that he would lead one of the Spanish armies after the French invasion of his country. By the time of Talavera he had already been humiliated by three resounding defeats by the French at Cabezon, Medina de Río Seco, and most recently, on 28 March 1809, at Medellin at the hands of Marshal Victor.

At the time of the spontaneous uprisings that followed the French seizure of power in Spain, Cuesta was the governor general of Old Castile. Reluctant to put himself at the head of the mob that summoned him, he was threatened with being hanged by them before he finally agreed. As Oman suggests, 'Remembering the awful slaughter at Cabezon, Río Seco, and at Medellin, which his incapacity and mulish obstinacy was destined to bring about, it is impossible not to express the wish that his consent to take arms had been delayed for a few minutes longer.'[8] By the time of Talavera, Cuesta was in an awkward political position. He had many enemies in the Central Junta who viewed him with suspicion and dislike. He had been placed at the head of the Extremaduran Army with great reluctance, and only kept his job after his defeats because of the support of some of the conservatives and clerical party. He was also the target of much jealousy from other Spanish generals who were contemptuous of his poor record and who could not understand why he was still in command after the humiliation of Medellin. Indeed, far from disgracing him and removing him from command, the junta actually rewarded him for this defeat. Judging that he had fought gallantly they granted honours to all those whom he recommended, and promoted him to captain general of Extremadura. However, it was common knowledge that his enemies in the junta put Venegas in command of the Army of La Mancha, with whom Cuesta would have to cooperate during the upcoming campaign, because he was known to be an enemy of the elder general.

Cuesta is described by Charles Stewart, later Lord Londonderry, at the review of the Spanish army that he had specially laid on for Wellesley just a few weeks before Talavera:

> Nor was Cuesta himself an object to be passed by without notice: the old man preceded us, not so much sitting on his horse as held on it by two pages [he was still suffering from the bruising he received when he was ridden over by his own cavalry during the defeat at Medellin]. His physical debility was so observable as clearly to mark his unfitness for the situation which he held. As to his mental powers, he gave us little opportunity of judging, inasmuch as he scarcely uttered five words during the continuance of our visit: but his corporal infirmities were ever at absolute variance with all a general's duties.[9]

An officer in the 3rd Guards pointed out, 'General Cuesta is said to possess the entire confidence of his troops, and this may be the reason why he has been selected to command an army of patriots, which ought to have an officer of youth, vigour and talent at its head.'[10]

As a general, Cuesta seemed to swing from a tendency for rashness (Oman, admittedly no admirer of Cuesta, describes his enthusiasm to attack at Medellín as 'that of a criminal lunatic')[11] to one of apathy. Like an insecure lover he almost inevitably adopted the opposite course to the one Wellesley advised, so that when Wellesley urged caution he tended to rashness, and when Wellesley urged him to move onto the offensive he automatically lapsed back into apparent apathy. Despite his record of catastrophic defeats he appeared to harbour an irrational disrespect for French military prowess, and in Wellesley's presence maintained an equally irrational overconfidence in his own army which was only exposed when he was left to face the French alone.

Although Cuesta's tenure in command was somewhat insecure, he seemed less concerned with the possibility of being replaced by a younger, more capable Spanish general than by Wellesley himself, whom some were pushing as a possible 'generalissimo' of all the Spanish armies. The fact that Wellesley's name was being suggested to the Central Junta would soon have become known to Cuesta given the allies that he had there. In truth, Wellesley's nomination received little support and, though Wellesley himself would have welcomed the appointment purely for the unity of command that would have resulted, he did not actively push the idea. But the simple fact that this possibility was being mooted goes a long way to explaining Cuesta's surly and uncooperative behaviour towards Wellesley during the coming campaign.

Oman suggests that:

> He disliked his destined colleague not only because he was a foreigner, and because he showed himself strong-willed and outspoken during their intercourse, but because he believed that the Englishman was intriguing behind his back to obtain the post of Generalissimo. This belief made him determined to assert his independence on the most trifling matters, loathe to fall in with even the most reasonable plans and suspicious that every proposal made to him concealed some trap.[12]

If this is really how Cuesta felt, and it must be remembered that Oman was no fan of the Spanish general, then it is little wonder that his relationship with Wellesley was such a stormy one. To be fair to Cuesta, we must remember that he was considerably senior to Wellesley and no doubt felt, justifiably, that he had much more experience fighting the French. We should not be surprised if he felt somewhat jealous of this arrogant and self-confident officer who always seemed to be calling the shots.

While British officers were prone to accuse Cuesta of pride, stupidity and obstinacy, and each of these words was used by Wellesley himself on different occasions, the truth was that the dominant feelings were resentment, jealousy and suspicion. Interestingly, Wellesley seems to have thought that Cuesta's behaviour was part of his character rather than being derived from a deep personal enmity. In 1833 the then Lord Wellington said of him:

> He did not want courage nor sense either, but was an obstinate old man and had no military genius ... if he would have fought when I wanted him at Talavera [here he presumably means when they faced the forces of Victor on 23 July], I have no hesitation in saying that it would have been as great a battle as Waterloo and would have cleared Spain of the French for that time.[13]

Whatever Wellesley's true feelings, the difficulties he had with Cuesta and the Extremaduran Army in this initial joint venture were to shake his trust in his Spanish allies for many years.

The French Commanders

After the French invasion of Spain in 1808, Joseph had been ordered onto the throne by his younger brother Napoleon. A rather reluctant monarch, he had been quite content as king of Naples, the previous throne thrust upon him by his brother's thirst for conquest, and it was only the thought that he might reign over both kingdoms that had encouraged his move to Spain.

Joseph's parents had hoped for him to go into the church, but he himself planned to follow his younger brother into the army. Napoleon, who was then at a military school at Brienne aged only fourteen, wrote to his uncle, 'He [Joseph] lacks the necessary boldness to face the perils of battle and his feeble health could never sustain the rigours of a campaign.'[14] Having finally been admitted into Brienne, Joseph was forced by the death of his father to head the family back in Corsica. Although he later worked as a commissary in the army he was most successful as a diplomat, and in 1800 he became an elected member of the Corps Législatif.

When Napoleon was made first consul for life, Joseph demanded that, as his elder brother, he should be appointed his natural successor. Napoleon declared that a ruling dynasty could only be founded on military glory, and that Joseph would have to learn how to command an army. Consequently, Napoleon appointed him colonel commandant of the 4ème de ligne with the army training to invade England. However, after showing initial zeal and enthusiasm, he tired of his duties and left the army without Napoleon's permission.

After his victory at Austerlitz in the latter part of 1805, the Emperor decided to occupy the kingdom of Naples as a punishment for its flagrant violation of a treaty of neutrality that it had signed with him. He proclaimed his brother

Placed on the throne of Spain by his brother, Joseph was a reluctant, if well-intentioned, king. However, his lack of military experience meant he never had the respect of the French army and was rarely able to impose his authority over it.

commander-in-chief of the French forces in Naples and later informed him that he wished him to become king. Joseph hurried to take over his new command and Naples was invaded on 8 February 1806. The plan was not his, however, as he was in nominal command only and deferred totally to Marshal Masséna, the senior French marshal. Naples was entered with hardly a shot fired and, despite the need to pacify the whole country, Joseph was happy to leave that to the professionals while he concentrated on establishing his rule.

When the French took over Spain, Napoleon decided that Joseph should become king and summoned him from Naples. Joseph entered Madrid on 20 July 1808. He was quick to complain to his brother that the French generals were acting independently but Napoleon was aware of this, and regularly sent them instructions of his own without informing his brother. The inference of this is clear: all the generals that Napoleon had in Spain were very experienced, and he had no intention of allowing Joseph to disrupt their operations.

The personal interference of Napoleon had several detrimental effects on the French war effort in Spain. The problems of communicating between the

Napoleon's short time in Spain gave him a distorted impression of the realities of campaigning in that country and the nature of the fighting. His constant advice and orders were often out of date or impracticable, and only complicated the difficulties experienced by his brother and his generals.

various armies was bad enough without deliberately giving instructions to one general without informing the others of what he proposed. This unsatisfactory situation was exacerbated when Joseph, the nominal commander-in-chief, was left in the dark with regard to the orders Napoleon was sending his generals. This lack of unity of command, a generally accepted principle of war, was to be a major cause of French failures in the Iberian Peninsula.

After his intervention in Spain in 1808, Napoleon left a detailed plan of how the campaign should be continued. Unfortunately, this was based on his limited experience in the theatre of war and proved unrealistic and unworkable. He always held a distorted impression of the true situation there and badly miscalculated the character of the Spanish people. To make matters worse, he continued to send orders to both his brother and his generals based on out-of-date information, so that his plans were often impracticable or even impossible by the time his direction arrived.

This was inevitable given the time it took for correspondence to travel between Spain and wherever the Emperor happened to be at the time, although he never seemed to appreciate the fact. For much of the campaign that led to the battle at Talavera he was in Austria fighting Archduke Charles, and hardly able to give the complex situation in Spain the attention it required if he was to have any constructive influence on what was happening there.

Joseph constantly begged for more troops and his concerns were confirmed when the corps of Dupont was defeated and captured at Bailén. In a panic Joseph left Madrid but planned a counter-offensive that was supported by his chief of staff, Marshal Jourdan. Napoleon, however, ridiculed his plan, complaining that he made war 'like a postal inspector',[15] and sent a string of correspondence criticizing his tactics and telling him what he should do. Needless to say, this criticism was deeply humiliating to Joseph, who realized that he was virtually powerless. He wrote to his brother, 'Yesterday and for the last four years I was able to command an army. Today, I have not the authority of a second lieutenant.'[16] Of course this rather exaggerated his responsibilities as a commander in Naples, and Napoleon only half-heartedly encouraged his brother.

Joseph complained that Napoleon had not officially appointed him as commander-in-chief in Spain, and so it was no surprise that he was not treated as such. Wherever the French armies met those of Spain they were victorious, but Joseph had no part in these triumphs. When Napoleon brought his army into Spain to re-establish his brother on the throne after Bailén, he had no intention of allowing Joseph any active part in the campaign. Having retaken Madrid and thrown Moore's British army out of Spain, he returned to France to plan the coming campaign against Austria. After he left, the lack of unity and the petty jealousies of the French commanders continued, but Joseph was powerless to stop them. It can be no surprise that Joseph found the situation intolerable and threatened to abdicate on a number of occasions. Napoleon, naturally, bullied him into continuing.

Joseph was in fact a conscientious king who worked hard to improve the lot of 'his' people, and gained a measure of support and even popularity in Madrid. But this support never extended far beyond the city limits mainly because of the influence of the juntas and church, but also because of the terrible behaviour of the French troops whose rapacious habits were not calculated to win them many friends among the local population. His case had not been helped by his brother's policy of terrorizing the population into submission by arrests and executions. This contrasted sharply with Joseph's own efforts to win the people over by showing himself to be a liberal and enlightened monarch. Napoleon's behaviour when he reoccupied Madrid was to provoke the first of a number of Joseph's offers of abdication: 'I blush with shame before my so-called subjects. I beg Your Majesty to accept the renunciation of all my rights to the throne of Spain that you have given me. I will always prefer honour and probity to power so dearly bought.'[17]

Joseph must have been pleased to see Napoleon leave, but he was to be disappointed if he believed that he would now be left alone to rule as he thought fit. The Emperor continued to send advice and censure to his brother that sapped his confidence and inevitably led to further frustration. Joseph never seemed able to understand that what his brother wanted was a compliant king of Spain to do his bidding, not someone with his people's interests at heart.

The arrival of Wellesley and his army in Portugal made Joseph more reliant than ever on the conduct of his generals. However, after Soult's humiliation at Oporto, Joseph's frustration finally drove him to take action: if he was to be dependent on the army for his throne he determined to put himself at its head and prove his military capacity. This sudden burst of action brought the rest of the French commanders to heel, and a coordinated plan was agreed that would defeat Wellesley's small army and its Spanish allies. Ironically, Talavera was to be not only Joseph's first major battle in command, but also the first major battle at which he was present. It is no surprise that he showed so little composure and authority.

Marshal Jourdan was Joseph's chief of staff at Talavera, having been appointed to this post by Napoleon when Joseph became king of Naples. There can be no doubt that the Emperor made this appointment on the basis of his considerable military experience but also as a senior officer who was past holding an active command. Having joined the army in 1778, Jourdan enjoyed a rapid rise and was made *général de division* in 1793 having fought in a number of important battles of the Revolutionary Wars. He was appointed commander-in-chief of the Army of the North the same year, and won the battles of Wattignies and Fleurus. He enjoyed further success as an army commander until suffering defeat at Würtzburg and Stockach.

After a brief ostracism, Jourdan was rehabilitated and briefly became the commander of the Army of Italy in 1804 and a marshal of the empire in the

Marshal Jourdan was an experienced officer who had tasted considerable success as an independent army commander in the Revolutionary Wars. However, as Joseph's chief of staff, though he gave 'King' Joseph sound advice, he was never able to impose the King's authority on the other French commanders, which resulted in the disjointed efforts that went a long way towards ensuring failure at Talavera.

same year. This honour was awarded for his past exploits rather than his potential, but Napoleon believed he would give Joseph wise council as his brother's chief of staff. His abilities were not taxed in Naples, though it seems he did little to try to impose Joseph's authority over the other French generals. He followed Joseph to Spain in 1808 and again seemed unable to exert any influence over the other French marshals and generals, who each seemed to be fighting his own personal war rather than working to a coordinated plan. It was only when Joseph himself finally exerted some authority that a cohesive strategy was implemented to stop the Anglo-Spanish invasion led by Wellesley. Throughout the campaign it appears that Jourdan gave the King sensible but generally cautious advice. As an inexperienced commander, Joseph appears to have been happy to tread this path; however, this inexperience also made him prone to submit to Victor's aggressive demands.

Jourdan was made the scapegoat for the defeat at Talavera and was replaced by Soult. However, when this marshal was recalled by Napoleon for his planned invasion of Russia, it was Jourdan who was reinstated as Joseph's right-hand man. In 1813 he advised Joseph against battle at Vitoria, and as they rode away from that crushing humiliation Jourdan is reported to have said, 'Well Sire, you have had your battle and it seems it was a defeat.'[18] Despite his opposition to fighting the battle, Napoleon again held Jourdan responsible for the catastrophe, and after being called back to France he was retired.

Marshal Victor, Duc de Bellune, was an able but impetuous corps commander. His lack of respect for both his commander and the British army resulted in unscientific attacks against a strong and determined enemy that met with well-merited failure.

If Jourdan represented the old guard of revolutionary generals, Claude Victor-Perrin represented the new generation of ambitious young officers who ascended to high command under the patronage of Napoleon. Enlisting as a drummer in 1781 just before his seventeenth birthday, Victor was given command of a division just three years later, although he was not made *général de brigade* until two years after that. He saw plenty of action throughout his early career and came to Napoleon's attention in Italy, where he was promoted to *général de division*. He distinguished himself at Marengo and was present at Jena, Pultusk and Friedland, where he again distinguished himself at the head of I Corps. He was created marshal immediately afterwards.

Victor led his corps into Spain, where he defeated a Spanish army at Espinosa at the end of 1808. He accompanied Napoleon at Somosierra and entered Madrid with him. In 1809 he won decisive victories over the Spanish at Uclés and Medellin. At this latter battle he defeated Cuesta's army of 35,000 men with just his own corps of 16,000. By the time of Talavera, Victor had a reputation for outstanding bravery and impetuosity which no doubt went a long way in ensuring he got his way with the rather weak-willed Joseph and cautious Jourdan. There can be no doubt that such a strong-willed and successful marshal gravely underestimated his British opponents at Talavera and paid a heavy price. His night attack on 27 July came close to success, but his stubborn determination to succeed the next day drove him to repeated and costly attacks.

After a subsequent defeat in Spain at Barrosa, Victor returned to France and commanded a corps during Napoleon's invasion of Russia. He again distinguished himself at the crossing of the Beresina, reputedly using Wellesley's reverse slope tactics. In 1813 he fought at Dresden and Leipzig, but it was becoming increasingly clear that he had lost his appetite for war and unwavering belief in Napoleon's star. In 1814 he failed more than once in independent command and was eventually sacked from his command of II Corps. However, he was immediately given command of two divisions of the Young Guard and was badly wounded at the Battle of Craonne. He swore allegiance to the King on Napoleon's abdication and tried to organize resistance to his march on Paris in 1815. Having failed, he joined Louis XVIII in his exile and was struck from the list of marshals by Napoleon. He served in the royal government and died in 1841.

Victor was one of Napoleon's most consistent marshals but was not in the same league as Masséna or Davout. He was never given the same large independent commands and served most effectively under his Emperor's eye. Undoubtedly brave and aggressive, he used tactics at Talavera that lacked sophistication. His succession of heavy frontal attacks allowed Wellesley to maximize his advantages of terrain and firepower, and it was this that lost the day for the French.

Horace-François-Bastien Sébastiani commanded the IV Corps at Talavera. He was a Corsican, like Napoleon, and was commissioned into the army in

Général de division *Horace-François-Bastien Sébastiani, commander of the French IV Corps. He was a cavalryman by trade, and his corps performed well under his command in Spain. The corps suffered heavy casualties at Talavera, but it was they who came closest to winning the battle for the French.*

1789. He served in the cavalry in the Army of Italy and commanded the future Emperor's escort during his overthrow of the Directory. Few could claim such association in the early years of Napoleon's meteoric rise that guaranteed a place in the Emperor's affections. This often spared his reputation from the glaring inadequacies of his performance that regularly followed.

After serving at Marengo, Sébastiani went on his first diplomatic mission to Turkey and Egypt, before becoming *général de brigade* in 1803. He was wounded leading a cavalry brigade at Austerlitz and was subsequently promoted to *général de division*. He then returned to Turkey as ambassador at Constantinople, returning in 1808 to command an infantry division in Lefebvre's IV Corps in Spain. He fought with his division in the victory at Zornoza in October of that year and gained a minor victory on his own account against a Spanish brigade the following month. At the end of the year he was made the IV Corps commander after Lefebvre was sacked for continually disobeying orders.

In early 1809 the IV Corps was deployed to the south of Madrid, protecting it against Cartaojal's Army of La Mancha. In March, Sébastiani made a surprise attack on this army and routed it at Ciudad Real. However, the majority of the Spanish army escaped and Cartaojal was replaced by Venegas. Recalled to join Joseph against Wellesley's advance, Sébastiani skilfully but easily stole away from Venegas and joined Joseph and Victor to fight at Talavera. Despite the heavy casualties suffered at this battle his corps remained effective, and in August he returned to confront Venegas, whom he defeated after a stubborn fight at Almonacid.

Sébastiani continued to command his corps in Spain until recalled by Napoleon to lead a cavalry division into Russia in 1812. His performance during this campaign was less than impressive, and he held the dubious distinction of having his division surprised and mauled by the Russians on two different occasions. Despite this he commanded the II Cavalry Corps in 1813, during which his corps was routed at the Katzbach and he was wounded at Leipzig. As the French army straggled homewards after this defeat, Sébastiani was able to go some way to repairing his reputation by taking a key role in the Battle of Hanau. Leading his much reduced corps in a number of decisive charges he made a significant contribution to the French victory against Wrede's Austro-Bavarian army.

In 1814 Sébastiani commanded the skeleton V Corps in the death throws of the empire. Despite another lacklustre performance he was appointed to the prestigious post of commander of the Imperial Guard cavalry after the Battle of Craonne. This he led with rather more distinction at Reims and particularly at Arcis-sur-Aube, where he again showed himself at his best when leading cavalry to the charge. It was not enough to save Napoleon, but he rallied to the Emperor on his return in 1815, and we can only speculate as to why he was given the responsibility of organizing the national guard rather than a field command. Having retired from the army after Napoleon's second overthrow, he entered politics and held a number of important posts, including those of foreign minister and ambassador to London. On his retirement in 1840 he was made marshal of the empire, though it is likely that this honour was for his service to the King rather than his less than spectacular military career under Napoleon.

Sébastiani was more suited to leading a cavalry charge than high command. His corps at Talavera acted with little 'ensemble', though it was his own division that came closest to winning the battle for the French. While, like many other French generals, he was quite capable of defeating the Spanish, he was rarely able to distinguish himself against more able opponents.

Chapter Four

Tactics

The tactics of the two major protagonists are studied in this chapter in some detail, because it is vital to fully understand how the two sides fought if we are to try to visualize the real dynamics of the battle as we work through the narrative, and particularly important if we are to follow its ebb and flow during a visit to the battlefield. Furthermore, many myths and much ill-informed and jingoistic bias have grown up around this subject, which initially appeared in contemporary accounts and have sadly been reproduced right up to modern times without being contested by further research until relatively recently.

By 1809, while French tactics had been proven in the hard school of battle, the tactics that Wellesley was to use with such great effect in his later campaigns were still to be clearly defined. We shall see the foundations of his future tactical system working at Talavera, but we shall also note that the lessons that Wellesley and his army learnt the hard way at this battle clearly contributed to their further development. As it would be invidious to say that British soldiers were any braver than French ones, we must examine why the British were so successful against the French, who had crushed, with apparent ease, all the other major powers in Europe.

The Development of Napoleonic French Tactical Systems

The tactics that Napoleon's armies used with such success in the early years of the empire had been inherited from the French armies of the Revolutionary Wars. They had evolved in response to the unique make-up and dynamics of the French armies of that era. The parade-ground drill and linear tactics that had been in use in the armies of all the major European powers since the time of Frederick the Great were beyond the capabilities of the large numbers of volunteers and conscripts that were hastily called up for the defence of *La Patrie*. It was therefore necessary to develop a new tactical system that required less training and was better suited to the much larger armies that were created from the *levée en masse*. The two main innovations that made their appearance during this time were the employment of large numbers of skirmishers and the attack column.

The use of light infantrymen trained to fight in open order was nothing new: what was new was the scale on which the French employed them. The French discovered that the new type of soldier the revolution had provided them with – a less disciplined, but more intelligent and free thinking volunteer or conscript – was well suited to fighting in these looser formations. Clouds of skirmishers were successfully used to overwhelm the thin line of enemy light infantry and then to harass the opposing rigid lines of infantry, picking off officers and gunners. They could also provoke them into wasting what was universally accepted as the most effective volley, the first one, against an elusive and open-ordered body. The impact of these skirmishers was as much moral as physical: the opposition stood immobile under a galling fire without being able to reply effectively. This moral effect was not an end in itself but was to have a decisive influence over events that followed: in this case the attack that was subsequently launched against them.

The formation used in this attack was the second innovation. No longer were their assaults delivered in a solid wall of soldiers formed in lines three deep that were difficult to move quickly and maintain in order. Instead, the French developed the attack column, a tactic that has generated, and continues to generate, considerable debate as to its advantages and disadvantages.

Battalion-sized columns had many advantages. With their narrow front they could move quickly around the battlefield, even over difficult terrain, allowing the French to get a decisive force to the critical place at the critical time. Being more compact than line they were easier to keep in order, as the officers and NCOs could more easily maintain control. The flanks of the column were also much more secure than those of a line, and by closing the intervals between the companies the column quickly became a viable square against cavalry. Finally, a flank attack by infantry could also be more effectively countered, as the column was so much deeper than a two- or three-deep line.

The major weakness of the column was, of course, its lack of firepower, and for this reason the line remained the preferred formation for use when on the defensive, even by the French. However, even when on the offensive, Napoleon's well-drilled soldiers were able to deploy quickly from attack column into line if required. In fact the early proponents of these tactics envisaged these columns advancing under cover of the clouds of skirmishers and then deploying into line at a musket's effective range, before overwhelming the opposition by fire after it had been shaken and demoralized by the skirmishers. The decisive attack would then be launched in line with the bayonet.

Despite British propaganda to the contrary, this is exactly what happened at the Battle of Maida. This battle has long been held up as the first example of British lines defeating French columns. In fact, although the French may have manoeuvred in column at this battle, British eyewitnesses agree that they attacked in line. It appears that having received specific orders from their commander (General Reynier) to attack *à prest*, that is without firing, they were relying on a moral ascendancy and the threat of the bayonet to overthrow their enemy. Instead they were met by steady and determined British infantry and drawn into a one-sided firefight that they were psychologically unprepared for.

During their period of victories over other European armies the French realized that success could be achieved much quicker without the need to deploy into line and enter into a firefight. Indeed, experience showed that by deploying into line and firing, it proved difficult to get the troops to resume the advance to deliver the *coup de grâce* with the bayonet. Consequently, there are recorded incidents of attacks being made with unloaded muskets to encourage the troops to close with their enemy. It is perhaps natural that even brave troops were happier firing, when they felt they were hitting back, rather than getting involved in the bloody business of hand-to-hand fighting which history shows rarely actually occurred. Instead, if a heavy artillery barrage had preceded the attack and the skirmishers had done their job well, the steady and resolute advance of a seemingly overwhelming body of men and the threat of cold steel were enough to break the resistance of all but the most stubborn troops. If this coordination had been successful, the enemy line would break and run before the two forces came into physical contact. It was actually this that Reynier was trying to achieve at Maida.

This then was the key to the tactical use of columns by the French, and however much British military commentators have derided it, these tactics had proved successful against all the major military powers of Europe. After their humiliation by Napoleon, the Austrians, Prussians and Russians all copied the use of attack columns in the tactical reforms that were instituted following their defeat. Furthermore, Wellesley's assertion that 'the column could and would be beaten by the line'[1] has been interpreted as meaning that troops in line will always defeat troops in column. Those who wish to interpret it this way seem to have forgotten that the Austrians, Prussians and Russians all fought in line against French columns and were decisively beaten. What Wellesley did not specify when he said this was that there were certain conditions that needed to be met before this would be the case, and as we shall see, it was Wellesley's own tactical innovations that actually generated these.

The French attack column was a simple and flexible formation. It was constructed by each of the battalion's six companies forming into a three-deep line and arranging themselves in a strictly observed order one behind the other. In fact there were two options for this: the preferred option was the *colonne par division*, which had a frontage of two companies and a depth of three (see Diagram 1 overleaf). The other (*colonne par peloton*) had a one-company frontage and a depth of up to six (see Diagram 2).

1. Colonne par division *(two-company frontage)*.

The distance left between each company and the one in front was also significant. If the commander expected to deploy into line, this interval was made big enough to allow the companies to wheel out into this new formation. If the commander wanted to maximize the psychological impact of his formation, or felt there was a significant threat from cavalry, he could close the companies up immediately one behind the other (known as *serrée en masse* or *colonne serrée*: see Diagram 3). It seems, however, that the most popular interval

2. Colonne par peloton *(single company frontage)*.

3. Colonne serrée *(closed column)*.

was a compromise between these two, a half distance. This gave the commander the option to expand or contract his formation, depending on the circumstances, without a considerable time penalty.

As we have already discussed, the light company of a French battalion was normally detached into a skirmish line and the grenadier company could well be incorporated into a combined elite battalion. This would leave only four companies in the battalion. In this case an attack column would form *colonne par peloton* with the companies one behind the other, giving a formation with a frontage of about forty men and a depth of twelve (Diagram 2).

Despite the predilection of the French generals for the use of assault columns, Napoleon often expressed his own preference for *l'ordre mixte*, mixed order. This saw a three-battalion regiment drawn up with one battalion in line and the other two in column on either flank (see Diagram 4). This formation offered the firepower of the line and the mass and flexibility of the column, and promised to go some way towards countering the ascendancy of fire enjoyed by the British. It is strange that this formation was very rarely used in the Peninsula, and it is intriguing to consider whether its use at Talavera would have influenced the result.

To the use of assault columns and strong skirmisher screens, Napoleon added a tactical refinement of his own: concentrated artillery fire on the point at which he planned to make his decisive attack. This often involved the use of 'grand batteries', consisting of concentrations of up to a hundred or so guns designed to batter a single point in the enemy's line. This would remove the need for the attacking troops to use their own fire to set the conditions for the final assault. Napoleon wrote: 'the general who has the skill to unite an imposing mass of artillery, suddenly and without his adversary's knowledge, in front of some point of the hostile position, may be sure of success'.[2]

Although the number of guns used in the Peninsular War did not approach those used in central Europe, the Emperor, in one of the many letters of

4. L'ordre mixte *(mixed order)*.

Battalion in Line

Battalion in Column
(two-company frontage)

Battalion in Column
(two-company frontage)

castigation he sent to Joseph after his defeat by the British, reinforced the need for thorough artillery preparation. He wrote, 'Columns do not break through lines, unless they are supported by a superior artillery fire.'[3] Napoleon himself was clearly well aware that the column relied on a strong skirmisher screen and a powerful artillery to provide the firepower that it lacked itself in order to set the psychological preconditions for a successful attack. Thus the number of muskets in a column that could fire was irrelevant, as there was no intention of it firing at all.

But the efficacy of French low-level tactics was not the only, or the most important, reason for their success. Napoleon had used these methods in his defeat of Austria, Prussia and Russia, but his victories on the battlefield were really the result of the brilliance of his strategic manoeuvres. These put his opponents at such a great tactical disadvantage when it came to battle that they were already half beaten before the fighting started. Napoleon did not generally bother himself with the tactics used by his subordinate commanders and rarely dictated what formations or tactics should be used. The low-level psychological advantages that were inherent in the use of columns by the French were merely further exploiting the psychological superiority that had already been established through Napoleon's strategic combinations and his (and his army's) growing reputation of invincibility. With this psychological advantage, French battlefield tactics then exploited the weaknesses inherent in many of the archaic military institutions of their opponents. Unfortunately for the French, Napoleon's appearance in the Iberian Peninsula was brief, and he never faced the British in battle there himself. His marshals and generals all lacked his strategic brilliance and drive, and were consequently unable to fight the stubborn and confident British with the same psychological superiority.

The Development of British Tactical Systems
It is these psychological aspects of French tactics that Wellesley seems to be addressing in comments he made before leaving London to command in the Peninsula. He is recorded as saying:

> They [the French] have besides a new system of strategy, which has outmanoeuvred and overwhelmed all the armies of Europe. 'Tis enough to make one thoughtful; but no matter, the die is cast: they may overwhelm me but they will not out manoeuvre me. First, because I am not afraid of them, as everybody else seems to be; and secondly, because, if all I hear of their system be true, I think it a false one against steady troops. I suspect all the continental armies were more than half beaten before the battle was begun – I at least, will not be frightened beforehand.[4]

It is the last two sentences of this passage that are the most significant and once again emphasize that it is the psychological dynamics of battle that are the most decisive. As an army's tactics are designed to give it an advantage over its adversaries, the psychological advantages that they offered could be more important than such physical advantages as bringing more muskets to bear. As we study Wellesley's tactics we will see that the power of British musketry, while it earned a fearsome reputation, was not necessarily their most decisive aspect.

Early studies of British tactics attribute their success to a simple and rather crude comparison of the frontages and firepower of the formations used by the opposing forces. Their logic was based on the argument that a British infantry battalion of 600 men deployed in a two-deep line would be able to bring all its muskets to bear, while a 600-man French battalion deployed in a nine-rank column could bring, at best, only 200 to bear. Therefore, given an equal rate of fire the outcome was inevitable. However, I hope that it is clear from the preceding section that those historians who argue this line have missed the point: the column that stopped to fire had already admitted defeat.

Another advantage that is given to the line is that as its frontage would be greater than that of the column, it would be able to 'wrap' around the flanks of the column and pour in a devastating flanking fire. Such a simplistic approach ignores the reality. The French never launched a single-battalion column at British lines that gave the opposing British battalion the opportunity to wrap around its flanks. At the minimum, using the French three-battalion regiment at Talavera as an example, the attack would consist of all three battalions, possibly in a line of three columns or with two forward and one in support. In either of these alternatives a British line would be either unable or foolish (because of the risk of being taken in flank themselves by the support column) to try to wrap around any single battalion's flanks. And even this example is unrealistic because few armies if any would launch an attack in a major action with so weak a force.

A deliberate attack would consist of at least a division (as in all the attacks at Talavera), and the three-battalion columns of a French regiment, depending on the interval between its columns, could be equal to the frontage of a single British battalion. In theory the French force would then be able to almost match the number of muskets in the front rank and have the advantage of the immediate physical support, as well as the psychological support, of the other ranks of the column pushing it forward.

It was standard operating procedure in all armies of the period to protect the vulnerable flank, or flanks, of any attack with a physical feature, cavalry or another infantry formation held back in echelon. If the French failed to take these elementary precautions there was every chance that a British unit, which was not attacked or threatened on its own front, could wheel onto the attackers' flank. This happened most famously at the climax of Waterloo, when the 52nd took the Imperial Guard in the flank, but also at Talavera. However, the flanks of any attack or formation are vulnerable, and in fact the depth of a column actually makes it better able to meet this kind of threat than a two- or three-deep line.

The argument is not whether a line was the best formation for the defensive, as this was generally undisputed (though in the later years of the Napoleonic Wars most countries other than Britain also defended in column because of the poor quality and lack of training of their conscripts). At this time of the wars even the French adopted the line on the few occasions they found themselves on the defensive. The real argument is whether the defensive line was a stronger battlefield tactic than the attack in column, which we must now define as including the psychological 'shaping' of an enemy line by the firepower of skirmishers and massed artillery. French experience had seemed to prove that the attack in column was superior to the defence in line as practised by the Austrians, Prussians and Russians. When the British proved successful where others had failed, the natural conclusion was that this was due to the British use of a two- rather than three-deep line, as even Oman concludes.

It is instructive to look at the introduction of the two-deep line into British battlefield doctrine. In fact both Dundas's regulations for the British infantry (issued by command in 1792) and *Rules and Regulations for the Formation, Field Exercise, and Movements of His Majesty's Forces* (1807) laid down that the line should form up in three ranks, and nowhere in the regulations or orders does it appear that any historian has found it stipulated that they should form in only two. Even in contemporary times, the usefulness of a third rank was a topic of much debate. Its stated use was as a reserve to replace casualties in the front two, to pass its muskets to those in front in order to cut down on the time required to reload and to add some substance to the line. Some nations used the third rank to provide its skirmishers (so almost by definition the rest of the unit actually fought in two ranks). Most nations agreed (except rather interestingly Britain) that the third rank was not to fire its muskets, as not only was the fire unlikely to be effective because of the difficulties of aiming between the two ranks in front, but also because experience showed that it could cause considerable casualties to these troops. The British stipulated that if firing in three ranks the front rank should kneel. However, other countries found that if troops were ordered to kneel it was very difficult to get them to stand back up and advance. In 1813 Napoleon repeatedly recommended to his generals that lines should consist of only two ranks.

In his book *Wellington's Army* Oman states that the use of two ranks had been a tactical innovation used by the British during the American War of Independence. However, he does not make clear why this tactic was developed, though we can be sure that it was not as a counter to the American use of columns as these were not employed at that time. When Dundas's regulations, which laid down a line composed of three ranks, were introduced, he claims that this was accepted only with reluctance by the British infantry, who had to be reminded a number of times by the Commander-in-Chief himself, the Duke of York, that this should be followed. It was only in 1801 that an order allowed two ranks to be acceptable.

Given the apparent lack of any official and specific tactical reasoning for the use of two ranks by the British army, it seems logical that its adoption was driven by necessity and experience rather than the discovery of a brilliant tactical innovation. In fact the only time that any regulation or order specifies the adoption of two ranks is when a battalion's strength has dropped so far that it can no longer maintain the laid down frontage, and it is here that we find the probable explanation. A British battalion had an established strength of 1,000 men broken down into ten companies. Dundas's regulations state that a company should have a minimum frontage of twenty men (that would be sixty men remaining in the company after casualties, the sick and stragglers had been taken into account), so that a battalion's minimum frontage was 200 men (in each of the three ranks). This would mean that in order to occupy its prescribed frontage in three ranks a battalion would have to have a minimum strength of 600 men. Once its strength went below this it was to form in two ranks in order to maintain that frontage.

In the previous chapter we explored the problems the British army had keeping its regiments up to strength without conscription, so it is no surprise that we find a high percentage of battalions on campaign quickly dropping below the 600 mark. By the time of Talavera 20 per cent of Wellesley's army were sick, and after a comparatively short campaign ten of his battalions were below 600 men and a further four only just above. It seems that after years of campaigning through the Revolutionary and Napoleonic Wars, British battalions were more used to forming in two ranks rather than three, and that possibly only later might it have become apparent that it offered incidental tactical advantages.

So it seems that the argument is actually all to do with frontages. After all, in a continuous line, as Wellesley's was at Talavera, it really made little difference whether the line was in two ranks or three, except that a two-rank line could cover a greater frontage. In fact, it can be argued that the three-rank line had the advantage of being able to replace casualties in the front two ranks with men from the third. The problem of his frontage was no doubt a much greater concern to the British commander than how many ranks his men formed up in, and this is well illustrated by the fact that at Talavera he was unable to cover his complete line without having to ask for assistance from his Spanish allies.

So having established that the use of two ranks was not a calculated innovation at the heart of Wellesley's tactical system it is necessary to identify some other reason why he was so successful against the French. What we shall see is that the secret lies in a combination of a number of minor innovations rather than merely the fact that his firing line was deployed in two ranks.

The future Duke of Wellington has often been described as a purely defensive general. This is inaccurate. It is true that in many of his battles in the Peninsula he was forced to fight defensively, even while on a strategic offensive as at Talavera. However, this was generally forced upon him when he suffered from a considerable numerical inferiority. When this was the case he was always very careful in the selection of the battlefield. Given that a battalion volley was unlikely to cause significant casualties on an enemy much more than 100 yards away, he deemed it useless to site troops where they could see much further than this, as it would inevitably expose them to a very heavy artillery fire to which they would not be able to reply. The French were always superior in artillery and, as we have seen, concentrating heavy fire at the point they planned to attack was a central pillar of their tactics.

Wellesley therefore always tried to place his infantry on a reverse slope position, where the lie of the ground provided substantial protection from the fire of artillery that had only a limited capability to drop projectiles into ground that could not be observed. This tactic protected both the numbers and morale of his troops. Eyewitness accounts testify that being caught in accurate artillery fire, and watching your comrades die an ugly death while being unable to reply, is one of the most demoralizing situations for a soldier. Adopting a reverse slope position also had other advantages: it concealed the defender's strength and dispositions from the enemy and forced him to launch an attack with only a sketchy idea of where the opposition's line was. Lying down, a tactic that would have been frowned on as cowardly fifty years earlier, was a further way to reduce casualties from artillery fire. Wellesley insisted in his infantry doing this if they were not threatened directly by attack and particularly if they did not have the added protection of a reverse slope position.

At Talavera it is interesting to note that the ground chosen by Wellesley offered few reverse slope positions to the British troops. However, there were some on the Cerro de Medellin, and an eyewitness tells us that during the intense artillery fire that preceded the first French attack Wellesley ordered both of Hill's brigades to move back from the sky line and lie down. We can only speculate as to whether the heavy casualties that his other troops suffered in this battle from artillery fire helped him to determine on the use of this tactic in later battles.

Having protected his line from the powerful French artillery, Wellesley then had to counter their strong line of skirmishers that protected the vulnerable columns and set the ideal conditions for a successful attack. He did this simply by using an even denser screen of skirmishers himself. Indeed, so strong did these lines of skirmishers become that on occasion the attacking French mistook them for the main line. This actually happened during the main attack at Talavera when the French claimed to have surrounded and captured a

British unit in front of the main British line. It was common to find the light infantry companies of a division amalgamated into a composite light battalion. This would be allocated its own command structure in order to improve their coordination across the whole divisional front. When the army reorganized into divisions at Abrantes, Lord Munster reports: 'The light companies of the regiments composing them [the divisions] were formed into a battalion, which under some intelligent officer, ever marched at the head, and to which was added a company or more of the deadly riflemen of the foreign corps, the 60th.'[5]

The effectiveness of his skirmisher screen was increased by the employment of riflemen. Although the rifle was slower to load than the musket, its superior range and accuracy ensured that the British skirmisher screen was usually able to outmatch its French equivalent. The 95th Rifles are perhaps the more famous of the two regiments of British riflemen, but only a detachment was present at Talavera. However, Wellesley did have the 5th Battalion of the 60th (Royal Americans) Regiment with his army, and, as we have heard, five of its companies were distributed among the infantry brigades to increase the strength of their own integral light infantry.

This combination of the careful use of ground and the employment of a strong light infantry screen as a central plank in his tactical system is well explained by Wellesley himself:

> We place our main bodies, indeed our whole line, behind the heights, at least the summits of them, and cover our front with light troops. [The French] place their lines on the heights, covering them with light troops. The consequence is that not only their light troops, but their line is annoyed by our light troops and they make a bad defence. On the other hand, with us it is an action of light troops only, and if we want the line we bring it on in succession into the position or such parts as is most wanted, still keeping it as a sort of reserve. A [French] general who is thus dealt with knows not where to apply his force, or what is against him except the exposed part of the line; and it is not very easy to make out where it is most vulnerable.

The key to Wellesley's argument against the use of assault columns was: 'I think it a false one against *steady* troops' (my emphasis). The use of the reverse slope, a readiness to get troops to lie down and the employment of a strong skirmisher screen allowed Wellesley to achieve two vital contributing factors to the defeat of the French columns. Firstly he protected his main line from suffering heavy casualties from the French superiority in artillery and the fire of their skirmishers, and, more significantly, from the demoralization that these casualties would have caused. In other words, the French were unable to achieve the vital psychological preconditions that an assault in column required for success.

The other way that Wellesley achieved this 'steadiness' was by a strict discipline: 'the ingrained habit of unhesitating obedience'. He was notoriously contemptuous of the quality of many of his troops and their reasons for volunteering. He therefore firmly believed in the need for the regular use of corporal punishment in order to ensure they did their duty. In battle the main responsibility of the sergeants was to keep the troops in the line, and it is no coincidence that the outdated weapon that they carried, the halberd, was particularly useful for holding horizontally and pressing against the soldier's backs to keep them there.

So having kept the British line intact by not suffering the psychological preconditions that the column depended on to break the will of the defender to resist, the next step was to ensure its defeat. One of the most significant ways of doing this was through superior firepower. Of course the red-coated British infantry was most famous for its disciplined and devastating musketry. As we have discussed, convention has it that the main reason why it appeared that the line always triumphed over the column was that the two-man line enabled every man to bring his musket to bear: the densely packed French columns meant a much higher proportion of shots found a target, and the lower number of French muskets that could fire ensured the contest would always be one-sided. However, although much of this may be true, there are actually two other reasons why the British tactics were so decisive.

The inherent inaccuracy of a technologically unsophisticated, smooth-bore musket meant that an average soldier was quite unsure of hitting a target much further away than a hundred yards. It was therefore generally accepted that in order to have any significant effect muskets needed to be fired in volleys. The idea was that if a sufficient number of muskets were fired at more or less the same time, in more or less the same direction, the law of averages would ensure sufficient hits to have an impact on the target enemy formation. This impact could be manifested in a number of ways. The most obvious was the number of casualties caused could be significant enough to disorder and demoralize the opposition. Equally a decisive psychological advantage could be derived from the fear caused by facing the incredible noise, belching flame and dense smoke that such a volley produced, as well as the dropping of casualties and the screams of the wounded.

From the days of Frederick the Great it was reasoned, therefore, that it was the side that could maintain the quicker rate of fire that would be victorious. The process of taking careful aim was pointless (as the chances of hitting what you were aiming at were small) and time-consuming, so a high rate of fire was considered more effective than slower, aimed fire. The muskets of most nations were therefore not equipped with any sights, and great efforts were made to increase the rate of fire through the design of better ramrods and slicker reloading drills. It was only in the British army that this belief was challenged, at the end of the eighteenth century. In its training camps at this time the troops were trained to level and aim their muskets. Furthermore, like all other armies they were taught to load quickly, and, perhaps more significantly, they trained more regularly with live ammunition. Indeed, many European armies used only blanks during training, as these were considered sufficient to ensure that the load had been effective, and to get the troops used to the sounds and sights of battle. Therefore it appears that only the British army was properly trained in marksmanship. The officers were also taught the importance of levelling and aiming the musket, so that they would ensure that even in the heat of battle the soldiers applied what they had learned.

It is significant that so many contemporary accounts of battle describe apparently devastating volleys that actually caused few casualties, the firing almost inevitably going high. This tendency was the norm when muskets were not held firmly into the shoulder and pointed only rather loosely in the direction of the enemy. The British were taught to aim low down the body to ensure that the chances of hitting the target were increased. It was also widely appreciated that the first volley was the most effective. This was essentially because the musket had been loaded before the battle and was therefore more likely to have been done so correctly. Also, the barrel was not yet fouled by heavy use and the aim was not so rushed because the musket was not being brought up quickly having just been reloaded. The British took care to reserve this most effective volley to the last crucial psychological moment and at a range where it was bound to be devastating. Being on a reverse slope position helped in this regard, as it reduced the temptation to fire too early.

The most critical point that most commentators have missed when discussing the dynamics of the line against the column is the event that caused the catastrophic breakdown of order within the column and which sent it back in rout. The devastating volley, or volleys, was just the psychological 'shaping' of the enemy's morale. The decisive action was the bayonet charge that followed the crushing psychological impact of the volley. It was this that was the final straw that broke the column's will to stand and slug it out at close quarters. Time and again the British line would stop the momentum of the column with a well-timed and accurate volley but rout it by sweeping down on it with levelled bayonets and a rousing cheer. Column versus line was merely a game of chicken in which each side used musketry, skirmishers, heavy artillery fire, surprise, weight of numbers or ground to gain an advantage over its opponents and ensure it was their morale that cracked first and saw them break before contact was made.

Throughout the Napoleonic Wars there were very few occasions when troops actually crossed bayonets. The few bayonet wounds that are recorded were inevitably taken in the back after one side had broken and run, and the pursuers had caught it up. Thus the initial, most effective volley was designed to halt and disorder the column, and the aim of the bayonet charge was more to break its will to resist and to send it scurrying back to its own lines than it was to inflict casualties.

Towards the end of the campaign it seems that the British had identified that a single devastating volley followed by a charge was the most effective tactic. However, there are many instances when several volleys were fired before the charge. This could be because the effect of the initial volley had not stopped the column or that the officers believed that the effect had not been sufficient and further fire was required. There were certainly instances when the conditions were not perfect and the British superiority was not decisive. For instance, at the crisis point of the Battle of Albuera, although the fire of the greatly outnumbered British line did stop the French, they held their ground and returned an effective fire that did not allow the British to execute a charge. The battle at this point degenerated into a close-range firefight, and it was only the superiority of British marksmanship that slowly pushed the French back, with very heavy casualties on both sides. Perhaps it is significant that this battle was one of the few recorded occasions that the French used *l'ordre mixte.*

It was therefore the bayonet charge that followed the musket volley that was the decisive aspect of the British low-level tactics. But one more point must be made. Just as their failure to rally after a charge was the undoing of the British cavalry, so the bayonet charge of the infantry had to be carefully controlled to ensure the line did not lose its cohesion and order that would make it vulnerable to counter-attack by French reserves. It was vital that it was in a fit state to be able to retire and refill the gap left in the line by its charge. A failure to maintain the order of the charge could have catastrophic consequences, as we shall see at Talavera.

The final verdict in the 'column *v.* line' debate is that 'the column could and would be beaten by the line', providing a number of specific conditions had been met. Wellesley repeatedly beat the column through a combination of his carefully chosen reverse slope positions, his strong skirmisher screens, the superior firepower of the two-deep line (which was made up of well-trained and well-disciplined men), and a closely timed and controlled charge with levelled bayonets against a column whose own preconditions for success – an enemy line that had suffered heavy and demoralizing casualties through the combination of a heavy preliminary artillery barrage and an active and elusive skirmisher screen – had been effectively countered, thus leaving the column itself to suffer heavy casualties and the loss of both its cohesion and morale, leading to inevitable defeat. As Talavera was one of Wellesley's earlier battles, it is interesting to note to what extent this successful formula was applied at this battle and which aspects needed further refinement.

Even after Waterloo, when to all British military minds the superiority of the line over the column was an article of faith, many respected European military strategists such as Jomini, who had fought throughout the wars, still advocated the column as the 'default setting' of offensive battlefield tactics. It remains difficult for those of us with an Anglo-Saxon military tradition to accept this, fed as we are on a staple diet of Wellington's victories with a small British army in the Peninsula and at Waterloo. But we forget that the largest and most cataclysmic of Napoleonic battles were all fought in central Europe without British involvement. While the British were unable to put more than 50,000 of their own soldiers in the field, the central European powers, from 1809 to 1813, fought with up to 300,000 on each side. This hardly qualifies us to be the final arbiters of which tactics were the best. What the British army did do was to find a tactical system which best suited its own unique military system and the geography of the countries in which it fought.

Chapter Five

Plans

The Anglo-Spanish Plan

The day after Wellesley had reviewed the Extremaduran Army, 11 July, he had a long meeting with Cuesta to agree the plan for the advance on Madrid. The locations and strengths of the French forces were reasonably well known, thanks to the effectiveness of the guerrillas in collecting such intelligence. Victor's I Corps lay behind the Alberche river just to the east of Talavera with about 20,000 men, Sébastiani's IV Corps was at Madridejos with another 20,000 (although Wellesley believed it was rather less than this) and King Joseph remained in Madrid with a reserve of around 12,000.

Wellesley and Cuesta also had to take into account the French forces to the north, in the Douro valley, as there was the possibility that they could move south against the allied lines of communication in the event of an advance. They knew Soult was at Zamora, still recovering and reorganizing after the humiliation of his defeat at Oporto and his subsequent traumatic retreat. Ney was supposedly far to the north in Galicia, though some reports placed him at Zamora with Soult, and Mortier was at Valladolid. However, neither Wellesley nor Cuesta believed that all these forces could concentrate and pose a threat to their plans. They believed that if Soult was to act it was likely to be against northern Portugal, and if he was to be able to interfere with their operation it would be by moving on their communications. Plans were put in place to cover the defiles at Perales and Baños in the Sierra de Francia to guard against this. To give a little added security to this flank, Sir Robert Wilson's Lusitanian Legion of 1,500 men, reinforced by two Spanish battalions and a squadron of cavalry, was to observe any French forces around Avila, and if there were none around that town, to make a feint on Madrid.

To ensure that Sébastiani was unable to add his forces to those the allies expected to meet before Madrid, they relied on the activity of General Venegas. This general, with the 23,000 Spanish troops of the Army of La Mancha, was to advance on Madrid from his position at Santa Cruz and deny Sébastiani the opportunity to join the remainder of Joseph's forces.

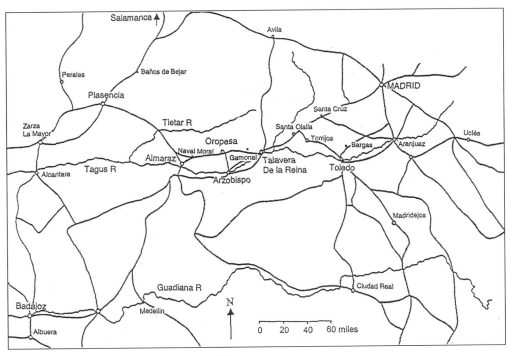

The Talavera Campaign, July–August 1809.

Unfortunately, this plan was based on their belief that the French IV Corps was only 10,000 strong, rather than the 20,000 men Sébastiani actually had. If they had had a clearer idea of the true odds facing Venegas, perhaps they would have been less confident about this aspect of the plan. However, even if the true state of affairs had been known they should still have been reasonably content that Venegas would be capable of fixing Sébastiani in place without getting decisively engaged.

If this strategy was successful, Wellesley and Cuesta would advance on Madrid expecting to meet only Victor's 20,000 and Joseph's 12,000 men, with 56,000 of their own. They could be confident that they would win a pitched battle or, if Joseph chose not to fight, that they would at least force him out of his capital. In the unlikely event that Sébastiani did move to reinforce Joseph, then Venegas would have a virtually unopposed march on Madrid that would force Joseph to turn back or divide his army. What they could not foresee was that Venegas would let Sébastiani slip away without trying to hold him on that front, and then waste critical time in inexplicable marches when there were only 3,000 men between him and the capital.

With the plan laid, Wellesley had only one major concern, and that was the supply situation. He had committed himself to this operation only after the Central Junta had promised to supply his army with the rations and fodder it required and the transport to move it. Although his army was still only at

Plasencia, it was already beginning to experience shortages, and his dispatches of 13–18 July display growing concern about this situation. Although some corn was available there was absolutely no transport – the whole area had already been swept clean of this commodity by the Spanish and French armies who had been operating over this ground for some months.

Wellesley did not fully understand the limited resources of this part of Spain, and if he was inclined to believe that the authorities were being treacherous it was actually merely the fact that the junta was making promises that it was just not able to keep. It is clear that the junta was well intentioned but that from its home in Seville it was as ignorant of the prevailing conditions in that part of Spain as Wellesley was. The consequences were to be serious, but for the time being it appears that Wellesley was hoping that his constant complaints would eventually improve the situation. In a final effort to force the Spanish to take action he wrote to O'Donoju, the chief of staff of the Extremaduran Army: 'If the people of Spain are unable or unwilling to supply what the army requires, I am afraid that they must do without its services.'[1] However, for the present at least it was an empty threat, and he gave the army, now a little over 21,000 strong, orders to march on Oropesa.

The French Situation

Before we look at Joseph's plans in detail it is necessary to quickly examine the situation he now found himself in. While Wellesley and Cuesta were planning the advance on Madrid, Joseph sat in blissful ignorance of the threatening storm. Indeed, on 1 July he received a dispatch from Napoleon directing that Soult's, Mortier's and Ney's corps should be combined into a new army under command of Soult. Their mission was to be another invasion of Portugal in order to throw the British out of the Peninsula. Written on 12 June, this dispatch was hopelessly out of date, as the situation had changed dramatically with Soult's defeat and retreat from Oporto. Despite this, Soult was delighted with his new command, and with Joseph's encouragement started the necessary planning and preparation. In reply to this dispatch, Joseph wrote to his brother, 'I am not in the least disquieted concerning the present condition of military affairs in this part of Spain.'[2] His main concern up to this time had been the rather haphazard manoeuvres of Venegas well to the south of Madrid.

On 9 July, Joseph wrote to Napoleon that the British army had made no significant movement and was still in the neighbourhood of Lisbon. In fact on that day Wellesley and his army were at Plasencia, 200 miles from Lisbon and only 125 miles from Madrid. This lack of intelligence was a feature of the campaign in the Peninsula where the guerrillas kept the allies well informed while the hostile population ensured the French were never able to get a clear picture of where the Anglo-Spanish armies were or what they were planning. Until 22 July, Joseph remained in complete ignorance of Wellesley's move to Plasencia, and devoted most of his time to curbing Soult's ever more ambitious plans. It was on this day that Victor came into contact with Wellesley's advance guard near Talavera and informed him that the British army had joined Cuesta and was advancing on Madrid.

Joseph's Plans

By a quirk of fate, on the same day that Joseph received this news, General Foy, one of Soult's brigade commanders, arrived at his headquarters. This marshal had also received news of the British move along the Tagus and refreshingly, given the constant quibbling that had gone on between them, proposed to move immediately to support the King. He suggested that he should manoeuvre his concentrated army against the British line of communications at Plasencia via Bejar and the Puerto de Baños, while Joseph covered Madrid with the I and IV Corps. If the allies did not immediately move against him then they would be caught between the two French armies and destroyed. The only thing that would stop him moving immediately was the need to await the arrival of an artillery train that was expected from Madrid to replace those guns lost during the retreat from Oporto.

Joseph agreed to this proposal as Soult's forces would have an effect quicker by pursuing this option than if Soult were to move to join up with him near Madrid. Foy was sent back the same day with an order for him to move with the greatest possible haste on Plasencia via Salamanca, where it was hoped he would arrive by the 27th or 28th. Meanwhile it was necessary to concentrate an army that was strong enough to hold the allies until Soult's manoeuvre could take effect. Venegas's failure to press Sébastiani made it perfectly feasible for this general to move the IV Corps to Toledo without any immediate danger, and Victor was ordered to fall back from his exposed position on the Alberche to the same town. Meanwhile, Joseph would leave only a very weak force to protect his capital while he joined Victor and Sébastiani with the forces he had held in Madrid. In this way the French succeeded in concentrating 46,000 men on 25 July at Toledo, a feat that Wellesley and Cuesta had not given them credit for.

The Allied Advance on Madrid

After Wellesley's meeting with Cuesta the British army did not resume its march until 17 July, in order to give the Spanish time to start their own advance. The British crossed the Tietar river and on the 18th entered Talaguela, on the 19th Castinello and on the 20th Oropesa, where the junction of the two allied armies was to take place.[3] The outposts were already in contact with Victor's force whose main body lay around Talavera, only 19 miles away. On the 21st, while waiting for the remainder of his army to come up, Cuesta was invited to review the British army. Soon after, he hurried off to meet up with the portion of his army which had marched from the bridge of Almaraz, by the road through Naval Moral, at Villada. The two armies were now in their predetermined positions.

On the 22nd the Spaniards took the high road towards Talavera, and at the small village of Gamonal, about halfway between Oropesa and Talavera, came into contact with the dragoons of Victor's advance guard. Albuquerque's cavalrymen, who formed Cuesta's advance guard, skirmished with this force, but although they considerably outnumbered the French they made no attempt to force them back. Even when Zayas's infantry division came up the Spanish made no effort to push forward, and one observer declared: 'it is my belief that they would have continued [skirmishing] until now if we had not aided them'.[4] The main body of the British army moved on the French left by a parallel route that took it through the mountains in the direction of San Roman.[5]

After the French cavalry had scurried away, the allied advance found Victor's numerically inferior force in a relatively weak and extended position beyond the River Alberche, 3 miles east of Talavera. Victor thus presented Wellesley and Cuesta with an ideal opportunity to defeat him in detail. Wellesley's proposal for an attack the following day, the 23rd, was received coolly by the Spanish commander, who would agree only to consider the idea. In order to be ready for the attack, throughout the night the British moved their troops forward into position, but to their great amazement and frustration Cuesta's tardy agreement allowed Victor to slip away, and the opportunity was lost. An officer of the 3rd Guards records, 'the disappointment of the troops at not being led against the enemy, whom they had made so many harassing marches to come up with, was very apparent'.[6]

Most contemporary accounts written by British soldiers state that Cuesta had agreed to an attack, but the Spanish commander wrote in his memoirs that only a reconnaissance was planned for that day. Claims that he refused to attack because it was a Sunday are refuted by Wellesley himself: 'he made many other foolish excuses, but that was not one of them'.[7] Meanwhile, Victor had withdrawn towards Torrijos having received Joseph's orders to join him at Toledo.

In another of his mood swings, Cuesta now believed that the road to Madrid was open and he rediscovered the indomitable spirit that he had lacked the day before. Wellesley, however, lacking information on the movements of the French troops around Madrid, and the army finding itself on half rations because of the continued failure of the Spanish to provide either the rations or the transport to move them, declared that he was not prepared to move any further. Furious that his allies were abandoning him, Cuesta determined to push for Madrid alone, confident that Victor's withdrawal had left it uncovered. Wellesley was now in an uncomfortable position. He was not prepared to advance further in the current circumstances, but neither did the situation merit a withdrawal that would inevitably have serious diplomatic implications. Without the direct support of the Spanish army he was left rather isolated and did not have a clear picture of where the enemy was and what he was doing. Obliged to offer Cuesta a measure of support, he pushed Sherbrooke's and Mackenzie's divisions with some cavalry forward to the

Alberche, and searched the Talavera area for the best available defensive position to occupy in case he was attacked.

On the 25th Cuesta was dismayed to learn that Victor's I Corps had been joined by Sébastiani's IV Corps and King Joseph's Guard. He now faced 46,000 men on his own. The French, having learnt that it was only Cuesta that was before them, advanced on the morning of the 26th hoping to defeat the Spanish, whose advance guard had reached Santa Olalla, before Wellesley was able to come to his support. The Spanish general, however, realizing that he had no hope of defeating such a force on his own, gave immediate orders for a retreat. Although his rearguard suffered a mauling at the hands of the advancing French cavalry, Cuesta's main body was able to conduct a rather disorganized but unhindered withdrawal, the French failing to take advantage of a significant superiority in both the quantity and quality of their cavalry. A more determined action from Victor's troops would undoubtedly have brought them significant benefits; instead Cuesta was allowed to withdraw to the Alberche, where he met Sherbrooke's and Mackenzie's divisions. The Spanish army bivouacked on the eastern bank of the river.

With the Alberche still between him and Wellesley, Cuesta and his army were still in a potentially perilous position. Again, Victor did not seem to realize the opportunity that had offered itself: with only the smallest amount of energy and determination he could have destroyed the Spanish army without Wellesley being in a position to significantly assist his allies.

Wellesley, realizing what a critical situation Cuesta was in, visited him in an effort to persuade him to cross the Alberche and join his own army at Talavera. Despite his precarious situation, Cuesta had one more trick to play on his helpless ally: having concentrated his army on the east bank of the Alberche, Cuesta refused to contemplate joining Wellesley's main position. As even a general of Cuesta's limited ability could see that staying on the banks of the river was extremely hazardous with a superior army approaching, there can be no doubt that his refusal was just another example of the bad feeling that existed between the two commanders. Having finally given in to Wellesley's pleadings, he was later to boast that he only consented after making 'the Englishman go down on his knees'.[8] Whether he meant this metaphorically or literally is immaterial, for Wellesley was well aware that his own position was untenable without the support of the Spanish troops, and that the dent to his pride was a price worth paying.

Chapter Six

27 July 1809

The Preliminaries

Early the next morning the Spanish troops filed across the Alberche bridge covered by the two British divisions. It was not until midday that the first French cavalry patrols were seen and the last British troops moved to the western bank. Sherbrooke led his troops back to the main position while Mackenzie's two brigades, with Anson's light cavalry, took position around the Casa de Salinas, a derelict fortified house, as the rearguard.

There then followed an incident that illustrates how the British army of 1809 was not yet the instrument with which Wellesley was destined to push the French out of the whole of Spain and Portugal. The area that Mackenzie's brigades occupied was covered in woods and olive plantations that were not dense, but gave poor visibility. For this reason the light cavalry was sent to the rear as it could neither manoeuvre nor observe the enemy. It can be presumed that the position was occupied only because it offered protection against the cavalry that was the only French force that had so far been seen.

Little did the British know, however, that the tardy pursuit of the Spanish by the French cavalry meant that the French infantry had had time to catch up with their fellow cavalry. The division of Lapisse had now closed up on the Alberche and was able to ford the river further to the north and then deploy unseen by Wellesley's forces. Some British officers claim that their movement was hidden by the smoke of burning huts that had been built by the French on the east bank of the river when they occupied the area, and set alight by the British on their withdrawal, but the truth is easy to find. The regimental history of the 2/87th records: 'There was no gunfire to be heard; it was a hot afternoon; and lulled by a false sense of tranquillity, Donkin apparently let his men lie down in the shade of the trees without having taken any adequate defence measures.'[1] Schaumann, a commissary with the King's German Legion, admitted, 'These troops ... if the truth be told, had actually surprised our light [*sic*] division.'[2]

This print well illustrates the formal posting of sentries in the French army, each placed in view of the next and briefed by an NCO. It was the failure of the British to carry out this procedure properly that resulted in a number of incidents that were to reflect badly on the army at Talavera.

Having successfully crossed the river unseen, Lapisse wished to take full advantage of his good fortune before he was discovered. Rather than waste the advantages of achieving surprise he launched the three battalions of the 16ème légère into the attack before the rest of his troops were up. At the time of their attack, Wellesley himself was in one of the towers of the Casa de Salinas, looking out for the French. The assault caught Donkin's brigade completely by surprise and it is reported that some of its troops were killed before they were able to form up. Wellesley himself was unaware of the French attack until the first volley of musket fire, and was forced to rush to his horse and ride to safety as the French light troops reached the house. He narrowly avoided being captured, the consequences of which, had it happened, would be hard to imagine.

The 2/87th and 1/88th of Donkin's brigade, and the 2/31st of Mackenzie's, were all broken by the initial onslaught and 'were driven in disorder from in the forest',[3] leaving behind about eighty prisoners and many casualties. Fortescue is perhaps a little generous to the 2/31st when he states, 'The 31st, though only a second battalion, behaved remarkably well, bearing apparently the brunt of the fight, for it lost over 100 killed and wounded.'[4] Only the steadiness of the two most experienced regiments of the division averted a complete catastrophe. The half battalion of the 5/60th of Donkin's brigade was beyond the frontage of the French attack and able to open fire on its flank. The other, the 1/45th, which had fought valiantly at Vimeiro – 'a tough old regiment, was never shaken for a moment'[5] – also held the French up while Wellesley and their own officers rallied the routed regiments. Facing these two steady regiments, the French I Corps was introduced to British firepower for the first time. Although the 9ème légère could not see this engagement, the sound of it in the distance still made an impression: 'It was the first time that we had heard the noise of an English fusillade ... indeed, never had we heard a rolling fire as well fed as that.'[6] Once the initial impetus of the French attack had been halted and the disordered regiments rallied, the British carried out an orderly retreat covered by the 1/45th and 5/60th and Anson's light cavalry, which had been sent back when the sound of musketry was heard.

The French did not give up the assault after their initial success, and two batteries of horse artillery were brought forward which continued to harass the British withdrawal. However, the steadiness of the two rearguard units had saved the division from a more serious mauling and they were able to move back to the main British position without further mishap.

This episode revealed the inexperience of some of the British troops who had allowed themselves to be surprised even while their commander-in-chief was in their midst. The history of the 45th says, 'our troops were quite unprepared for such an event; some young corps were surprised, and consequently did not behave well'.[7] Their failure had cost them dear: over 90 soldiers remained in the hands of the French and well over 300 men were killed or wounded; the 2/87th alone had lost 198 men. Colonel Guard of the 45th was among the wounded. It is estimated that the French losses were about 100, but in the absence of any figures this is clearly no more than a guess. The consequences could have been worse still if Lapisse had felt he had the time to commit his entire division to the attack. In the event, a single regiment of three battalions had been sufficient to disorder an entire British division. This action should have served as a lesson for the British, as it exposed the failure of their pickets to give the main body sufficient warning of the French attack. But as we shall see, this was not to be the only example of this failing on the 27th.

On its arrival at the main British line Mackenzie's brigade was allocated a position forming the second line on the centre right of the British position. However, no staff officer appears to have met Donkin to give him any directions, and on his own initiative he took up position on the southern slopes of the Cerro de Medellin, a hill at the northern extremity of the British position, where he seconded the KGL brigades of Löw and Langwerth. Meanwhile, Victor pushed his troops forward after the retiring British rearguard, and when he saw that they had taken up position on the Medellin he called forward his corps artillery. These guns quickly deployed and opened fire on the British line. In the gathering gloom of the evening this fire was not very effective, and though the British artillery replied, it also rather wasted ammunition in a pointless exchange.

While the positions taken by the British redcoats on the higher ground were clear to the French, further down the hill the allied line could not be so clearly made out through the olive groves, orchards and undergrowth that bordered the Portiña brook. As Victor's corps settled into position opposite the Medellin, with the infantry divisions and the corps cavalry under Beaumont drawn up behind the artillery, Latour-Maubourg's six regiments of dragoons took position opposite the Spanish part of the line in the south. Not long afterwards they were joined by Merlin's cavalry that had been sent forward by Joseph. The King was still some distance behind with Sébastiani's troops. In an effort to establish the extent of the allied lines Merlin sent some of his cavalry forward to reconnoitre.

At this time Wellesley was at the southern tip of his own line behind Campbell's brigade and had a grandstand view of what happened next. The artillery duel thundering in the background clearly unnerved some of the Spanish soldiers, and when the French cavalry patrols appeared through the olive groves to their front they panicked. Four battalions unleashed a tremendous volley and, seemingly scared by the noise of their own muskets, broke ranks and rushed to the rear shouting 'treason'. Wellesley described what happened in a letter to Castlereagh:

> Two thousand of them ran off into the evening of the twenty seventh, not 100 yards from where I was standing, who were neither attacked, nor threatened with attack, and who were only frightened by the noise of their own fire. They left their arms and accoutrements on the ground, their officers went with them, and they plundered the baggage of the British army, which had been sent to the rear. Many others went who I did not see.[8]

The battalions who ran were the 1st Battalion Leales de Fernando VII, the two battalions of the Badajoz Infantry Regiment and the battalion of the Imperial de Toledo. The last three battalions had been hastily reconstituted after being almost destroyed at the Battle of Medellin, and were made up of young conscripts lacking proper training. These battalions were part of Portago's division that was in the Spanish front line. The battalion of Leales de Fernando had been part of the garrison of Badajoz, and now formed part of Manglano's division in the Spanish second line. Their lack of experience in the field no doubt contributed to their being swept away by the flight of the others.

Some of these fleeing Spanish units were met by other British troops hurrying forward the next day, one of whom reported: 'I wish I could assert with truth that this retrogression was confined to our Spanish allies. But the truth must be told, and I regret to say that stragglers from the British army were among them, taking a similar direction to the rear. As they passed, they circulated reports of a most disheartening nature.'[9]

Given the strength of the cavalry patrols that appear to have prompted this rout and the fact that the remainder of the Spanish army held its position, there was never any danger that the French could exploit the situation. However, the occurrence can hardly have enhanced the already poor opinion that the British had of the Spanish soldiers as they contemplated the coming battle. Cuesta, no doubt humiliated in the eyes of his allies by the actions of these battalions, decided after the battle to execute 200 of the men who had been rounded up. Wellesley spoke up on their behalf in an effort to spare them, but a member of the 7th Fusiliers reported after the battle: 'Early in the morning some twenty five Spanish soldiers, dressed in white, attended by several Popish priests, were marched in front of our regiment and shot ... These unfortunates belonged to regiments that had given way in the late battle.'[10]

The growing darkness put an end to the useless waste of artillery ammunition and both sides appeared to settle down for the night in preparation for the mighty clash that was inevitable the next day.

The Battlefield

It is now necessary to consider in detail the ground that Wellesley had carefully chosen to fight the coming battle. At first sight it does not suggest itself as a particularly strong position, and indeed it is not. However, in the circumstances it was the best available: Wellesley had had sufficient time in the area to look at all the options. Although the Alberche had offered a tempting obstacle to fight behind, the British commander had discounted it, writing to O'Donoju (one of many Spanish officers of Irish descent whose predecessors had fled to France and Spain to fight the British): 'no position could be worse'.[11] The eastern bank, which the French would have occupied, dominated the west, and the river itself was little use as a barrier as it could be forded almost all along its length. However, the ground Wellesley selected for his line of battle offered a number of advantages that may not be immediately obvious.

The town of Talavera, lying along the River Tagus, provided a secure anchor for his right flank. Talavera was only a small town of about 10,000 inhabitants, most of whom had fled when the French had occupied the area prior to the arrival of the allied army. The old part of the town was surrounded by a considerable wall which, although crumbling, would still provide reasonable protection if it was needed. Many of the buildings had been looted and ransacked by the French soldiers.

Wellesley's position was roughly along the line of the Portiña brook that runs down from the mountains and meets the Tagus in Talavera. As we shall see, the allied line crossed this stream about midway down its length, as it is only in its upper reaches, as it runs between the high ground of the Cerro de Medellín and Cerro de Cascajal, that it becomes significant. Here the banks are steep and quite high and it forms a substantial obstacle. Further south the stream bed is insignificant and other features offered better protection to the troops in the line. In the summer of 1809 the stream was virtually dry and contained only pools of brackish water.

For about a mile to the north of the town the ground is virtually flat, 'covered with olive trees, and much intersected with banks and ditches',[12] but then starts to rise with the slightest of slopes to where there is a small but perceptible rise at a place called the Pajar de Vergara. This feature has been variously described as a 'hillock' or 'large mound'; however, both these descriptions are something of an exaggeration, and many modern historians admit to being unable to locate it at all. Wellesley himself described it as 'a commanding spot of ground',[13] and another eyewitness a 'small eminence'.[14] The Pajar marked the point where the ground levelled off into a plain. The first part of this plain was also covered in olive groves, but before the ground started to rise again towards the Medellin it was 'perfectly open and covered with long grass'.[15] Thus most of the southern half of the battlefield made both observation and manoeuvre in compact formations difficult. Beyond the plain an increasingly steep climb starts up the Cerro de Medellin. This hill forms part of a ridge that runs roughly north-east to south-west and parallel to the River Tagus.

The Medellin is the highest point of this ridge and its summit offers excellent observation across all the surrounding countryside, right down to Talavera itself. It is no surprise that Wellesley placed himself here for most of the battle. The history of the 45th describes the Medellin as 'impregnable when held in force',[16] but although it is a challenging climb to a body of men in formation while under fire, perhaps 'impregnable' is a little too strong a description. To the north-east of the highest point is another, lower, height that rises between the summit and what were the French lines on the Cerro de Cascajal on the far side of the Portiña brook. This small ridge-line is not clearly shown on many maps of the battlefield and tends to be ignored by most commentaries, yet it is clear from visiting the battlefield that it must have been here that the British line deployed.

To the north of the Medellin ridge-line lies a long and shallow valley which then rises steeply to the rugged mountains of the Sierra de Segurilla. This valley offered an attractive avenue of approach to attack the Medellin without having to negotiate the Portiña and the steep, broken and narrow approach from the east; the history of the 45th Regiment describes it as the 'weak point in the line'.[17] The only obstacle along the valley appeared to be the line of the Portiña brook. Although here in its upper reaches it was a water obstacle of no consequence, particularly at this time of year, one of its small tributaries had cut a ravine into the softer ground of the valley floor which presented an obstacle that was difficult to spot and negotiate. The British cavalry were to discover this obstacle rather late and to their cost.

Deployments

Although the town of Talavera was small, its buildings and its crumbling but substantial walls offered excellent cover. To the north on the gentle slope, enclosures, olive groves and gardens also offered excellent protection. It was therefore here that Wellesley deployed Cuesta's Spanish troops. The problems of their inability to manoeuvre on the battlefield and brittle morale would be nullified to a large extent by deploying them on the defensive behind good cover. This portion of the line was little more than a mile long, a relatively short frontage for Cuesta's 30,000 men. He was therefore able to deploy his troops in three lines, giving his position plenty of depth, a vital ingredient in a defensive position. His Vanguard Brigade of light infantry and Zayas's 1st Division occupied the eastern outskirts of Talavera, with a brigade of four regiments of cavalry on the flat open ground next to the river. Forming a second line behind them in the town itself was Iglesias's 2nd Division. The 3rd and 4th Divisions of Manglano and Portago were in a double line to the north

An old British map of the battle showing the action of the 27th, the French counter-attack in the centre and the final French attack in the north. The Portiña brook met the Tagus in the town of Talavera and not as shown here.

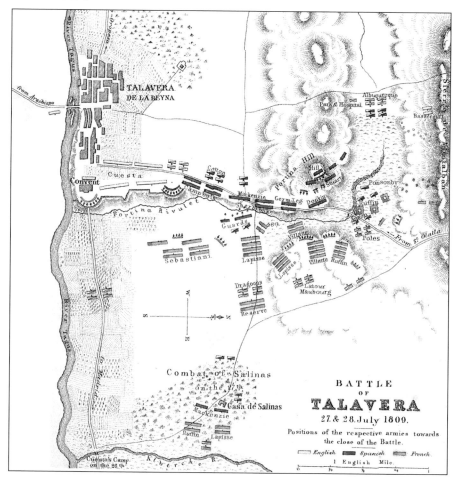

of the town. Here they occupied very strong positions, with the front line protected by a sunken lane and walls.

The second line was behind the Portiña: though it was no obstacle in itself, the wooded banks offered some protection. The whole front was covered by olive groves and enclosures that were occupied by skirmishers and denied both sides much room to manoeuvre, fields of fire or observation. The main drawback to the position from a defensive perspective was the lack of good shoots for the artillery, so the batteries were spread along the line where they offered the best protection for the infantry. The army reserves, consisting of Bassecourt's 5th Division and Albuquerque's cavalry division, formed up behind Manglano's and Portago's troops, with the cavalry in the second line and the 5th Division in the third.

The British sector of the line started at the Pajar de Vergara feature that lay on the French side of the Portiña brook. This had been strengthened by an earthworks designed to take a battery of guns. It was not particularly impressive; a space had been levelled 80 yards long and 20 feet wide, and the dirt thrown up into a wall 3 or 4 feet high. It seems that this work was never completed, 'having been interrupted by the unlooked-for rapid advance of the enemy'.[18] Into this redoubt was placed Lawson's battery of 3-pounders. To the immediate left of this battery was General Alexander Campbell's 4th Division; firstly his own brigade of the 2/7th and 2/53rd, and to its rear, forming a second line, was Kemmis's brigade consisting of the 1/40th, 97th and the 2nd Battalion of Detachments. These troops stood astride the Portiña.

To the north of Campbell were the four brigades of General Sherbrooke's 1st Division. These provided the centre of Wellesley's line and all stood behind the Portiña. They extended across the most exposed part of the plain and up the eastern slopes of the Medellin in the order: Henry Campbell's (1/Coldstream Guards, 3rd Guards), Cameron's (1/61st, 2/83rd), Langwerth's (Light Companies and 1st and 2nd Battalions KGL) and Löw's (5th and 7th Battalions KGL). Across the front of the KGL brigades the banks of the Portiña were steep and high and posed a substantial obstacle to an attacker.

Forming the second line of this part of the front were General Mackenzie's 3rd Division and all the British cavalry. Mackenzie's brigade of the 2/24th, 2/31st and 1/45th stood behind Campbell's Guards brigade, and to their left was the light cavalry brigade of General Cotton (14th and 16th Light Dragoons). Further back was the rest of General Payne's cavalry division, consisting of his own heavy cavalry brigade (3rd Dragoon Guards and 4th Dragoons) and Anson's light brigade (1st Light Dragoons KGL and 23rd Light Dragoons). Mackenzie's second brigade, that of Donkin (5/60th, 2/87th and 1/88th), which had suffered so badly that morning, stood on the southern slopes of the Medellin, directly behind the KGL brigades of Langwerth and Löw.

General Hill's 2nd Division was committed to the defence of the key to the British position, the Cerro de Medellin. The northern slopes of the hill were to be defended by Stewart's brigade (1/29th, 1/48th and 1st Battalion of Detachments), and the eastern slopes by that of Tilson (1/3rd, 2/48th and 2/66th). As the rest of the army occupied their positions, Hill's division remained encamped on the reverse slopes of the Medellin. The consequences of this oversight we shall see later.

The 5/60th Regiment of Donkin's brigade, as a rifle-armed battalion, was trained to fight both in line and as skirmishers. They had therefore given up a company to each of the brigades of H. Campbell, Cameron, Tilson, A. Campbell and Kemmis to thicken up the skirmisher screens made up of their own brigade's light infantry companies. This left the battalion with only five of their ten companies in line (although no doubt at least one of these would have been used with their own brigade's skirmishers). A company of KGL light infantry provided Langwerth's skirmishers (who were also uniformed in green and armed with rifles). These were some survivors of the KGL Light Battalions that had formed part of Moore's army the previous year. This left just the brigades of Löw, Stewart and Mackenzie having to rely only on their own light infantry companies to provide their skirmisher screen. Whatever the logic behind the distribution of these specialist companies, we do know that a thick line of skirmishers covered the complete front of the British army.

Wellesley's left flank, therefore, rested on the Cerro de Medellin, a strong, but by no means impregnable, position. The valley that ran to the north between the Medellin and the Sierra de Segurilla appears to be an excellent approach, and, though the mountains would have made a better anchor for his left, Wellesley felt they 'appeared too distant to have any influence on the expected action'.[19] Although he was proved to be wrong in this assumption he had no troops to further extend his line anyway. In order to cover a potential flanking move from this direction, some of Stewart's troops on the Medellin faced north and half of Rettberg's battery was later placed on the northern slopes to cover against this threat. However, an attack from this direction remained a concern for Wellesley, and it is no surprise to find that later he was to obliged to weaken other parts of his line in order to send troops to strengthen this flank.

Rettberg's battery was initially placed in line 'between the first and third divisions',[20] covering to the east from where it would be able to supplement the fire of Heyse's KGL battery positioned to the rear left of Löw's brigade. Eliott's battery covered the front of Cameron's brigade, sited in a strong position above the Portiña. The final battery, that of Sillery, was left in reserve in the second line behind the 1st Division.

At this time the allied army had only Victor's corps before it. The heads of Victor's columns had appeared about 7.00 pm, closely following the horse artillery that had continued to harass the withdrawal of Mackenzie's division after its earlier skirmish. King Joseph and the rest of the French army were still some way behind and only crossed the Alberche, $4\frac{1}{2}$ miles to the east, as Victor drew up his troops opposite Wellesley's line.

The ground facing the position of the allies generally reflected that on which they stood. To the south was flat ground or gentle slopes, covered by olive groves, enclosures and brushwood. Because of this the French were unable to see the Spanish army in any detail, and Latour-Maubourg's six regiments of dragoons (the 1ème, 2ème, 4ème, 9ème, 14ème and 26ème Regiments) were drawn up to observe this area of the line. This cavalry force was soon to be joined by Merlin's light cavalry division (10ème and 26ème Chasseurs à Cheval, Polish Lancers and Westphalian Chevaux-Légers). Their job was to reconnoitre the Spanish position, and it was one of their patrols that had provoked the Spanish panic that evening.

Victor's three infantry divisions all took post facing the British sector of the line. Ruffin's division (9ème légère, 24ème and 96ème de ligne) occupied the Cerro de Cascajal hill which lies opposite the Cerro de Medellin on the other side of the Portiña. This hill is considerably lower than the Medellin and in contrast slopes far more gently down to the stream that runs between them. However, although the ground occupied by the British line dominates its rather flat top, it makes an excellent location for drawing up a considerable force of artillery. From here it could hammer away at the high ground opposite and cover the attack columns formed up behind. Villatte's division (27ème légère, 63ème, 94ème and 95ème de ligne) followed Ruffin's troops onto the flat ground of the Cascajal. Further to the south, Lapisse's division (16ème légère, 8ème, 45ème and 54ème de ligne) formed up facing Sherbrooke's brigades on the lower ground opposite the British centre. The corps cavalry under Beaumont (2ème Hussars and 5ème Chasseurs à Cheval) halted in a second line behind Lapisse.

The Night Attack

As Wellesley's troops started to settle down for the night, Victor, on the high ground opposite, had no intention of ending the day's fighting just yet. Having occupied Talavera and the surrounding area in the previous weeks he was well acquainted with the ground, and fully realized the importance of the Cerro de Medellin. Understanding that it was the key to the British position and would therefore feature prominently in the coming battle, he resolved to seize it by a surprise night attack.

Victor's decision has been criticized by many commentators on the battle. Oman writes: 'To attack in the dark across rugged and difficult ground was to court disaster.'[21] However, it was clearly a courageous decision that, had it succeeded, would have made Wellesley's position untenable and forced him to withdraw if he had been unable to recapture it with an immediate counter-attack. Night attacks were a rare occurrence in the warfare of that era, as it was believed that it would be impossible to maintain control and order in the darkness. However, achieving surprise and taking risks often produce results out of all proportion to the potential consequences of failure. As we shall see,

Victor's gamble came within a whisker of success, and even its eventual failure could hardly be called a disaster.

While waiting for his whole corps to come up Victor had had plenty of time to establish the British deployment. For some unexplained reason, Hill's division, which was responsible for this vital piece of ground, had not fully occupied its position. His two brigades had stopped on the reverse slope of the hill about half a mile short of their battle positions, where they had bivouacked and sent only pickets forward. The only troops that can be said to have truly occupied the hill were those of Donkin's brigade who were established on the southern slopes, but not the summit, after moving back from their earlier scare on the Alberche. The two KGL brigades of Löw and Langwerth were further down the slope to the south-east.

It is quite possible that Victor had noticed that the hill was not strongly held and it could have been this that determined him on such a hazardous but potentially decisive attack. To him it appeared that the summit was virtually bare of troops. Hill, who as Wellesley's most trusted and experienced subordinate had been given the task of holding this key terrain, admits that he dined in Talavera and arrived to find his division misplaced only late in the evening. He was in the process of sending it forward when the French launched their attack. If he had been very much later what followed would almost certainly have been dramatically different and possibly even catastrophic for Wellesley.

Victor did not discuss his plan nor seek permission for its execution from his commander-in-chief, King Joseph. In his history of the campaign Oman suggests this was because he held the military prowess of the Emperor's brother to no account and did not want his opportunity for a stunning success vetoed by his nominal superior. However, as Joseph was still some way behind with the main body, and it was likely that the British would surely move more troops onto such vital ground sooner rather than later, Victor may well have felt that he had to seize the opportunity while it was there. Delay caused by trying to locate his commander and then discussing his hazardous plan would reduce the chances of success even if he agreed.

Victor's plan was to use Ruffin's division for the assault on the Cerro de Medellin, while that of Lapisse launched a noisy demonstration against the British centre further to the south. Ruffin's division was to advance in three regimental columns: the 9ème légère in the centre, the 96ème de ligne on its left and the 24ème de ligne on its right. It is not clear what time the assault started, but Sergeant Nicol of the 92nd (Gordon Highlanders), a member of the 1st Battalion of Detachments who was an eyewitness to this attack, described Lapisse's demonstration as taking place 'after dark'.[22] It clearly distracted the British centre from what was about to strike to the north, as the same witness states that 'the French made a charge of infantry without success. From the place where we stood we could see every movement on the plain.'[23]

But of course the real assault was not coming from across the plain, and Ruffin's division achieved complete surprise when it launched its own attack at 10.00 pm when it was 'very dark'.[24]

An officer of the 9ème légère, Lieutenant Girod, reports that the regiment formed three battalion columns for the attack: two in the front line marched level with each other, while the third moved behind to act as the reserve. Meanwhile, on the British side, the 7th KGL was settling down for the night, lying in its battle position on the lower slopes of the Medellin. Their own pickets had not been thrown forward very far and consequently were not in a position to give their unit much warning of the tempest that was about to descend on them.

Some commentators suggest that this failure was because Löw believed that Hill's division was providing outposts across his front, and that this is why he did not take what would have been more adequate security measures. This task was normally carried out by the division's own battalions and it seems strange that he thought that this would be done by troops from another division.

Whatever the reason for the misunderstanding, the German unit was totally unprepared for the audacious French attack and was therefore quickly broken. The history of the King's German Legion states that the 7th Line and part of the 5th were 'thrown into confusion by the suddenness of the attack, were charged by the French column and gave way'.[25] In a matter of minutes the 7th Battalion lost 150 of its 557 men, half of whom were prisoners. The other KGL battalion of Löw's brigade, the 5th, lay to the right of the 7th, and although it was not in the direct path of the French it was bundled back down the slopes of the hill and was not rallied for some time.

Having reorganized themselves after their initial success, the men of the 9ème légère continued the climb up the hill with shouts of 'Vive l'Empereur!' Their encounter with Löw's brigade had taken place somewhat to the south of the highest point of the Medellin, but now they slightly changed their direction to head for the summit. Unwittingly, this change in direction ensured that most of the regiment avoided a head-on collision with Donkin's brigade, which occupied the second line behind the Germans, and gave them a route almost clear of British troops. However, at least one of the battalions came into contact with this brigade, and after an exchange of fire and a 'brilliant charge'[26] was repulsed. The story is taken up by Lieutenant Girod:

> We had already reached two thirds up the height without meeting any enemy when suddenly we received a terrible discharge of musketry, that in an instant caused us to suffer a heavy loss: nearly 300 men and 13 officers, among which our Colonel, my Chef de Bataillon, our two Adjutant-Majors and our two Carabinier captains, in a nutshell, the principle commanders of our two columns were put *hors de combat*.[27]

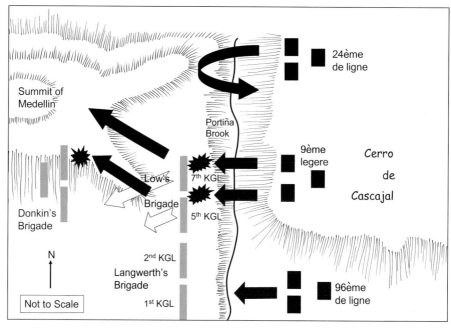

The Night Attack, 27 July.

However, Donkin's brigade did not block the route to the summit and the 9ème légère worked round his flank and carried on up the hill. By this time the French light infantry was in some disorder, and it can have been little more than a crowd of men who made the summit.

As the sounds of this attack reached the ears of General Hill he was just forming up Stewart's brigade in order to lead it forward into its battle positions. Not believing that there was a substantial attack, he nevertheless warned the brigade to be prepared to support the Germans. 'Not having an idea', he wrote, 'that the enemy were so near, I said to myself that I was sure it was the old Buffs, as usual, making some blunder.'[28] However, seeing the flashes of firing on the summit of the hill he moved forward with Brigade Major Fordyce to see what the commotion was. Approaching the crest he shouted for the men to cease firing, only to find himself among the skirmishers of the 9ème légère: 'a French soldier got hold of my right arm and would have secured me if my horse had not at that moment sprung forward'.[29] This soldier then fired at him but only succeeded in wounding his horse. Unfortunately, Fordyce was killed in this fracas, but Hill managed to make his way back to the safety of his own men.

The first unit Hill met was the 1st Battalion of Detachments and he sent it up the hill to confront the French. On the outbreak of firing Stewart had established that this battalion was the closest to the summit, and to cries of 'The hill! the hill!'[30] it was sent forward. The battalion arrived on the summit before the main body of the 9ème légère, but was facing due east while the

French attack was coming from the south-east. Thus the French regiment, having recovered some order, came up at an oblique angle, and some of the British troops found themselves in its rear. The French opened a heavy fire on this single battalion and were able to grab a large number of prisoners. Nicol reports, 'they seized some of our men by the collar and were dragging them away prisoners'.[31]

The Detachments suffered seventy casualties in this engagement as well as losing the prisoners. Lieutenant Girod claimed: 'We had found and made

Lord Hill, commander of the British 1st Division. One of Wellesley's favourite and most able subordinates, he must nevertheless take much of the responsibility for how close the French came to success during their night attack on the evening before the battle.

captive approximately 200 Scots in kilts (these were the first we had ever seen) and we had also seized two cannon.'[32] This number of prisoners may have been taken, but many of them were able to escape in the darkness and inevitable confusion. It is also quite possible that the French had overrun some of Heyse's battery, which was deployed just to the north of Löw's brigade, but were subsequently unable to drag the guns to their own lines when they were thrown back.

Lieutenant Girod claims his regiment occupied the summit of the Medellin but, seemingly unsupported by the rest of the division, his commanding officer 'was soon convinced that it was impossible to hold this position; indeed, masses of enemy infantry advanced in the darkness threatening to surround us'.[33] To the British challenges the French tried to trick the lead British troops by replying 'Españioles' and 'Allemands',[34] and those who were fooled were captured or killed.

As the 1st Battalion of Detachments engaged the French, Hill, without changing his wounded horse, put himself at the head of the 29th and led the men forward. They advanced in column of companies and quickly came up behind the Detachments, which was just as well. Although this battalion was made up from companies of experienced soldiers, the fact that they had no great loyalty to their present temporary unit meant that they lacked the cohesion and ethos that was the very strength of the British regimental system. This lack of unit cohesion, and the confusion of the fight in the dark, began to tell, and they were in danger of breaking. Nicol admits, 'affairs hung in the balance'.[35] As the 29th came up one of its officers recalled of the Detachments: 'The soldiers seemed much vexed, we could hear them bravely calling out "There is nobody to command us! Only tell us what to do, and we are ready to dare anything." There was a fault somewhere.'[36]

The 29th, which had fought with distinction at Roliça and Vimeiro, came through the thinning and increasingly disorganized ranks of the 1st Battalion of Detachments. The forward company delivered a volley into the leading French troops and then charged forward with bayonets lowered. The French unit did not wait to meet the charge and the 29th 'sent them into the valley below', despite the best efforts of their officers to 'slow the race of our men'.[37] As the 29th advanced to follow up its success the men became aware of another French column moving across their front. Wheeling into line to face the new threat they delivered a telling volley into their flank. Unable to reply effectively to this threat, and perhaps already aware of the disorganized retreat of their comrades, they also beat a hasty retreat back down the hill.[38]

This was most likely the 9ème légère's third battalion advancing in support of its comrades. However, it could also have belonged to one of the other regiments of Ruffin's division. The 96ème de ligne was to have turned the Medellin on the left flank of the 9ème légère. However, after crossing the Portiña brook the men found themselves faced by a particularly steep slope that held up their advance. As they attempted to negotiate this obstacle the KGL light companies of Langwerth's brigade engaged them. This contact developed into a ragged firefight that caused the German light infantry quite heavy casualties, but did not involve the 1st and 2nd battalions of the KGL who were in line behind them. As it became clear that the main attack had failed, the 96ème withdrew without substantial loss.

The 24ème de ligne was supposed to assault the Medellin from the valley that ran to the north of this hill. However, it appears that no attack developed from this direction. The reason for this is unclear. Most accounts claim that the men were disorientated in the dark and, unable to find the point of attack, gave up the attempt. This is unlikely as the ground had been seen in daylight, and the Medellin was a very distinctive feature only a few hundred yards from the French lines. This explanation seems little more than an attempt to support the argument that the night attack was ill-conceived from the start, rather than a genuine attempt to explain its failure. It is more likely that the natural aversion to night attacks, the confusion caused by trying to maintain formation over difficult terrain, and then the uncertainty caused by the sound of heavy fighting on the hill all combined to ensure that the attack was not pushed forward with any resolution.

So ended the controversial night attack; Nicol claims it was eleven o'clock when the firing finally ceased.[39] Although it had failed, it had surely been rather too close to succeeding for Wellesley's liking. The reason that it came so near to unhinging the British commander's plans was evident: the negligence of one of his most trusted subordinates. It was probably to protect his friend that this daring attack gets only a passing mention in his dispatch covering the battle and actually portrays Hill as the saviour. Wellesley stated: 'Early in the night he [the French] pushed a division along the valley on the left of the height occupied by ... Hill [of course it was not actually occupied] of which he gained a momentary possession; but ... Hill attacked it instantly with the bayonet, and regained it.'[40]

The French admit to losses of about 300, including 65 prisoners. The commander of the 9ème légère, Colonel Meunier, was struck three times in the encounter with the 7th KGL and taken prisoner, but he was recovered from a hospital when the French reoccupied Talavera six days after the battle. The British loss was higher. In his dispatch on the battle, Wellesley wrote: 'We lost many brave officers in the defence of this important point.'[41] Löw's two battalions lost 187 men, 88 of whom were prisoners; the light companies of Langwerth's brigade lost 36 men; the Battalion of Detachments, 69 men; and the 29th, 55. In total the British loss in this action is given as nearly 400.[42] It could well have been worse, for, as we have seen, Girod claims to have captured substantially more prisoners but admits that many escaped in the confusion of their subsequent repulse.

There is no doubt that the British had suffered a scare, and the first priority was to secure the Medellin against another attempt. Consequently, Stewart's brigade occupied the summit of the hill. Because of the potential for chaos caused by moving troops in the darkness, the brigade was not formed up in its proper order of seniority, which was the strictly adhered to norm. Instead, the brigade deployed into its battle positions in the order that required the least amount of swapping battalions around in the dark. Thus the 29th ended up on the left, with the 1st Battalion of Detachments in the centre and the 48th on the right. Hill's other brigade, that of Tilson, carried the line on from Stewart's right to Löw's brigade, which closed up on Langwerth's, so that they ended up a little further south than their original deployment.

To increase security further, the British pickets were sent forward to the banks of the Portiña brook. Here they were so close to their French counterparts that they could hear the challenge of 'Qui vive?' called by their sentries as the French officers and NCOs conducted their rounds. On a number of occasions the outposts fired on each other, and the sound of this firing often forced the British units to 'stand to' in case it heralded another French attack. Such was the British nervousness that at one stage the whole of Sherbrooke's division opened fire on an imaginary French assault. An anonymous sergeant of the Guards noted in his memoirs:

> By a sudden impulse on the left the ranks commenced a kind of firing resembling a *feu de joie*, which communicated from one battalion to the other and ran down with the rapidity of lightening, and by this our battalion alone had one lieutenant colonel mortally wounded and our adjutant was also wounded in three places and expired in the hands of the French.[43]

A number of other men who were out on picket duty were killed and wounded, and it was only the quick thinking of some of the NCOs who, seeing the rolling fire coming towards them, got their men to lie down and consequently avoided even greater casualties.

Wellesley settled down for the night with his staff on the Medellin, wrapped only in their cloaks. The whole night was to be marked by uneasiness and nervousness – the bickering of the outposts, the regular 'stand to arms' and the sound of French artillery being deployed on the far side of the Portiña, their positions marked by burning torches. This was hardly the psychological preparation a soldier needed prior to his first major battle.

Chapter Seven
28 July 1809

After a much-disturbed night the British officers awakened their battalions well before daybreak in order to be in position in case of a dawn attack by the French. Deserters that had come across the lines during the night had warned them that such an attack was planned. The dull morning light revealed the majority of the French army deployed before the British lines. It was clear that they had every intention of leaving only a small holding force of cavalry in front of the Spanish army in order to concentrate all their infantry to smash its way through the fragile looking red-clad line. Victor's divisions occupied the area of the Cascajal, with Ruffin on the right opposite the British left, with Villatte's division behind him in the second line. The corps cavalry of Beaumont was in a third line. To Ruffin's left, opposite Sherbrooke on the lower slopes of the Cascajal, was Lapisse's division with Latour-Maubourg's six regiments of dragoons in support.

To the south of Lapisse and Latour-Maubourg, opposite the right of the British line, the Pajar de Vergara and part of the Spanish army, was Sébastiani's corps. The French division commanded by Sébastiani himself formed the right next to Lapisse, and to his left was the division made up of Dutch and German troops commanded by Leval. Behind Leval were two battalions of excellent Polish troops of Valence's division, the other four battalions of which had been left behind to help cover Madrid. Next to the Poles in the second line was Merlin's light cavalry division. Further south, facing virtually the whole of the Spanish army were just some light infantry companies from Leval's divisions and 2,300 cavalry commanded by General Milhaud. Finally, the army's reserve consisting of Joseph's brigade of Guards, the brigade of Dessolles and two regiments of cavalry were well back towards the Casa de Salinas.

Of particular concern to the British must have been the number of guns that faced them, given the meagre means at their own disposal. This powerful artillery was well placed in a seemingly endless line across the front of their position that was not covered by olive groves. With a distance between the two protagonists of 600 to 800 yards (Nicol claims it was only 200 yards!)[1] they

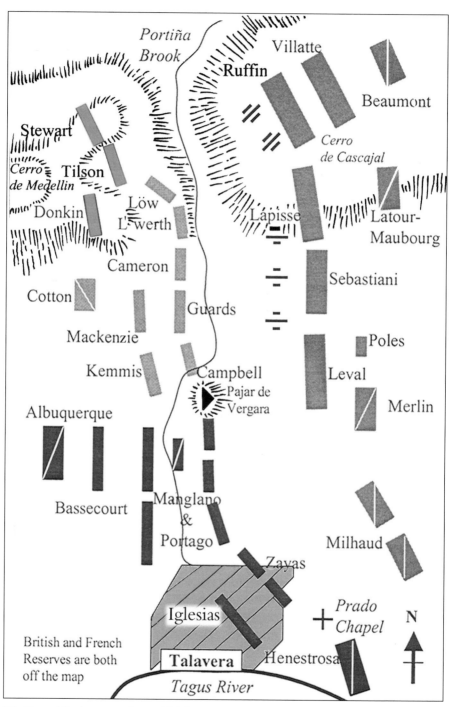

The General Deployment at Dawn, 28 July.

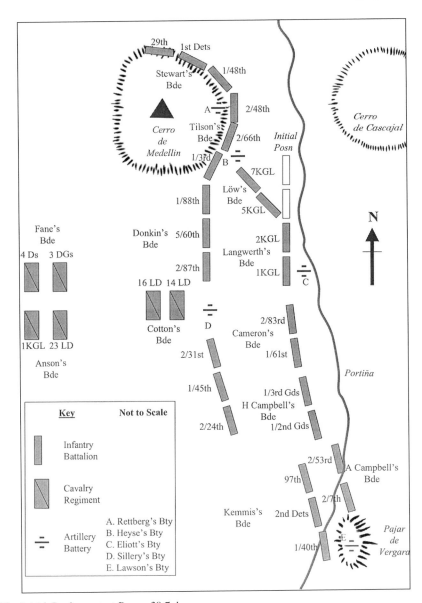

The British Deployment at Dawn, 28 July.

were well within their maximum range, and the lack of cover for the British soldiers did not bode well.

Wellesley's tactic of placing his troops on a rear slope was not appropriate on much of the terrain that was available at Talavera, and this early in his career it must be doubted whether he had fully refined this tactic. Even on the Cerro de Medellin the main ridge-line ran north-east to south-west, so even here there was not the same amount of cover that was evident in Wellesley's later defensive battles in which his deployments ran along distinct ridge-lines. There can be little doubt that the pounding his troops received at Talavera helped to determine him on this aspect of the tactics for which he became famous.

Despite the seeming inevitability of battle, the truth is that as dawn broke King Joseph had not yet decided on a general action, still hoping that Soult's manoeuvre would force the allies into a withdrawal without a battle. Given the British shortage of supplies and diminishing confidence in their allies, news of such a move would inevitably have forced Wellesley to abandon his march on Madrid and head back towards Portugal. There was no real need, therefore, to waste soldiers' lives trying to gain an advantage that would be achieved without the shedding of blood.

After his check the night before, Victor had sent his chief-of-staff, General Châtaux, to report what had happened to the King, and to inform him that he planned to renew the attack the next morning if he did not receive orders to the contrary. General Châtaux takes up the story: 'I arrived at midnight close to the King to give him an account of the situation of I Corps and to take his orders. I was given nothing.'[2] I suspect that Victor was not too upset by this lack of direction as it gave him carte blanche for his actions on the morning of the 28th. He probably had the suspicion, even if he was not sure, that, apart from the King, both Marshal Jourdan and General Sébastiani were likely to be against an attack. However, Victor was determined not to miss the opportunity to destroy the small British army. He seems to have been determined to win the laurels that would come from capturing the strongest point of the British line and no doubt gain prestige in the eyes of his Emperor.

At first light Joseph and his headquarters were still not on the battlefield. Once again Victor sent General Châtaux back to him, this time to explain his plan to renew the attack and to request that Sébastiani and the Reserves support him. Both the King and Jourdan feared the wrath of the Emperor if they cancelled the attack, as the Marshal would surely write to Napoleon describing how they had wasted the opportunity of destroying the British army. Therefore, instead of countering Victor's plans, Joseph decided to endorse the attack but to exert a certain measure of control and authority over his difficult subordinate by refusing to commit any other troops than the I Corps until there was some evidence of success.

Napoleon's own grand strategy prescribed the destruction of the enemy's field army as the first objective of a campaign, followed by the occupation of his capital. It is therefore fair to assume that he would have supported Victor's proposal for a battle rather than a plan that envisaged a strategic manoeuvre that would force Wellesley's retreat, but leave his army intact. In his later correspondence Napoleon poured scorn on Soult's movement on Wellesley's rear, and castigated his brother for not uniting that Marshal's troops with his own and destroying the allied army by the use of overwhelming force. Soult's manoeuvre on Wellesley's communications was not calculated to destroy the

British army, which would continue to be a threat to French ambitions in Spain as long as it remained in being. By the destruction of the British army as Napoleon would have wished, the French would have secured Madrid and then had the option of invading a weakly defended Portugal or defeating the unsupported and still disorganized Spanish armies.

The First Attack

Alexander the Great's favourite battlefield tactic was to attack the most strongly held point of his enemy's line, as he reasoned that this was where their commander most feared an attack. Therefore, if he was to prevail by concentrating all his combat power on this single point he would win the battle without heavy fighting and casualties elsewhere. In a decision reminiscent of Alexander, Victor again planned to attack the strongest point of the British line, the Cerro de Medellin. The difficulties of attacking the hill, up a steep, rocky slope and on a relatively narrow front, were obvious, but it remained the key to Wellesley's line and thus 'the grand object of their desire'.[3] He who remained in control of the Medellin would probably win the battle, and so Victor was seduced into an unsophisticated frontal assault on this vital ground.

No thought was given to manoeuvring the British off the heights. Although Jourdan was opposed to an attack as he thought the Medellin was 'impregnable to a frontal attack',[4] he made clear in his memoirs that after the failure of the night attack the army should have formed up in the valley to the north of the British position, which was then unoccupied by any allied troops, and the Medellin should have been attacked from that direction at daybreak. This would have approached the hill from a less difficult direction and threatened the exposed flank of the British left. The assault would have been supported by a deception attack on the shaky Spanish army to the south. This plan offered the possibility of securing the hill without risking what would inevitably be heavy casualties. It is quite possible that Victor may have supported such a move in other circumstances, but he was still to fully appreciate the capabilities of the British army; after all, their performance in the previous twenty-four hours had been less than inspiring.

Victor's plan was to launch a diversionary attack with Lapisse's division, supported by Latour-Maubourg's cavalry, on the lower, southern slopes of the Medellin, while Ruffin delivered the main attack on the heights. Villatte's division would provide the reserve. Ruffin deployed his men with the 24ème de ligne on the left, so that they faced Tilson's brigade, and the 9ème légère on the right opposite Stewart's. The 96ème de ligne remained in reserve.[5] In this encounter the French would have an advantage in numbers of about 1,000: 4,900 Frenchmen against 3,700 British.

Oman states that the attack was made in three large regimental columns, but this is unlikely. Usual French practice would have had them in individual battalion columns, and Fortescue states, 'We know for certain that each battalion was in close column of double companies',[6] although he does not give his source. The Earl of Munster has them in this formation,[7] and the regimental history of the Buffs has them in 'nine ranks',[8] suggesting the same. The only possible advantage of regimental columns was if the advance was restricted to a narrow frontage or in the hope of intimidating the opposition by conveying an image of irresistible force. Individual battalion columns would have been easier to control and maintain in order. What is certain is that an advance in line would not have been able to keep its dressing and order over such ground, even if the French had been inclined to use it.

By launching such a localized attack and committing a relatively small proportion of his troops to the actual assault, Victor would get neither the benefit of surprise nor concentration of force, both of which can be vital to the success of an attack. Wellesley, meanwhile, would quickly be able to identify where the attack was coming and concentrate solely on that point. To believe that such a strong position could be taken in this way can only be the result of breathtaking overconfidence on the part of the French Marshal.

At 5.00 am a signal gun on the Cerro de Cascajal initiated a tremendous artillery barrage from over fifty French guns: 'Their guns began to pour grapeshot and shell into our lines.'[9] Wellesley, with only eighteen guns of his own on this part of his front, was unable to respond effectively, and the French pummelled away at the British line. It was only on the Medellin that the troops were able to drop back behind the slope and escape the fire that was proving very accurate. A witness describes how: 'they served their guns in an infinitely better style than at Vimeiro: their shells were thrown with precision, and did considerable execution'.[10] The history of the 24th also relates that 'The men fell fast from shot and shell', but goes on to say that 'The brigade was therefore ordered to lie down, and then the roundshot did little damage.'[11] An ensign in the 3rd Guards also described the effect of this barrage on the troops:

> a tremendous cannonade – shots and shells were falling in every direction – but none of the enemy were to be seen – the men were all lying in the ranks, and except at the very spot where a shot or shell fell, there was not the least motion – I have seen men killed in the ranks by cannon shots – those immediately around the spot would remove the mutilated corpse to the rear, they would then lie down as if nothing had occurred and remain in the ranks, steady as before. The common men could be brought to face the greatest danger, there is a spirit which tells me it is possible, but I could not believe that they could be brought to remain without emotion, when attacked, not knowing from whence. Such, however, was the conduct of our men I speak particularly of the Brigade on 28 July, and from this steadiness so few suffered as by remaining quiet the shots bounded over their heads.[12]

Initially this barrage was very effective, but by giving orders for the troops to lie down the casualty rate was reduced considerably. It appears that the brigades of the KGL suffered the most from this fire as they were ordered to throw back their left. This produced something of a dog-leg in the British line but brought them 'close under' Heyse's battery.[13]

Firing artillery between hills meant that the solid iron balls tended to bury themselves straight into the ground rather than bounce in the way they did on flat ground. This considerably restricted their effectiveness, as unless the shot was very accurate it would cause few casualties. A bouncing cannon ball, however, could continue to cause casualties until it finally came to a stop. Even a seemingly innocuous rolling ball could take off a man's foot. For the troops on the lower slopes of the hill and the gentle slope down to Talavera, where the ground allowed the French artillery to maximize their effectiveness, there was no escape other than to lie down. Once this had been done, the effect of the bombardment was largely psychological.

We do not know how long this morale-sapping barrage went on. Oman reckons on about forty-five minutes before the French assault columns began their attack on the Medellin. The smoke from the French guns hung low in the damp, early morning air, and a gentle easterly wind blew it into the faces of the British line, obscuring their view. Because of this the British heard the French advance, rather than saw it. The sound of the French drums beating the attack through the veil of smoke must have been quite disconcerting to the troops who could not see what was happening ahead of them, especially as for many of them this was their first real battle. Their feelings of anxiety could not have lessened as the sounds of firing came ever closer, as the skirmishers of each side fought for an advantage. However, pushed on by the inexorable advance of the columns behind its opponents, the British skirmish line was reluctantly and slowly pushed back. Working in pairs, with one loading while the other chose a target, the British line slowly retired with great control and maintaining a steady fire.

General Hill sat on his horse on the Cerro de Medellin trying to make sense of what was happening in the smoke that obscured his view down towards the Portiña. He could have been in little doubt that his division, and the hill upon which it waited, was the objective, but as he heard the bickering of the light troops in front of him he was probably still unsure of the strength of the attack. Because the British line was above them, the French artillerymen were still able to fire on the heights over the heads of the advancing infantry columns.

By the time the first of Hill's skirmish line came into view through the smoke, he must have been getting quite frustrated. By now the enemy artillery would have been forced to cease its fire or switch it against other targets so as not to endanger its own men. It was clear that the British skirmish line successfully held up its French counterparts and was still not pressed too closely. The men were determined to make an impression on the enemy, retiring in order and continuing to fire and manoeuvre in their pairs as if at drill. Hill was known as a mild-mannered man, not prone to outbursts of anger or frustration, but as the tension mounted his impatience got the better of him. Wanting his frontage cleared to receive the French with his fire he ordered the light infantry bugles to sound the recall, and was heard to shout: 'Damn their filing, let them come in anyhow.'[14]

Now the French artillerymen had ceased fire the smoke slowly cleared, and their infantry columns could be seen moving up the hillside. This must have been a hard climb: the slope is steep and rocky. It was inevitably very difficult to keep any semblance of order, and the pace of the advance must have been slow.

As the heads of the columns approached within 100 yards of the ridge-line, Hill gave his battalions the orders to stand up and advance so they looked down on the advancing French. The six battalions delivered a shattering volley that brought the columns to a standstill, as the front ranks fell in disordered heaps and the following ranks hesitated. The stunned survivors returned what was obviously a ragged and uncoordinated fire as they attempted to wrest back the initiative.

But this running fire was never going to be able to subdue the regular, crushing volleys that erupted from the British line. The French momentum was blunted by this devastating fire, and their formation fell apart as the rear ranks, unsighted by the men in front of them and hidden from the British line by the increasingly thick clouds of smoke from the musket fire, pushed forward to join the fight. As they pushed forward, the wounded and less stout-hearted of the front ranks started to drift to the rear. Despite having begun their attack with a numerical advantage, the numbers were quickly levelled out by the terrible toll now being taken, and as casualties mounted, particularly among the officers and NCOs, the order and cohesion of the columns was lost.

On this part of the field, where Hill's division had the benefit of high ground, the defence was conducted in almost textbook fashion. Wellesley's defensive system is perfectly illustrated by the actions of the 2/66th who were part of Tilson's brigade. Ensign Clarke describes his battalion's actions:

> Our orders were to lie down behind the ridge until the enemy's column had reached the top, then to rise, deliver a volley, and charge. I was sent to the summit by the commanding officer to let him know where the enemy were and returned with the intelligence that a strong column was only fifty yards off. The volley was delivered and we rushed on them with the bayonet. At first they appeared as if they would stand the charge, but when we closed they wavered, and then turned and ran down the hill in the wildest confusion.[15]

It is interesting to note that in nearly every case of a column disintegrating, the first soldiers to run were those from the rear. Eyewitnesses testify that the column tended to get narrower at the front as it advanced. It seems that the less determined soldiers in the front ranks slowly started to drop back towards the rear. Once the column came under fire, those in the front ranks, unable to turn back because of the press of the ranks behind them, soon became embroiled in a fight for their lives. The braver men coming up behind replaced those who had fallen and spread toward the flanks in order to be able to fire, temporarily at least expanding the column's frontage. The men behind, who actually might have had every intention of doing their duty, were unable to advance because of the mass of men in front, no doubt frightened by the noise and confusion ahead and aware of the wounded and more cowardly moving past them to the rear. Unable to occupy themselves by firing and perhaps suddenly pushed back by the men at the front facing a determined bayonet charge, it was these men who were most likely to have broken first. It is hardly surprising, then, if the front ranks, having suffered much from the deadly volleys and aware that they were being deserted, turned about rather than face hand-to-hand combat in which they would be at a considerable disadvantage.

Meanwhile, just to the south of this attack, it quickly became apparent to Sherbrooke that his front, though covered by the division of Lapisse, was not in danger of attack. He therefore ordered the 5th KGL to pivot to the left and take the columns of the 96ème in the flank. Had Lapisse advanced in echelon in support of the attack as we have heard was Victor's plan, Sherbrooke could not have dared to do this, but now was the folly of Victor's unsupported attack fully exposed, as the 5th KGL opened fire on the vulnerable and already shaky flank of the 96ème. Not even the French accounts offer an explanation for Lapisse's inactivity and apparent ignoring of his orders.

The sudden fire from an unexpected direction put the French in an impossible position, and at this point Stewart's brigade on the left of the British line was ordered to charge, apparently by Wellesley himself. The consequence of this charge is well described by a participant: 'on we went, a wall of stout hearts and bristling steel. The enemy did not fancy such close quarters, and the moment our rush began they went to the right-about. The principal portion broke and fled, though some brave fellows occasionally faced about and gave us an irregular fire.'[16]

The momentum gained by charging down such a steep slope and the adrenalin of success took all six of Hill's battalions down the hill to the Portiña. The more enthusiastic even crossed the stream and started up the more gentle slopes of the Cascajal. However, here they came under fire from the French artillery and Villatte's uncommitted division, and they scampered back to safety and reformed on the lower slopes of the Medellin. One can assume only that Villatte's division was unable to take advantage of the disorder in the British ranks caused by this charge because of the debris of Ruffin's division that was falling back towards it. Once they had reorganized their ranks the

British fell back on their original line and stood ready to face a second attack.

A French account of this attack has Colonel Jamin, commanding the 24ème de ligne, shouting 'Au revoir Messieurs les Anglais' as he retired with his survivors, and receiving a mocking reply from a British officer of 'Au revoir Monsieur le Colonel; au revoir messieurs!'[17]

As can be imagined, Ruffin's division suffered heavy losses in this ill-conceived attack. Oman calculates them as fully 1,300 men in an action that took no more than forty minutes. But the losses were not all one-sided, and Hill's brigades returned to the high ground about 750 men shorter, including the commanding officer of the Buffs, Lieutenant Colonel Muter, who was wounded during the attack and died of his wounds the following day. Hill himself also received a wound from a musket ball to the head that forced him to hand over command of his division to Tilson and retire from the field, though it did not turn out to be serious. Despite the ratio of nearly two to one, this hardly reflects badly on the outgunned and outmanoeuvred Frenchmen in an encounter that is often depicted as a one-sided slaughter. Lord Munster recalls:

> The dead of the enemy lay in vast numbers on the face of the hill, and had been tall, healthy, fine young men, well-limbed, with good countenances; and as proof of their courage, (the head of their column having reached within a few yards of the top of the hill before being arrested,) the bodies lay close to our lines.[18]

The charge of the 29th Foot at Talavera: 'on we went, a wall of stout hearts and bristling steel'. The 29th had earned an excellent reputation fighting at Roliça and Vimeiro, and had saved the situation during the French night attack on the 27th. They were highly regarded by Wellesley, who regretted having to send them back to England to recruit, as they had no second battalion to draw on. (Courtesy of the Regimental Headquarters of the Worcestershire and Sherwood Foresters Regiment)

As the weather was very hot, the men were immediately set to work to bury the dead and this work commenced even as the French artillery continued its fire on the British line.

There are few battles in history where modern authors do not criticize the tactics used by the losers. This is very easy to do with the benefit of hindsight and without having had the experience of command in battles of this time, with all the difficulties that were inherent in trying to control events while surrounded by both the physical and psychological 'fog of war'. However, even Victor's supporters must find it difficult to understand how he could have believed that such an attack, on the strongest point of the British line, effectively unsupported and with such a fraction of the overall French forces, could really have had a reasonable chance of success.

Oman's verdict on this attack is not flattering: 'It was a rash and unscientific operation, and received a merited chastisement.'[19] An hour and a half after their advance, Victor's men were back where they had started, licking their wounds and no doubt reflecting on the large numbers of their comrades that had fallen. It was clear to the French chain of command that the British were not going to be frightened off the hill, and if they were to achieve this it would need a rather more coordinated and synchronized operation than the one that had just failed so dramatically. But in the light of this latest failure the first decision that needed to be made was whether another assault should be launched.

While the senior French commanders gathered on the Cascajal to discuss their next move, the French artillery fire died down and the French soldiers were fallen out to prepare their breakfast, covered by a strong line of pickets. The sight of the French troops preparing their food 'was a painful sight to us, who felt acutely for our starving soldiery, who began to experience the most pinching want'.[20] The same commentator tells us that Wellesley himself was approached by a soldier who requested the order to attack, 'for when engaged they forgot their hunger'.[21]

This pause in the battle also saw a temporary, undeclared truce break out that marked the fighting in the Peninsula from that in central Europe. From early in this war the soldiers of each side developed a mutual respect for each other that lasted throughout the fighting in Spain and Portugal. Men from both sides went down to collect water from the Portiña brook; it was developing into 'an intensely hot' day.[22] In no time the men who had so recently been killing each other were communicating as best they could and were soon joined by their officers. Nicol recalls, 'both armies went for water as if a truce was between us, looking at each other, drinking, and wiping the sweat from their brows, laughing and nodding heads to each other; all thoughts of fighting for the time forgotten'.[23] A young officer of the 29th even returned two crosses of the Légion d'Honneur taken from the bodies of French officers that had fallen close to the British lines.[24] After a short conversation it was agreed that each could cross the small stream to collect their wounded from the earlier fighting, and soon there was confusion as blue and red uniforms passed each other as they moved backwards and forwards searching for their wounded comrades.

Interlude

While these acts of mercy were being played out below them, the French commanders argued whether the bloodletting should continue. For his part, and no doubt feeling somewhat humiliated by his earlier failures, Victor was determined to continue the struggle. No doubt this was motivated as much by his thirst for revenge as a real belief that the British could be forced to abandon their positions. Now they had come forward, both Joseph and Jourdan could see the strength of the British position for themselves.

Joseph was unconvinced that a further attack should be attempted, but if it was, it should be mounted against the British left using the shallow valley between the Medellin and the Sierra de Segurilla as an approach. Jourdan, in contrast, favoured moving onto the defensive, as he felt the French were there to stop the Anglo-Spanish advance on Madrid and not attempting to invade Portugal. As Wellesley was on the strategic offensive, it could be argued that he had rather tricked them into an attack in the first place. Jourdan's preference was for a withdrawal to the line of the Alberche to adopt a defensive line on the eastern bank of this river.

Victor declared that the reason that he had failed previously was because he had been left to conduct the attack unsupported; if the attack was made with the efforts of the whole army then success was assured. Although he was right to suggest that a concerted effort would greatly improve the chances of success, he seems to have forgotten that he had launched the earlier attack with less than a third of his own forces. Determined to get his way, he swore to take the Medellin if Sébastiani's two divisions attacked the centre of the allied line at the same time, and that if they could not take the Medellin, 'we ought to give up soldiering'.[25] However, with Sébastiani supporting Jourdan's defensive proposal, it seemed that Victor would not get the opportunity to have another crack at the British.

However, it was while the generals were debating their next move that two dispatches arrived with news that would significantly change the strategic situation. The first came from General Valence, the governor of Toledo, who announced that Venegas had appeared before the town and his troops were already skirmishing with the Polish outposts. This was the first news that Joseph had received about this Spanish army for some time, and until now he had been unsure of its whereabouts. Venegas was now only two days' march from Madrid, and Valence had only four battalions of Poles with which to oppose the 23,000 men that made up the Army of La Mancha.

The second dispatch came from Marshal Soult: in it he complained that he had still not received the artillery reinforcement he had been promised. He declared that he would not be able to move until it had arrived and that he was also still awaiting the arrival of the VI Corps from Astorga. He would therefore be unable to reach Plasencia until 3 August at the earliest, and possibly up to three days later. This news meant that he would not be in a position to directly threaten Wellesley's rear for up to six or seven days.

These two pieces of news forced Joseph's hand. If he did not immediately attack the Anglo-Spanish army he would have to march against Venegas, who posed the most immediate threat to Madrid. In order to be sure of having sufficient force to beat the Army of La Mancha he would not be able to leave behind a force stronger than 30,000 in front of Wellesley. However, this force was threatened with defeat by the British general, who now had no immediate need to draw off to confront Soult and would, with his Spanish allies, have a considerable advantage in numbers. If, however, Joseph were able to defeat Wellesley on the 28th, his army would still be strong enough to frighten off or even dispose of Venegas. He finally concluded that he now had no option but to attack.

The French commander resolved not to make the same mistake that Victor had made in the morning, and planned to concentrate all his combat power against the British portion of the allied line. Joseph does not appear to have contemplated attacking the Spanish, although suggestions that the reason was that they occupied such strong ground hardly seem plausible, given the many occasions that the French triumphed over them in stronger positions than they now held. Joseph ordered Victor to storm the Medellin, this time by outflanking it to the north so as to turn the British line and manoeuvre onto a more advantageous approach that would minimize the advantage that the hill offered to the defence. Victor's assault on this key position was, however, something of a diversionary attack. The main effort would be an attack on the British centre and right by Sébastiani's IV Corps, whose two divisions numbered 14,000 men and had not yet been engaged. If all went well, Wellesley's position on the Medellin would be made untenable by penetrations of his line to its north and south. The Spaniards would be left in their strong positions with only Milhaud's dragoons to observe them and cover the exits from Talavera.

Even after the losses of his two earlier abortive attempts on the heights, Victor still had 16,000 men available for his part in the assault. Ruffin's division, which was now about 3,700 men strong, was sent to the extreme right of the French line, into the shallow valley. His mission was the turning movement around Wellesley's left flank. To reinforce him, and no doubt to stiffen his tired and much depleted troops, Victor sent Cassagne's brigade of Villatte's division (consisting of the 27ème légère and 63ème de ligne). To support Ruffin's attack Joseph also attached Merlin's division to him, consisting of four regiments of light cavalry, and these formed up in the valley behind the infantry.

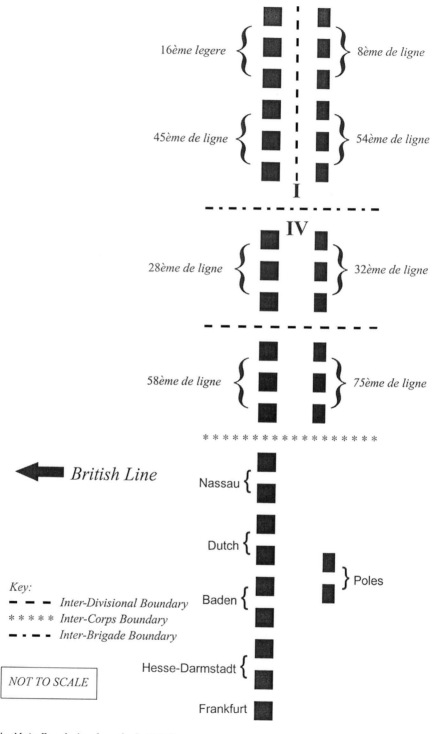

16ème legere

8ème de ligne

45ème de ligne

54ème de ligne

I

IV

28ème de ligne

32ème de ligne

58ème de ligne

75ème de ligne

British Line

Nassau

Dutch

Poles

Baden

Hesse-Darmstadt

Frankfurt

Key:
– – – Inter-Divisional Boundary
* * * * * Inter-Corps Boundary
– · – Inter-Brigade Boundary

NOT TO SCALE

The Main French Attack on the British Centre.

After Victor's initial attack, Wellesley had reinforced the Medellin by pulling Donkin's brigade further up the southern slopes towards the summit of the hill in case the French should make another attempt on this vital ground. Victor could see these movements, and it became clear that a third frontal assault would be yet another costly failure. He therefore decided to mask it for the time being and left only the strong battery of artillery and Villatte with his 2nd Brigade (the 94ème and 95ème de ligne) on the Cerro de Cascajal, supported by his corps cavalry under Beaumont.

Lapisse's division was moved from the Cascajal to face the two brigades of the KGL and the 2/83rd that was the left-hand battalion of Cameron's brigade. He deployed Laplannes's brigade in the first line with his battalions in column, but each column closed up to within six paces of each other,[26] proving that there was never any intention of deploying into line. Solignac's brigade provided the second line and was drawn up in battalion mass, allowing Lapisse to bring up his supports quickly, and in good order, to exploit any breakthrough gained by the first line.

Facing H. Campbell's Guards brigade and the 1/61st of Cameron's brigade in the centre of the British line was the 1st Division of Sébastiani's IV Corps. As well as being the corps commander, this general also personally commanded this division, which was the strongest in the army with over 8,000 bayonets. He formed his twelve battalions in two lines of columns like Lapisse, but with the difference that instead of having his brigades one behind the other, he arranged them side by side. Each brigade had one regiment in battalion columns in the front line and the second regiment, in the same formation, in support.

Sébastiani's 2nd Division was represented by only the 4th Polish Regiment, which consisted of two battalions; the rest of this division had been left to cover Madrid under command of General Valence, who, as we have heard, was currently in contact with the Spanish General Venegas at Toledo. These two battalions were used as the reserve for General Leval's division, which consisted of a rather diverse selection of troops – the 2nd Nassau Regiment, the Hesse-Darmstadt Gross und Erbprinz Regiment, the 2nd Dutch Regiment and the 4th Baden Regiment, each of two battalions, and a single battalion from Frankfurt. As this division deployed in a single line of battalion columns it stretched across the frontages of A. Campbell's division, the Pajar de Vergara battery and the four Spanish battalions on the extreme left of Cuesta's line.

Latour-Maubourg's division of Dragoons was to support the main attack on the British centre, leaving the King's Guards and Dessolles's brigade as the army reserve. The latter was held well back, and it is highly likely that Joseph had no intention of using this final reserve during the battle, in order to ensure that he had some fresh troops available should the battle be lost.

The drawing up of the army into its assault formations and positions inevitably took some time and could be clearly observed by Wellesley on his dominating height. He was therefore in a good position to determine the likely

French points of attack and decide on what redeployments and counter-measures he should take. The first thing that needed to be done was to deploy some troops to cover the shallow valley on the extreme left of his line. As he lacked the infantry to do this, he moved Fane's and Anson's cavalry brigades from their position behind the centre of the British line to the left flank, where they could see straight down the valley. From here they would threaten the flank of any force that attempted to attack the British line from this direction. He also withdrew a half battery (of Rettberg's battery) to a small spur on the northern face of the Medellin from where it would be able to enfilade the valley.

Wellesley also sent a message to Cuesta pointing out that the Spanish forces were not directly threatened and requesting that he send some reinforcements to the most threatened parts of the line. Given the bad feeling that is supposed to have existed between the two commanders, it is interesting that Wellesley was not too proud to make such a request for soldiers from someone in whom he seemed to have such little faith, and that Cuesta was not so petty minded as to refuse. The result was that Cuesta sent his reserve division, that of Bassecourt, and a battery of 12-pounders which were considerably more potent than any of the artillery that the British owned.

Wellesley was able to deploy Bassecourt's troops on the lower slopes of the Sierra de Segurilla, which now ensured that the British position on the Medellin could not be outflanked with equanimity, and effectively anchored the left of the allied line. Four of the Spanish heavy guns under Captain Uclés were used to reinforce the British light artillery in the Pajar de Vergara, and the other two were positioned on the west of Rettberg's half battery to extend the coverage of the valley to the north.

A little later, and apparently without further requests being sent, the Duke of Albuquerque's cavalry division also moved to the assistance of the British and took position in a second line behind Anson's and Fane's cavalry. The horse artillery battery of this division deployed next to the two Spanish 12-pounder guns. These latest reinforcements finally ensured the security of the British left flank.

Chapter Eight

The Main Attack

We do not know if Joseph planned to launch his assaults simultaneously, but if he did, it did not happen that way. At about 2.00 pm the French artillery opened a tremendous barrage across the whole British front with virtually all their guns: 'The advance of French columns is invariably announced by a general fire of artillery throughout the whole extent of their position; and the ordinary custom was not omitted.'[1] As before, the British guns replied as best they could, but were too weak in numbers to be able to conduct effective counter-battery fire. Perhaps rather unfairly Nicol recalls, 'Our guns on the hill opened upon them, but did little execution to what we expected; it was said "They are the German Legion artillery."'[2] Furthermore, knowing the weakness of his artillery, Wellesley inevitably sited his guns to cause the maximum damage to the vulnerable French columns rather than their artillery.

With much of the British line in full view of the French guns and with little cover, the red-coated infantry could only lie down and pray. Because of the ground, the two lines were quite close to each other, particularly in the north where they stood on the two pieces of high ground. Consequently their fire was accurate and deadly, the 'thunder of the artillery [causing] the very earth, not to mention the heart in one's breast, to shake and quiver.'[3] Even Hill's troops, who had more protection than most, suffered many casualties during this time.

As Joseph's troops were concentrated almost exclusively against the British part of the allied line, he was aware that those on the left of his assault would have their flank somewhat in the air and be vulnerable to a Spanish counter-attack if they were to venture from their strong defensive positions. His plan, therefore, was for Leval's attack to be held back somewhat in echelon from Sébastiani's division in order to 'refuse its left'[4] to protect against this possibility. As it turned out, Leval's division was the first to come into contact with the allied line.

Leval's Attack on the British Right
The ground over which Leval was to launch his attack certainly presented him with many difficulties. Between his troops and the allied line in front of him

were olive groves, vines, patches of undergrowth and stone walls. These meant that he could not get a clear idea of his enemy's locations and strengths, and although movement was not overly restricted it would certainly be difficult to maintain strict order and control; the terrain would force his division to advance in rather looser order than was ideal, and this would make its evolutions less precise.

In an attempt to overcome these problems Leval ordered his troops to advance *en colonne serrée*, columns that would keep the companies closed up on the ones in front. This would make them easier to control and keep in order, but more difficult to deploy if the need arose. Rather more difficult to understand was his decision to adopt an unusual assault formation that had all his battalions in a single line. In this way he would inevitably rather blunder forward with little or no flexibility to react to the unexpected. Given the poor visibility caused by the olive groves through which he had to advance, the unexpected is exactly what he should have been expecting! This deployment also put everything 'in the shop window', leaving him with no reserves. It was most unusual to launch an attack with no uncommitted troops who could exploit any success of the first line or restore the situation by a counter-attack in the event of a repulse. We have no explanation why he did this, and many have speculated that it was due to overconfidence. Whatever the reason it was to have serious consequences. Although Leval had the two battalions of Poles in support, they did not move up behind the attack but remained at the line of departure to provide a force to rally on if the need arose.

The olive groves also made it impossible for Leval to deploy his artillery into a position from which it could fire on the British positions. Thus the British line would not be discomforted or suffer any attrition from a heavy preliminary artillery bombardment in the way the normal doctrine dictated. One of the preconditions for a successful attack by column would therefore not be met, and all Leval could do was move his guns forward behind the lead troops in the hope of finding a position from which they might support the final assault.

With no preliminary bombardment and with the closeness of the country blocking his view of the rest of the battlefield, Leval's division launched its attack prematurely. Struggling to maintain its orientation and order through the difficult going, and consequently afraid that it would fall behind its allotted place, the advance was pushed on. Despite the potential for chaos, the poor observation and what appears to be another example of poor British security resulted in an early and unexpected success. As the thick line of skirmishers crept forward through the trees and vines they succeeded in surprising some of the British outposts, and a number of men were surrounded and captured. (French claims that this was the whole of the 45th Foot can be discounted, as this regiment was in the second line and finished the battle with only thirteen men missing. However, the Nassau Regiment claimed to have retained sixty-seven prisoners even after many escaped during their precipitous retreat.

Although this number is also likely to be an exaggeration, the 97th of Campbell's 4th Division ended the battle with twenty-four men missing, which this incident might account for.)

Taking advantage of this early success the skirmish line quickly pushed back the rest of the British light infantry and rushed forward to the main line. The difficulty of the ground and the pace of the advance had totally disrupted the cohesion of the battalion columns by the time they broke out of cover into the clearing before the British line. Indeed, such was the disruption that they appeared to the British as a confused mass of skirmishers.

To prepare for the assault that the artillery bombardment elsewhere on the line inevitably heralded, A. Campbell had brought forward the 1/40th of Kemmis's brigade to reinforce the 2/7th and 2/53rd of his own. To his right were the six British and four Spanish guns in the Pajar de Vergara redoubt. The French advance brought the Nassau and Dutch regiments to face Campbell's troops, and the Baden regiment faced the redoubt. The Hessian Regiment and the Frankfurt Battalion faced the remains of the Badajoz Regiment, Imperial de Toledo (both of which had run away the night before) and the Provincial de Guadix. No doubt to strengthen their resolve as much as to make up for their losses, these had been reinforced by the Osuna Infantry Regiment and Voluntarios Estrangeros from Iglesias's division and the Provincial de Truxillo of Zayas.

The forward edge of the broken ground across which Leval's division advanced brought it out into a clearing about 200 yards from the British line. The difficult advance had already consumed all the momentum of the attack and there was no time to redress the ranks and recommence the assault. Perhaps in an effort to give themselves time to repair their formation, an eyewitness recalls they 'called out "Espanholas" [*sic*] wishing us to believe they were Spaniards. Our captain thought they were Spaniards, and ordered us not to fire. But they soon convinced us who they were by a rattling volley.'[5]

It is quite possible that the green uniforms of the Nassauers and the white of the Dutch confused the British at first, and the fire 'staggered our line and even caused them [the British] to fall back'.[6]

The Nassauers did not attempt to reform as the breakdown of the formation probably allowed more men to manoeuvre into a position to fire. Several times the Nassau and Dutch troops advanced a short way towards the British line, loading as they went and then delivering a volley. These cannot have been well controlled but despite this, no doubt because of the admirable discipline of the German troops, the situation hung in the balance for some time. The commanding officer of the 2/53rd, Lieutenant Colonel Sir George Ridout Bingham, admits that the 2/7th were driven back by an attack on its flank and that some Nassauers 'penetrated nearly to the work [the Pajar] in front'.[7] The 2/24th of Mackenzie's brigade that was standing in reserve was ordered forward to support the front line in this area. Advancing into the gap between

Campbell and Sherbrooke, it found itself on the flank of the Nassauers and was able to pour an effective fire into them, causing them to 'flinch away.'[8]

Further south the Spanish infantry was locked in an indecisive engagement with the Hessian and Frankfurt troops. Here the Spanish volleys were not so effective and the Germans were able to hold their own. However, the outcome of this attack was decided in the centre where the unfortunate Baden battalions found themselves looking down the barrels of ten artillery pieces at very short range. Although the six British guns were only 3-pounders, the four Spanish guns were heavy 12-pounders and the effect of grapeshot fired from behind the protection of the earthworks was terrible. With their musket fire largely ineffective because of the protection enjoyed by the allied gunners, the Badeners, who had proven themselves the bravest of troops on many battlefields, were mown down. When their colonel, von Porbeck, fell, it proved to be the last straw for the Germans; their morale broke and they 'melted away'.[9]

Judging the moment perfectly, General Campbell ordered the first line to charge. Colonel Myers of the 2/7th, having rallied his battalion but seeing the initial hesitation of his inexperienced troops, grabbed the battalion's king's colour and, calling out 'Come on the Fusiliers',[10] led his men forward in the charge. With the Badeners falling back on their left and with the levelled British bayonets closing in on them, the Nassau and Dutch battalions fell back into the cover of the olive groves and made for their own lines. The trees and bushes broke up the British line and the momentum of the charge was lost. However, as it advanced it came across a French battery of six guns that were being brought up along a narrow track to support the attack. Unable to be turned around, the guns were abandoned by their crews and captured by the British. These were spiked and dragged to the edge of the clearing. The German troops facing the Spanish line, seeing the hurried departure of the troops to their right and fearing that they would be outflanked, had no option but to withdraw also.

Anticipating the difficulties of controlling a pursuit through the difficult terrain in front of him, Campbell quickly recalled his front line before it was lost in the olive groves and vines, and beyond such control. The action had cost the brigade only relatively light casualties, and thanks to the discipline of the troops, and the prudence of their commander, the British line was quickly re-established and ready to face a second assault.

For their part, the men of Leval's division had pressed their assault bravely and given a good account of themselves. As they were not pursued closely they were able to rally on the two Polish battalions and were soon ready to make another effort if required. However, in the forty-five minutes that this action lasted, between 600 and 700 men had become casualties, well over half of them from the Baden Regiment.

The Crisis of the Battle

As Leval's division was fighting to press home its attack, what was to be the main French attack was finally developing against the centre of the British line. It was here that the most desperate fighting of the day took place, and where the British came closest to losing the battle. Sherbrooke's eight battalions first had to endure an hour of heavy bombardment as the French attempted to set the conditions for a successful attack by shattering British morale and causing as many casualties as possible. The flat, open ground on which it was deployed made the British line very vulnerable to this prolonged artillery fire – there was no cover along the centre of the British position. This hour must have seemed like an eternity as the men lay in their exposed positions. An officer of the 45th recalls, 'I regarded it as perfectly miraculous that any individual escaped.'[11]

At about 3.00 pm the divisions of Lapisse and Sébastiani started their advance. The forward line of battalion columns moved off in an imposing mass through the line of their own artillery. The second line also advanced but kept well behind to act as the reserve, finally stopping behind a stone wall. From here they could quickly move forward to reinforce success, and in the case of a repulse the forward line could move back through the intervals between the columns and reform behind them. This second line would be far enough behind the first to ensure that it would not be swept away by the broken battalions and would still be able to exploit the inevitable disorder in the opposition's line if it pursued too far.

On this as on many future battlefields, the end of the artillery fire was greeted with great relief by the British troops, as they would much rather have faced the French infantry than lie helplessly under a storm of shot and shell. Lapisse's lead brigade (six battalions of the 16ème légère and 45ème de ligne) was advancing against the front of the KGL battalions of Löw and Langwerth and the 2/83rd that was on the left of Cameron's brigade (a total of five battalions). Sébastiani's 28ème and 58ème de ligne advanced against the two Guards battalions of H. Campbell's brigade and the 1/61st, the right-hand battalion of Cameron's brigade. An ensign in the 3rd Guards recalled, 'The French came on over the rough and broken ground … in the most imposing manner and with great resolution.'[12]

The French skirmishers pushed back the British light troops with ease and crossed the Portiña brook without interference from the silent red line beyond. Sherbrooke's division covered more or less the same frontage as the two French divisions that were advancing against it. The British general had given strict orders that the first volley should not be fired until the French columns were only 50 yards away, and that this single volley was to be immediately followed by a bayonet charge, the essence of British tactics in the Peninsula. As the French columns advanced to within extreme musket range they would have expected the first volley, as less experienced troops were prone to fire early. When this fire did not come and the British line remained still and steady, the advance would have become more agitated, as the indicators of a breakdown in British morale appeared to become less certain.

A French officer described the attack:

> The French charged with shouldered arms as was their custom. When they arrived at short range, the English line remained motionless, some hesitation was seen in the march. The officers and NCOs shouted at the soldiers, 'Forward March; don't fire'. Some even cried, 'They're surrendering'. The forward movement was therefore resumed; but it was not until extremely close range of the English line that the latter started a two rank fire which carried destruction into the heart of the French line, stopped its movement, and produced some disorder. While the officers shouted to the soldiers 'Forward: Don't fire' (although firing set in nevertheless), the English suddenly stopped their own fire and charged with the bayonet. Everything was favourable to them; orderliness, impetus, and the resolution to fight with the bayonet. Among the French, on the other hand, there was no longer any impetus, but disorder and surprise caused by the enemy's unexpected resolve. Flight was inevitable.[13]

The front ranks of the two French divisions were cut down in the single tremendous discharge, and before the bewildered survivors could collect themselves the British charge broke through the smoke. Despite the best efforts of the French officers and NCOs to organize a measure of resistance, the columns broke up and their soldiers turned away in the face of British cold steel: 'The coolness on our part staggered the resolution of the enemy.'[14]

However, Sherbrooke's orders were not strictly obeyed by the whole of his line. In the Guards at least, the fire was reserved until after the French had been put to rout by a charge of levelled bayonets. An anonymous Guards sergeant recalled, 'instead of waiting to receive them, our centre advanced upon them with a cheer, which struck them with panic, they faced about, and received two vollies [*sic*] whilst retiring in confusion'.[15] A subaltern of the same regiment also remembered this variation: 'On their approaching within 200 yards we were ordered to advance without firing a shot and afterwards to charge this we did ... our fire was reserved until they were flying ... The enemy did not wait for us, we carried everything before us.'[16]

If further verification of this unusual tactic is required, it comes from the Earl of Munster, who also recalls the Guards advancing against the French without having unleashed a devastating, close-range volley first. The French broke and fled before contact was made.[17] Most contemporary commentators agree that hand-to-hand contact was almost unheard of on an open field of

The 3rd Guards at Talavera. (Courtesy of the Regimental Headquarters of the Scots Guards)

battle; the side with the weaker morale invariably broke and ran before bayonets actually crossed.

The French first line rushed back across the Portiña and began to reform behind their second line. The British general, however, had not given the same detailed orders for the control of this charge as he had for initiating it. Thus the majority of his troops, swept up by the excitement of their success, charged out of control after the fleeing Frenchmen. Only Cameron kept his brigade on a short leash and stopped it just beyond the Portiña. The rest of the division charged on to exploit its success, its order and cohesion breaking up with every step. The battalions of the KGL, having negotiated the Portiña, started to push north up the slopes of the Cascajal while the Guards pushed forward across the plain, seemingly oblivious to the fresh French troops formed up behind a wall beyond those fleeing before them.

With Cameron's men halting and redressing their ranks the brigades on either side of them found themselves in terrible disorder, with new lines of fresh enemy troops before them and both flanks in the air. The guns on the Cascajal opened fire on the advancing German troops and, with the Guards disordered after crossing the Portiña, the French second line 'gave them a tremendous volley and then quitting the enclosure charged in their turn'. The KGL were clearly routed:

the whole of their infantry fairly ran away. Poor Langwerth seized the colours and, planting them, called to the men to form. He was killed in attempting to rally them. Colonel Derenham was equally unsuccessful. He got 40 or 50 round the colours but the instant he went to collect others these set up [sic]. Had not the 16th [Light Dragoons] been moved up opportunely there would have been a gap left in the line. The Germans formed in our rear.[18]

'The period was critical ... the destruction of the whole brigade seemed inevitable.'[19] The crisis point of the battle had been reached, and it would be the reaction and decisions of the commanders of the two sides that would decide the day.

The Guards found themselves in a very dangerous position: on their left flank the KGL troops were in precipitous retreat, while on their right, two regiments of French dragoons advanced to try to exploit their disorder. The Guards blamed the KGL for their predicament: 'it was necessary for our brigade to retire. When we faced about, the enemy that were flying rallied and opened a heavy fire and we were taken in our left flank by that part of the enemy which ought to have been driven back by the Germans'.[20]

The British battalions were now forced into a fighting withdrawal in which they formed into small groups, each desperately fighting its way back towards its own lines. Cohesion had been lost but none of their fighting spirit. Cameron's still formed troops gave them some cover, but with both flanks in the air, these too were soon forced to fight their way back across the Portiña. The French, smelling success and pushing them hard, killed many and swept up those left behind as prisoners: 'the havoc was great, and we were thrown into momentary confusion',[21] recalled a participant. The French pursuers were confident of success and pushing triumphantly on across the Portiña. It appeared that the British centre had been 'broken beyond repair',[22] and even Napier admits that Wellesley's centre was 'absolutely penetrated'.[23] The French officers were heard to exclaim: 'Allons, mes enfants, ils sont touts nos prisonniers.'[24]

Two of the KGL battalions were particularly hard hit during this desperate retreat; in twenty minutes the 1st Battalion lost half its strength, 387 men, and the 5th Battalion lost over 100 men as prisoners alone. The Guards battalions also lost heavily: 611 men killed or wounded, but no men were taken as prisoners.

Seeing the catastrophe that was unfolding before him, Mackenzie, whose brigade had formed the second line behind the Guards brigade, sent a staff officer to bring back the 2/24th, who were ordered to occupy the original line of the Guards. This they were able to do before the 2nd Guards came straggling back. As these small groups approached their original position, the 2/24th wheeled back by companies to let them through and then reformed line

The 45th Foot at Talavera. Part of Mackenzie's division, the 45th had distinguished themselves at Vimeiro and during the surprise on the Alberche the day before the battle. The illustration shows them helping to repulse the French counter-attack at the crisis of the battle, a feat for which their brigade received little recognition because of the death of Mackenzie. They were to earn the nickname of the 'Old Stubborns'. (Courtesy of the Regimental Headquarters of the Worcestershire and Sherwood Foresters Regiment.)

to meet the advancing French with 'steady and destructive volleys'.[25] Behind Mackenzie's brigade the Guards 'rallied with astonishing rapidity'.[26]

The other two battalions of Mackenzie's brigade, the 1/45th and 2/31st, moved into line on the left of the 2/24th. These three fresh and steady battalions, supported by the 14th and 16th Light Dragoons, now faced the advancing six battalions of the French 32ème and 75ème Regiments. This unequal fight was desperate. The French appear to have followed up their success in a much more measured way, and the two sides now engaged in a fearful firefight which caused further heavy casualties to both sides. General Mackenzie himself fell, as did 632 men of the 2,000 that had gone into action in his three battalions. The casualties were such that the 2/24th found itself in a single rank, as the whole of the second rank had been absorbed into the first.[27] After half an hour of desperate fighting the rallied Guards regiments were able to retake their place in the line. The superior marksmanship of the British began to tell, and slowly but surely the French line was forced back.[28] The French resistance was finally broken by a manoeuvre of the Light Dragoons on the exposed flank of the 75ème de ligne, which broke to the rear dragging the rest of the French line with it.

However, further to the north the crisis was far from over, and Wellesley, watching this epic struggle unfolding below him, quickly realized that Mackenzie's single brigade would not be sufficient to rally the whole of Sherbrooke's division and to plug the large gap that had appeared in the centre of the British line. As Langwerth's routed brigade rushed back, pursued in its turn by the apparently victorious French, he might well have regretted pulling Donkin's brigade up onto the summit of the Medellin earlier in the day. However, he was still not prepared to weaken the key to his defensive line by such a strong force while fresh French troops stood in observation just a few hundred yards away. As he could not spare more than a single battalion he chose the 1/48th from Richard Stewart's brigade.

Still nearly 800 strong after their action the night before and the intense artillery bombardment, this battalion under Colonel Donellan, who had already had two horses killed under him, moved down from the Medellin and took position on the original line of the KGL brigades. As these battalions came streaming back in disarray, the 1/48th provided the rock on which they could reorganize themselves. 'A close and well-directed fire from us arrested the progress of the French ... The leading files of the French halted, turned and fled back and never made another effort.'[29]

Despite the disorganization of the KGL troops, the French do not seem to have followed up this success with quite the same determination as they did against the Guards, and the first volley of the 1/48th appears to have been sufficient to stop them. However, it is certain that the arrival of this single battalion was vital as without it it is doubtful that the KGL battalions would have been able to reorganize themselves sufficiently to offer Lapisse's counter-attack any substantial opposition. The history of the King's German Legion states that it was only their skirmishers that pursued too far and that the remainder 'fell back with little disorder',[30] but perhaps their level of casualties belies this. It is impossible to know who was stretching the truth, but Lieutenant Colonel Ridout Bingham states: 'This crisis might have been fatal; the enemy were near or rather beyond the centre of our position, when the 48th Regiment further to the left was thrown forward and brought on their flank, which movement was decisive.'[31]

Stopping to return the steady and accurate fire of the 1/48th, the momentum of the French attack was lost. Endeavouring to urge his men to restart their advance, General Lapisse was shot down. The discomfiture of the French was made worse by the batteries of British artillery on the Medellin that opened an enfilading fire into their vulnerable flank. As this force started to waver, the collapse of Sébastiani's division to its south finally broke its will to resist, and the leaderless division also turned and fled back towards its own lines.

Lapisse was not the only senior casualty of this action: as the 1/48th advanced Colonel Donellan had his knee shattered by a musket ball. 'Painful as must have been his wound, his countenance did not betray his suffering but preserved its usual expression. Calling Major Middlemore, the next senior officer, Colonel Donellan, seated erect in his saddle, took off his hat, bowed and said, "Major Middlemore, you will have the honour of leading the 48th to the charge."[32] The gallant Donellan was evacuated to a hospital but his leg was not amputated, and he died on 1 August.

Despite the timely and effective intervention of the 1/48th it was the action of Mackenzie's brigade that saved Wellesley from defeat. Sébastiani's division had come close to success and must have felt that victory had been plucked from its grasp. Schaumann recalled of the French assault, 'Even the oldest veterans could not remember ever having witnessed an attack delivered with such desperate fury.'[33] But they paid a terrible price: all four of Sébastiani's regimental commanders were casualties, as were seven of the twelve battalion commanders. Seventy other officers and 2,100 soldiers were killed or wounded, of whom sixty or so were prisoners. The wreck of his division fell back a full mile from the Portiña to lick its wounds.

The British troops in the centre left had suffered even more severely than their comrades on the right: Cameron's brigade, having stopped its pursuit and reformed, still lost 500 out of its original 1,400. The KGL brigades had suffered particularly: Langwerth had been killed and his brigade was reduced from 1,300 to just 650 men fit to fight on. Löw's brigade, after its involvement in the earlier French attacks, had faced this latest French assault with just 950 bayonets and had suffered a further 350 casualties, including 150 prisoners taken during their confused and disordered flight. It is no small wonder that the few exhausted survivors were able to retake their place in the line.

Leval Launches a Second Attack

At the height of the desperate battle in the centre, Sébastiani's other division, that of Leval, had been able to rally and reorganize itself without hindrance from Campbell's controlled pursuit. Hearing the sound of the intense fighting to his north Leval felt he should launch a second attack in the hope of relieving some of the pressure on his comrades who were still in contact. Although he had suffered a bloody repulse his casualties were sustainable and he felt his division was capable of another effort.

At about 4.00 pm Leval began his second assault, but the result was the same. Once again the difficulties of the ground disrupted the cohesion of his columns, so that when they broke out into the clearing before the British lines they were unable to reply effectively to the musket volleys and grapeshot that met his advance. Since the first attack, Campbell had brought Kemmis's brigade to reinforce his line and these fresh troops ended any hopes Leval may have had of achieving success. Still disheartened from their earlier failure the German and Dutch troops put up only token resistance, and 'speedily went to the right about'.[34] Spanish cavalry moved to threaten this withdrawal, and the

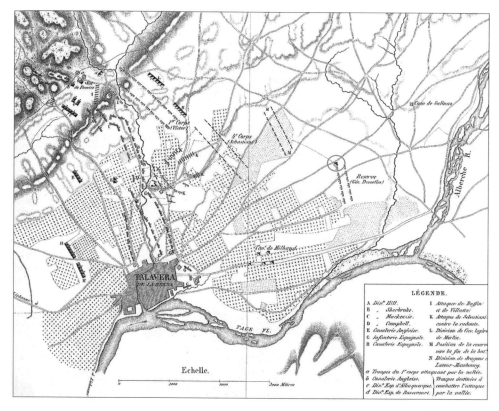

An interesting French map of the battle showing the attacks of Sébastiani's IV Corps in the centre and Ruffin's in the northern valley. Like most old maps, the elevations shown are confusing and often inaccurate. However, of particular note are the extent of the olive groves and the inclusion of Casa de Salinas (where Wellesley was nearly captured on the 27th) and the Alberche river.

Hessians and Frankfurters were ordered into square. However, they were unable to do this before they were successfully charged by the cavalry of the Regimiento del Rey (the King's Regiment), who sabred many. Nevertheless, the difficult terrain reduced the effectiveness of the charge and the Germans were able to gather in a tight mass and eventually gain the safety of their own lines. Even so, the Spanish cavalry regiment also managed to overrun a battery of artillery that was struggling to move up to support the infantry attack. Four guns, three from the Baden battery and one from the Hesse-Darmstadt battery, were captured and dragged back to the redoubt by a Lieutenant Piñiero. In this charge the Frankfurt Battalion lost an officer and thirteen men killed, and five officers, including the commanding officer, Lieutenant Colonel Welsch, and sixty-four men wounded.

This action was much to the credit of the Spanish cavalry who were generally considered as practically worthless by their British allies. Nor were these the only guns captured during this second attack: a howitzer and two guns belonging to a Dutch battery were abandoned in the precipitous withdrawal and were found after the battle by the British in the close country in front of their lines. Private Cooper of the 7th Foot, a young British soldier quoted earlier, observed: 'After these two attacks and smart repulses, we were not troubled by their company any more during the battle.'[35] The final casualty toll in Leval's division was 1,007, including the colonels of the Baden and Frankfurt regiments. It is likely, but impossible to confirm, that the unfortunate Badeners must have suffered a high proportion of these as a result of their close encounter with the allied artillery, but despite this and the fact that the division lost just over 1,000 men in the whole battle, only 6 officers and 97 men are reported as killed. In contrast Campbell had suffered only 236 losses, and the Spanish loss is estimated as not more than 150. Campbell was rightly praised for the effectiveness of his brigade and the shrewd way in which he handled it.

While the centre and right of the British line had been fighting for their lives, Hill's division had had a relatively quiet time. However, the French artillery had thundered on and there had been a steady trickle of casualties. Donkin's brigade was the most exposed, and although it did not fire a single shot during the day it suffered 195 casualties. Throughout the desperate fighting to the south, the men of Villatte's brigade stood idly on the Cascajal, waiting for news of their comrades' success so that they could seal the victory by finally seizing the key to the British line. But they too were exposed to artillery fire, and without any cover on the exposed Cascajal they suffered almost as much as Donkin's brigade. One can only surmise that they were required to provide protection for the artillery and that this duty did not allow them to pull back out of range of the British guns.

The Last Throw of the Dice

The French attack in the valley to the north of the Medellin was the last to develop. The columns of Ruffin and Villatte did not start to roll forward until the battle in the centre was reaching its climax. The battered regiments of Ruffin advanced on the French right along the lower slopes of the Sierra de Segurilla opposite the Spanish division of Bassecourt. To their left was Cassagne's brigade of Villatte's division. Moving behind them in support was Merlin's cavalry. In front of these 8,000 infantry and 1,200 cavalry stood 5,000 Spanish infantry and another 5,000 British and Spanish cavalry.

The French commanders faced a difficult dilemma in this part of the battlefield. They stood on the shallow floor of a valley that was about 1,000 yards wide and closed in on both flanks by high ground that was occupied by the enemy. An attack onto the north face of the Medellin would mean exposing their rear and flank unless a considerable covering force was warned off, and this would almost certainly mean that insufficient troops would be available to assault the still formidable and strongly held hill. The only alternative appeared to be to clear the valley of allied troops before an attempt was made on the heights of the Medellin, but even then they would have their southern flank open to a potentially heavy enfilading fire from the guns and troops that garrisoned the hill.

The French commanders decided on the former plan, but, given their options, it is perhaps not too surprising that their advance was rather tentative. No doubt their fears were soon realized as their troops came under a heavy enfilading artillery fire from the ten Spanish guns and Rettberg's half battery deployed on the northern slopes of the Medellin. Because of the acute angle at which they were forced to reply and because of the height of the allied guns, the French artillery that had accompanied the advance could offer their infantry little support.

Before the lead French troops were level with the British line on the Medellin, Ruffin deployed the 9ème légère to form a screen opposite Bassecourt's troops on the lower slopes of the Segurilla. The other six battalions of the 24ème and 96ème de ligne continued their advance down the valley, with Cassagne's brigade on their left nearest the Cerro de Medellin. Their reserve was a converged battalion of grenadiers, formed by amalgamating all the grenadier companies of each of the battalions into a single battalion. This followed up behind the rest of the division.

By the time the French were level with the Casa de Valdefuentes farm, at the base of the Medellin, the crisis at the centre of the British line had passed and Wellesley was able to turn his attention to this part of the field. Some of Cassagne's brigade sheltered behind the Valdefuentes farm buildings and sent forward their skirmishers, who started up the hill and engaged their British counterparts.[36] Perhaps identifying that the French advance was not pressed with determination, Lord Munster claims Wellesley gave the order 'either positive or discretionary' for Anson's brigade of cavalry to charge '*if the opportunity offered*',[37] supported by Fane's heavy brigade.

Most British commentators report that Wellesley gave a direct order for Anson to charge, and if this is the case we must assume that there was something that caught his eye that made him believe that the French were vulnerable. Although the French were advancing up a valley that was favourable for a charge, it was still a very risky venture: 900 light cavalry, supported by 1,000 heavy, were being asked to charge about 8,000 French infantry supported by artillery and a considerable force of cavalry. Not only was the charge to be made by light cavalry, whose whole *raison d'être* was not as shock troops (that was the role of the heavy cavalry who were supporting them), but it would be made with little chance of achieving surprise against infantry who would have plenty of time to form square. It was widely accepted that steady infantry formed in square were virtually invulnerable to cavalry attack, and although some of the French troops in the valley had suffered considerably earlier in the battle, they were experienced troops and certainly still battle-worthy.

It is difficult to believe that Wellesley would have given a direct order in these circumstances, and Lord Munster's account, though flying in the face of the majority of writers, seems the most credible. Fortescue suggests, 'It seems certain that Anson launched his men, or possibly they launched themselves, into action prematurely; for it can never have been Wellesley's intention that they should dash themselves against unbroken infantry in square.'[38] Whatever orders were actually given, they were interpreted 'into direct orders, or considered as definitive.'[39]

As soon as Anson's troopers started forward 'in the most perfect order',[40] the French infantry formed square. The 23rd Light Dragoons who formed the right of the brigade faced the large regimental square of the 27ème légère of Cassagne's brigade, with the 1st Light Dragoons of the KGL on the left opposite smaller battalion squares of the 24ème and 96ème de ligne. As the charge moved down the valley it came under fire from the French skirmishers on the lower slopes of the Sierra de Segurilla and artillery on the Cascajal, which made both regiments veer slightly to the left.[41] But it was not to be the artillery fire or the squares bristling with bayonets that were to bring the charge to grief.

British cavalry regulations laid down that a charge would start off at a walk, increase to a trot, begin to gallop 250 yards from the enemy and then break into

The Final Attack in the North.

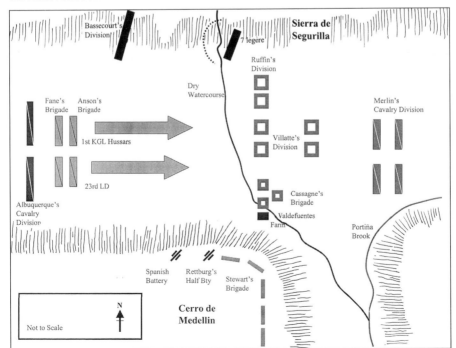

an all-out charge at about 80 yards. This gradual increase in pace would stop the horses from becoming too tired too early and ensure that the order of the troops was not lost, thus presenting an imposing and frightening wall of horses to the enemy. However, 'just as they were in full swing',[42] they came across an obstacle in the long grass of the valley that could not have been previously spotted. British eyewitnesses claim that about 150 yards in front of the French squares was a narrow but deep ravine that ran down from the Sierra de Segurilla to the Portiña. Gouged out by winter torrents from the mountains, but dry at this time of year, the ravine was described as about 15 feet wide and 10 feet deep in front of the 23rd Light Dragoons, and shallower but broader in front of the KGL Light Dragoons. Although a careful rider picking his route carefully could quite easily cross it in many places, this luxury was not available to the charging British cavalry.

Colonel Sir John Elley, who was the adjutant general of Wellesley's cavalry, rode ahead of the regiment on a conspicuous grey horse in order to set the line of the charge. He was the first to come to the obstacle. With the freedom he had riding out on his own on a good horse, he was able to jump the ravine without too much difficulty and then turned on the other side in order to try to stop the rest of the regiment, who would have far more trouble crossing it successfully. Unfortunately it was too late and the charging line had to do the best it could. Many crashed down into the ravine, some were able to slow down and negotiate the banks where they were not so steep, and others were able to jump it.

Most of the second line of squadrons were able to pull up and remained on the home bank, albeit in some disorder. It was at this time that the 27ème légère opened fire and completed their discomfort. The commanding officer of the 23rd, Colonel Seymour, rallied the survivors of the two right-hand squadrons and, with Colonel Elley, charged forward against the squares of the French light infantry. The left-hand squadron ran up against the French square whose 'well directed volley'[43] caused further heavy casualties and threw them back. However, the right-hand squadron found itself unopposed by infantry and charged on into the French cavalry behind.

This charge must have been rather ragged, although it was described as being delivered with 'irresistible impetuosity'.[44] However, it almost captured generals Villatte and Ruffin, who had not taken the precaution of taking refuge inside a square. The 10ème Chasseurs à Cheval, who were in the first line of the French cavalry, swerved aside rather than meet the charge, but reordered their ranks and then swung back into the rear of the 23rd as the British cavalry came into contact with the Westphalian Chevaux-Légers in the French second line. Surrounded and with their horses blown, most of the survivors were either cut down or captured. Elley himself escaped by cutting his way out and then making a circuitous route to the north of the French forces, and finally reached the safety of Bassecourt's Spaniards. He estimates that only seven or eight of the 170 that charged with him also escaped. Major Ponsonby, also of the 23rd, summed the experience up with typical British understatement: 'We had a pleasing amusement of charging five solid squares with a ditch in their front. After losing 180 men and 222 horses, we found it not so agreeable.'[45] It seems that the French were not the only ones to underestimate their opponents, as he concludes with apparent surprise: 'Frenchmen will not always run away when they see British cavalry.'[46]

Meanwhile the 1st KGL Light Dragoons, under the command of Colonel Arentschildt, suffered a similar fate. Captain von Linsingen, a squadron commander, recalled: 'Too late to pull up, the foremost horsemen rode headlong at the hollow and a fearful scene ensued. Some tumbled in and over the ravine, while others leapt boldly across the chasm and gained the other side; but great disorder was the consequence.'[47] Although the ravine was shallower across their front, it was considerably wider. They did not suffer as many casualties at the ravine as their British comrades, and more of the first line was able to pull up. While a fair number picked their way across, those that did not were further disordered by the arrival of the support squadrons who pulled up among them. Like his fellow commanding officer of the 23rd, Arentschildt claims to have gathered up what troops he could and continued the charge against the squares of the 24ème de ligne. However, their approach was in inevitable disorder, the square stood firm and they quickly gave up the attempt. Given the relatively light casualties they suffered (37 for the whole day), this attack could not have been pressed very far, if at all, for Schaumann, an eyewitness, states, 'The First [KGL] Hussars ... turned sharply about at the ravine, and came back, having suffered only trifling losses.'[48] Even the history of the King's German Legion states that the rear squadrons halted after the crossing, and that 'few of them arrived before the bayonets of the enemy, and no impression was made upon the squares.'[49]

Lieutenant Girod de l'Ain of the 9ème légère, who was on the lower slopes of the Sierra de Segurilla, had a perfect view of this charge and gives us an interesting perspective of it:

> this was a charge by some English cavalry, that we saw arrive from afar like a hurricane; it was a regiment of dragoons charging in order of battle and launched full tilt ... We observed this line of enemy cavalry, incapable of manoeuvre, following a single direction so blindly, that we shouted with one voice: 'They are deserting, they are deserting!' But soon saw one of our regiments of légère (the 27ème), which, marching in column close to an isolated house, found itself in the path of this cavalry; not having time to form square, it threw itself around this house, with their backs against the four walls; the square thus found itself naturally formed, and more solid ... The English line extended well beyond both sides, to right and left ... the two

wings, no longer master of their horses ... continued on their course straight ahead, always flat out. We then saw a line of French cavalry, which stationed in the rear, came up at the 'petit trot' before the English cavalry; it was the brigade of General Stroltz, composed of the 10ème and 26ème Chasseurs à Cheval. We anxiously wondered what would happen when these two lines of cavalry met; but the shock did not last long: we saw the English line pass through the French line, without stopping or losing their formation; we only had time to notice a few sabres flash in the air and the smoke of some pistol shots ... but soon our chasseurs remounted and, a little shaken, launched themselves at the gallop in pursuit of the English dragoons, which only stopped in the waters of the Alberche, where they were all taken prisoner.[50]

Apart from the admission that the first line of French cavalry was overthrown, it is interesting to note that no mention is made of the ravine to which so many British commentators refer. This ravine, and the British accounts that blame it for the calamity that it apparently caused, is the source of some controversy that is worth exploring. It is Oman who claims, without disclosing his source, that it ran 125 yards ahead of the French. However, in a letter written to Napier, whose work on the Peninsular War was long considered the authoritative account, Major Ponsonby specifies that the ravine was a mere 30 yards from the French.[51] As he claims to have inspected the site the day after the battle, we should perhaps give him credit for writing the truth. He goes on to say that it was far more of an obstacle in front of the KGL Light Dragoons who were consequently unable to cross and close with the French infantry squares. As if this does not confuse things enough, Oman claims that the KGL Light Dragoons did directly charge the French squares, using the colonel of this regiment as his source. However, given the relatively low casualties of the German cavalry, I believe the balance of truth lies with Napier.

The situation is further complicated by the fact that Spanish accounts claim that the ravine was not such a difficult obstacle as some British commentators would have us believe. Neither Lord Munster nor Sergeant Nicol, who were eyewitnesses, mentions it at all, while Lord William Russell, who took part in the charge, refers to it as 'a very small ditch, which threw most of the rear rank down, the front rank passing it without difficulty'.[52] Given that Colonel Elley implies that about 160 men were lost in the final stages of the charge and that others must have become casualties as a result of the French musket fire, this does not suggest that many of the regiment's 207 casualties could be attributable to a fall into the ravine. Furthermore, it is puzzling that if it was such a large obstacle it was not visible to Wellesley and the others on their commanding position on the Medellin. To say that it was hidden in long grass is hardly credible when one stands on the Medellin with a grandstand view over the ground across which the light dragoons charged. Oman visited the battlefield himself in 1903 and admits that, while the ravine appears virtually unchanged from its description from 1809 along the line of the KGL charge, it has virtually disappeared along the route taken by the 23rd Light Dragoons. This he ascribes to its being filled up so the area could be cultivated, but in the light of so much conflicting evidence we must accept that the whole truth may never be known.

Even putting aside the exact extent of the obstacle that faced the British cavalry, the 23rd must still accept some blame for the consequences of their ill fortune. It was common practice for cavalry units to send out small bodies of skirmishers, and even single officers, to reconnoitre the ground over which they might charge to avoid just this sort of disaster. It appears that Colonel Elley rode ahead of the regiment for this reason, but was clearly too short a distance ahead to give sufficient warning. Furthermore, while the gallantry the survivors of these two cavalry regiments exhibited by continuing the charge is to be admired, it must be questioned what they thought they would be able to achieve against a strong and fully prepared enemy: the price was inevitable failure and heavy casualties in the British cavalry regiment. The 23rd started the day about 450 strong, and at the ravine and in the subsequent combat their total loss was 207 killed, wounded or missing, of whom 105 were captured.

Sergeant Hamilton of the 43rd, who was part of the 1st Battalion of Detachments stationed on the Medellin, should have had a good view of the charge. He describes it as 'ill timed and injudicious. The ground had not been reconnoitered [*sic*]. Sir Arthur Wellesley's intention was that the cavalry should charge when the enemy by deploying, had extended and exposed their flank. When the charge was actually made, the enemy were still in column, and too strongly posted to afford any prospect of success.'[53] I find it difficult to argue with Hamilton's assessment, but we must be wary of crediting him with full possession of the facts. He does not claim to have watched the charge and therefore may not have witnessed it personally. If he did not, then he must have relied on others for some of the details he has included in his judgement. For instance, however plausible his explanation of when Wellesley planned the charge to be launched, that is, when the French had turned south against the heights of the Medellin and thus exposed their flank to the cavalry, I can find no corroboration for this in any accounts from even senior officers who were present with the commander-in-chief at the time. We can be reasonably sure that a sergeant who was later wounded with the light infantry screen was not in a position to overhear Wellesley, who spent most of the day on the summit of the Medellin 500 yards behind the front line.

In contrast to much of Wellesley's writings on his cavalry, which was generally negative, in a dispatch written after the battle to Castlereagh, the minister for war, he wrote: 'although the 23rd [light] dragoons suffered considerable loss, the charge had the effect of preventing the execution of that part of the enemy's plan'.[54] He also went on to thank Anson's brigade.

Putting aside the controversy surrounding the timing and advisability of the charge, the consequences for the British were ultimately beneficial and this may well go some way to explaining Wellesley's own reaction to it. Indeed it is possible that Wellesley's praise for the charge may be to cover a certain amount of responsibility for the catastrophe suffered by the 23rd Light Dragoons. Ruffin and Villatte had not suffered greatly by the time the British cavalry had been beaten off, but they faced the same dilemma as earlier. The western end of the valley was still held by a strong force of allied cavalry, most of whom had still not been committed. This would pose a significant threat should they try to wheel to the south to attack the Cerro de Medellin, and the 9ème légère would need to be reinforced if it were to risk exposing its rear to the 5,000 Spanish infantry of Bassecourt. As the allied artillery continued to 'pour a withering fire into the French squares'[55] and news of the disasters that had befallen their comrades across the rest of the front started to arrive, the two French generals rather tamely withdrew their forces back to their start lines. In the final analysis, the French ultimately abandoning their attack in this part of the field seems to have compensated for the heavy losses suffered by the 23rd. Joseph's last throw of the dice had failed.

The two sides now stood on exactly the same positions they had occupied at the beginning of the day. Both were exhausted and only the opposing artillery continued the fight. Their fire provided a gruesome finale to the battle, as the long dry grass between the lines was set alight. The fire spread quickly across the battlefield, and a number of the more badly wounded that were unable to move were burnt to death and many of the corpses set alight.

Wellesley's troops were certainly in no state to move over to the offensive, and the French too had few fresh troops available. After their bloody repulse the two divisions of Sébastiani had withdrawn a mile from the British line to regroup. Only the two brigades of Villatte maintained the combat power for offensive action, and on their own they were unlikely to succeed where greater numbers of troops had failed. Joseph still had Dessolles's brigade of 3,300 bayonets and the 1,800 of his own Guard held back in reserve, and for a time he actually considered committing them. Some commentators claim that he gave the orders for them to move forward before deciding that it was too risky to commit his last fresh troops. He had heard that some of Cuesta's units had moved forward, and although this was only an unsubstantiated rumour it was all the encouragement Joseph needed to determine on retreat.

If the Spanish general had felt confident enough to order a proportion of his army onto the offensive, the exhausted and battered French army could well have found itself in serious trouble with the Alberche river behind it. For his part, Wellesley claims he was satisfied that the Spanish did not attempt anything too rash, as he wrote: 'the ground which they occupied was so important ... that I did not think it proper to urge them to make any movement on the left of the enemy'.[56] The importance of this ground was that it secured the flank of his now exhausted army and, without confidence in the ability of the Spanish troops to manoeuvre, he felt it was better not to risk such a movement, despite its offering a potentially decisive outcome.

In the light of the rumour that the Spanish troops were manoeuvring, Jourdan and Sébastiani also advised a withdrawal, though it is no surprise to learn that Victor, incensed by their failure, was angrily demanding a final effort. For some time he sent increasingly acrimonious messages back to Joseph demanding that he release the reserves for a final assault. The truth was that as darkness approached there was no time to achieve a decisive result, and even news that the Spanish army was showing no sign of movement was too late to change the course that had been decided upon. The orders were given about 5.00 pm for a withdrawal to a position on the near bank of the Alberche, with the infantry moving back covered by the cavalry of Merlin, Latour-Maubourg and Milhaud. In a fit of pique Victor refused to obey his orders and remained on the Cascajal as the sun set on the sight of the remainder of the French army filing off to the rear. It was not until 3.00 am that he sullenly ordered his troops to retire, leaving the battlefield to the exhausted but unbeaten British soldiers: 'The retreat was made in the best order without leaving a single vehicle, nor wounded man, on the field of battle ... For by tradition the field of battle remains the bivouac of the victor.'[57]

Chapter Nine

Aftermath

The Butcher's Bill

'The battlefield presented a shocking spectacle. Corpses lay thickly all about for miles around, particularly on the hill which our troops had so bravely defended. Here, indeed, the dead were so plentiful that it looked as if several battalions were merely sleeping there.'[1] The next morning, the 29th, the British awoke to find the French army had gone and all that remained were scattered corpses. Their own heavy casualties and the exhaustion and hunger of the troops ruled out a pursuit, even if Wellesley had been inclined to order one.

'I never saw a field of battle which struck me with such horror as Talavera',[2] wrote an eyewitness. The British army had suffered a loss of a quarter of its strength: 5,365 casualties out of the 20,500 that were available at the start of the battle. The infantry, however, who had done most of the fighting, had lost a third. Not surprisingly the French had suffered even more, losing a total of 7,268 men and 17 guns, but this represented a percentage loss of only a fifth of their infantry (who did virtually all of the fighting) and only about a sixth of the army as a whole.

As all the French infantry were ranged against the British part of the allied line they had enjoyed an advantage of about 15,000 bayonets. The strength of the Medellin position alone should have been no counterbalance to such a numerical superiority, and anyway the main French attack fell primarily against Sherbrooke's and Mackenzie's 8,000 troops, who faced the 15,000 men of Lapisse and Sébastiani on virtually flat ground.

Of the 5,363 casualties suffered by the British, 801 were killed, 3,915 were wounded and 647 were listed as missing. Of the latter, 108 belonged to the unfortunate 23rd Light Dragoons and nearly 300 to the KGL. Two British generals, Mackenzie and Langwerth, were killed, and General Hill was wounded. Even Wellesley was struck on the collarbone by a spent ball: 'I was hit in the shoulder at the end of the action, but not hurt, and my coat shot through.'[3] Two of his ADCs were also wounded. Although the French casualties were substantially more, a few less were actually killed: 761. This probably reflects the high proportion of British casualties that were caused by artillery. The 206 listed as missing do not include a large number of wounded who were taken by the British and then subsequently recaptured in the hospitals when the French later reoccupied Talavera. General Lapisse was killed, as was von Porbeck, the regimental commander of the 2nd Nassau Regiment, who also acted as one of Leval's brigade commanders. The very high number of casualties among the French field officers bears testimony to their courage and leadership: all the regimental colonels and seven out of twelve battalion commanders in Sébastiani's division became casualties.

There is no accurate report of Spanish losses, so numbers cannot be established with any certainty. In one of his dispatches, Cuesta states that they were 1,201, but it is impossible to believe that these were all battle casualties given the relatively small amount of fighting they were involved in. Most commentators estimate that Spanish battle casualties are unlikely to have exceeded 400 or 500 men, and that the balance included the men who had fled on the evening of the 27th and were still unaccounted for after the action.

Despite some claims, the British captured no French eagles during the battle. The 5th Battalion KGL recovered three standards from among the bodies of the French 28ème de ligne that were reported as 'Eagles' and the 29th Foot two others on the Medellin. In 1808 Napoleon had reduced the number of eagles carried by the infantry from one per battalion to one per regiment. Each battalion still carried a standard but the pole no longer carried the eagle on the top, and it was these that the 5th KGL and 29th must have found. Even if one of them had been the regimental standard, the real prize, the bronze eagle fixed to the top of the flagpole, had obviously been removed and carried to safety.

The number of guns captured by the allied army was to be a source of much controversy after the battle. From the allied perspective, the number taken is not in dispute: however, from the French perspective the loss of any guns was significant. The scale of a victory during these times was measured more by the trophies that were taken, such as standards, flags and prisoners, rather than a straight comparison of casualties, which, as we have seen, is not necessarily a conclusive way of calculating who actually won. It was therefore in Joseph's interests to keep quiet the number of guns he lost so he did not incur the wrath of the Emperor. He wanted to describe the battle as a French victory; losing a considerable number of guns was always likely to undermine his case.

Unfortunately for Joseph, Napoleon read the British newspapers and they contained a claim that twenty guns had been captured. In fact the actual number was seventeen. Needless to say the Emperor wrote a scathing letter demanding to know whose guns had been taken. There was certainly some confusion in Joseph's staff as to the exact loss and it is clear that Sébastiani, whose corps had lost all the missing guns, and his artillery commander, General Sénarmont, had conspired to cover up their loss from Joseph. As the arguments raged the unhappy situation was resolved when fifteen of the seventeen guns, which Wellesley had presented to Cuesta, were recaptured a week later during the Spanish retreat. Thus Joseph was able to state honestly that he had only two guns missing, though Napoleon had Berthier write: 'Inform General Sébastiani that far from having captured thirty guns, as stated in his reports of our victories, he appears to have a deficiency of two, the value of which will be deducted from his pay.'[4]

Final Moves

On the morning of the 29th, Wellesley did not even feel strong enough to push forward a reconnaissance in force in order to locate the French army and try to divine its intentions. The first priority was to rest and resupply the army, something easier said than done. The appalling supply situation that the army had struggled with was not going to end just because they had gained a victory. The half ration that had been issued for the day of battle had to be reduced to a third of a ration the day after, and water was also scarce for the thirsty troops. One British soldier reported, 'nothing was served out to us from 2 or 3pm on the 27th, until about 10am on the 29th'.[5]

There was also much work still to be done: the wounded of both sides had to be collected and taken to the temporary hospitals that were set up in Talavera, and the dead needed to be buried. The plight of the wounded was particularly bad, as apart from their wounds there was virtually no water available. A sergeant recalled:

> notwithstanding the utmost tenderness was used, the removal of the wounded occasioned the most piercing shrieks – it was my lot to go with a Corporal of the company to the general hospital in Talavera, and I beheld what I never wish to see again – the road (about a mile) was covered with wounded, and wounded men dying while being carried there. Every street in the town was filled with them and absolutely impassable for no place had been prepared for their reception. Even burying the dead was no easy task; we had but few tools, and the ground was hard and rocky, therefore the dead were either thrown into the dry beds of winter torrents, etc, and scantily covered with earth; or, together with dead horses, gathered into heaps and burned. The smell was intolerable.[6]

In one of his dispatches Wellesley wrote, 'The extreme fatigue of the troops, the want of provisions, and the number of wounded to be taken care of, have prevented me from moving from my position.'[7] At 6.00 am he was encouraged by the arrival of reinforcements that went some way to make up for his losses of the previous day. Three experienced battalions of the Light Brigade and a battery of horse artillery came up under the command of Robert Crauford.

The wounded: 'Every street in the town was filled with them and absolutely impassable for no place had been prepared for them.' The plight of the wounded after every battle of this era was awful; neither army had a well-organized or proficient medical service. Fifteen hundred British wounded were left behind in Talavera and were taken prisoner by the French when they reoccupied the town several days after the battle.

These outstanding troops, who were to win many laurels in the following five years, had covered an incredible 43 miles in twenty-four hours after hearing the news of the impending battle.

Wellesley now presumed that Joseph would be forced to split up his army. To ensure the security of his capital the King would have to send a substantial force to intercept Venegas's army, which was surely strong enough to brush aside the weak forces currently before him. He would also be forced to leave a considerable force before Wellesley and Cuesta, and this would give them the opportunity to gain a decisive victory: 'We shall certainly move towards Madrid, if not interrupted by some accident on our flank,' Wellesley wrote.[8] The latter statement was not idle speculation: he was aware of the possible threat that Soult posed to his communications. However, he had been led to believe that the French Marshal would be unable to concentrate more than 20,000 men, and it may be remembered that the mountain passes at Perales and Baños were supposed to be guarded by Spanish troops.

On the 30th Wellesley received more specific information on Soult's movement on Plasencia, which informed him that the French had easily dealt with the weak Spanish forces at the passes. Given that the French had been able to concentrate their forces from around Madrid against him, it was logical to assume that Venegas had failed to tie even a modest force down between himself and the capital. Consequently, Wellesley now felt he had no option but to move to secure his communications by attacking Soult and to attempt to improve the supply situation which threatened to destroy his army.

While Wellesley remained at Talavera for three days after the battle awaiting further news and resting his troops, Joseph first withdrew and took up a defensive position on the eastern bank of the Alberche. However, once it became clear that Wellesley was not following up his advantage, Joseph was able to take the necessary measures to secure his capital. As his priority lay with Madrid, he left only Victor and the 18,000 troops that remained to him to contain Wellesley and Cuesta. This was a totally inadequate force should the allies advance against him, and Victor stayed on the Alberche in considerable trepidation while Joseph took the remainder of his army to confront Venegas. Victor, further disturbed by an exaggerated report of the movement of Sir Robert Wilson's small force of Spanish and Portuguese troops towards his rear, started a withdrawal towards Madrid.

With Victor's force withdrawing Wellesley now had some freedom of action to deal with Soult. He had a long discussion with Cuesta to discuss their future movements. It was always going to be a stormy meeting: 'I certainly should get the better of everything, if I could manage General Cuesta; but his temper and disposition are so bad that that is impossible'.[9] Wellesley was quite clear that his priority was the protection of Portugal rather than the taking of Madrid. This, however, caused considerable and understandable frustration to his ally, who wished to liberate his capital but understood that he needed British help in order to do this. It was finally agreed that Cuesta would remain at Talavera with the custodianship of the British wounded, while Wellesley marched west to confront Soult at Plasencia. Fearing that Cuesta might evacuate Talavera in his absence, Wellesley ordered that all of the 5,000 wounded and sick who were fit to travel were to be sent back towards Portugal.

During his march to Plasencia, Wellesley learnt from a captured dispatch, sent to him by Cuesta, that Soult had been able to concentrate 50,000 men rather than the 20,000 he had previously believed. Wellesley therefore halted his march before committing himself to an action he would have no chance of winning, and finally resolved to put the Tagus between him and the French by crossing the bridge at Arzobispo. This dispatch was also sufficient to unsettle Cuesta at Talavera. He therefore determined to retire to Oropesa in order to cross the Tagus at Almaraz. Much to the disgust of the British, this move left 1,500 of their wounded in the hands of the French when Victor reoccupied that town, but in the Spanish commander's defence he risked his army by staying there, and all the wounded that were left behind were unfit to travel.

Most of these unfortunate men, although well treated, were eventually sent back to France and remained in captivity until 1814 (Sergeant Nicol, whom we have heard from often, was one of these, and he left a very interesting account of his experiences).

Wellesley and Cuesta had a final, acrimonious meeting at Oropesa. Here the Briton declared his intention to withdraw south to seek safety and supplies behind the Tagus. Cuesta, who was keen to make a joint attack on Soult at Plasencia, decided to chance an offensive without British support. However, Cuesta's first brush with Soult's advance guard convinced him that he could not face the French alone, and he hastened after the British who crossed the Tagus at Arzobispo. Soult's lively and intelligent pursuit all but put Cuesta's army to rout, and Wellesley's army was too weak to be able to face Soult with confidence. Soult's manoeuvre offered up an opportunity to seize a large portion of Portugal almost without a fight, but Joseph, who was concerned that any further advance would leave Madrid isolated, stopped him.

The disappearance of the French came as something of a pleasant surprise to Wellesley, but he would not be content until he knew their intentions and had made provision for the protection of Portugal. Once it was clear that the French were making no threatening moves he could then see to the welfare of his men. Although the strategic situation had eased, his supply problems had not, and the fortnight that was spent behind the Tagus was a time of desperate shortage. Wellesley wrote:

> a starving army is actually worse than none. The soldiers lose their discipline and their spirit. They plunder even in the very presence of their officers. The officers are discontented, and almost as bad as the men; and with an army that a fortnight ago beat double their numbers, I should hesitate now to meet a French corps of half their strength.[10]

With the Spanish junta unable or unwilling to help and the countryside already stripped of all means of sustenance, on 20 August Wellesley felt he had no option but to retire to the Portuguese frontier. His army finally put into cantons around Badajoz as the fertile region around the Guadiana river was able to provide the supplies and the opportunity to rest that his army desperately needed.

Chapter Ten
An Assessment of the Battle

Talavera was one of the bloodiest battles of the Peninsular War, and one whose consequences are most debated. Despite the tactical subtleties and experiments that Wellesley was trying out in a major battle for the first time, it was still rather tactically unimaginative and something of a bloodbath when one takes into account the percentage of each army that became casualties. Only at Albuera did the British sustain a higher proportion of losses, although it was Beresford, rather than Wellington (as he was then), who commanded there. But not only was it bloody, like Waterloo six years later it was a rather 'close-run thing'. Although not an eyewitness, the celebrated General Sir Charles Napier wrote: 'Every officer I have seen and spoken to about the matter has told me the same story, viz. that the Battle of Talavera was lost if the French had made one more attack; and that the whole army expected to be beaten next day.'[1]

The British Perspective
Wellesley gave a rather sterile account of the battle in his official dispatch from Talavera dated 29 July. We have already seen how he covered up the negligence of General Hill, and his description of the crisis of the battle also rather underplays just how much of a crisis it was, although in an earlier letter he had admitted: 'The advance of the Guards to the extent it was carried was nearly fatal to us.'[2] As a great admirer of the Guards, he toned down this opinion in his official account.

We have also seen how cutting Wellesley was about the performance of his Spanish allies, and he was quick to point out who had done the lion's share of the fighting. He was not one to paint a dramatic picture of the intensity of the battle, or the exploits of his troops, and was economical with his praise. Indeed perhaps the closest he comes to praise is a description of the French withdrawal, 'which was conducted in the most regular order'.[3] He did, however, describe the battle as a 'long and hard-fought action', and admitted to 'the great loss which we have sustained … I have particularly to lament the loss of Major General Mackenzie.'[4]

It is one thing is to win a battle; it is another to be able to exploit your success. This Wellesley was clearly not in a position to do, and we should consider whether a small army that loses a quarter of its strength is actually a defeated army.

Wellesley's tactics went some way to ensuring that the battle turned out the way it did. By the time of Talavera, his recent experiences had convinced him of the unreliability of his Spanish allies in a pitched battle with the experienced and tactically efficient French. This fact, coupled with the relative numerical weakness of his British army in relation to his enemy, forced him to fight a defensive battle. But although the reasons he fought defensively are understandable, this type of battle rarely produces a decisive result unless it is accompanied by offensive action. By the end of 28 July he had no fresh British reserves (other than an inadequate force of cavalry) and the rest of his own troops were too exhausted to move over to the offensive. Rightly or wrongly, he was not prepared to risk launching the 35,000 virtually fresh Spaniards after the beaten and demoralized French (supposing he could convince Cuesta to do it), even though this offered the only chance of turning a tactical victory into something that could have been far more decisive.

Wellesley's aim in fighting at Talavera was to defeat the French and then continue his march to Madrid. While there is little doubt that he achieved the first, he certainly did not achieve the second. The history of the 45th summed it up rather well:

> A brilliant victory, it is true, had been gained, but no results had followed; the losses had been considerable, and a bitter hatred of the Spaniards had been engendered among our overworked and ill-fed soldiers ... But in spite of being a failure, the campaign had clearly proved two things – the steadfastness and ability under great trials of the English general and the stubbornness and capacity for fighting, under the most adverse circumstances, of the troops he commanded.[5]

Perhaps it was a pyrrhic victory rather than a 'brilliant' one, but it was a victory nevertheless and it was certainly of importance, if not for the reasons Wellesley fought the battle. While Roliça, Vimeiro and Oporto were all victories, Talavera was fought on a larger scale and with greater ferocity, and it was this victory that finally established the British army and its commander as a true match for the French. Any brilliance was not in the decisiveness of the result, nor even the tactics; the brilliance had been in the fighting qualities and stoicism of the British soldier, and perhaps the numbers of dead testified to the courage of the vanquished rather than to the scale of the victory. If Victor had directed the battle with a little more military art, sophistication and respect for his opponents, then it could have been a different ending altogether. The lack of real strength of Wellesley's position and the inexperience of his army made the outcome far less certain than in most of his later battles, and Fortescue reasons, 'The French ought to have won the battle; and if they were properly handled they must have won it, for their infantry counted nearly double that of the British.'[6]

The French Perspective

Needless to say, Joseph tried hard to hide the extent of his defeat from Napoleon. Coming after his hard-won victories over the Austrians it did much to undermine what the Emperor had achieved in the Wagram campaign, and his private secretary, Bourrienne, wrote, 'Napoleon, while in Vienna, heard of the affair of Talavera de la Reyna [*sic*] ... he was very much affected by the news, and did not conceal the chagrin it caused him.'[7] His brother's report claimed that 'the English army was forced from its positions ... the battlefield, of which we have possession, is covered in their dead ... If I have a regret, it is that we did not take the whole English army prisoner.'[8]

Napoleon was not fooled by this account, which can at best be described as wishful thinking. No doubt the Emperor heard the truth from others that were present, and sent back a scathing rebuke to his brother for trying to mislead him. However, although he castigated his brother, he made Jourdan the scapegoat. On 21 August he wrote to the Marshal, 'When one attacks good troops, like the English, in good positions, without reconnaissance, and without being certain of success, one only condemns men to death uselessly.'[9] Ten days later he followed this up with a second letter which gives us an interesting insight into his own philosophy on when to give battle, and also expresses the belief (while overestimating how many fresh troops Joseph had at the end of the battle) that one final effort should have been made to save the day:

> His Majesty finds besides, that once one has resolved to give battle, it is necessary to do so with maximum vigour and unity, and that it is to suffer an insult to be repulsed when one still has 12,000 men who have not fired a shot. The Emperor adds that one should not offer battle unless one is assured in advance that the odds in one's favour are three out of four ... but once it has been resolved upon, it is necessary to vanquish or perish.[10]

Joseph continued to claim that Talavera was a French victory, and while his report to Napoleon was largely fiction, we must be a little more wary of writing off this specific claim as a figment of his imagination. From his own perspective it is understandable how Joseph could interpret the battle as something of a success. He had fought to a standstill a British and Spanish force that outnumbered him by nearly 10,000 men, and this, combined with Soult's strategic manoeuvre, had forced them to renounce their advance on

Madrid. Furthermore, he had been able to concentrate 46,000 men against Wellesley and Cuesta, while successfully gambling that only 3,000 Poles could hold up Venegas's advance on Madrid with 23,000 men. Without the benefit of hindsight this would have been a creditable achievement. Not being a Napoleon, his aim was not to destroy the Anglo-Spanish army but to save his capital, and save it he did.

But if Joseph could try to claim a strategic victory he could certainly not claim a tactical one. This can essentially be put down to the French failure to obey two of the widely accepted principles of war, namely 'unity of command' and 'concentration of force'. The first is well illustrated by a quote from the famous French military historian Thiers, who says:

> the heroic soldiers lost the fruits of their heroism through the failure of leadership. Surely, King Joseph and Marshal Jourdan, the one acting in accordance with his good sense and the other from his experience, would have acted more appropriately if they had not been placed between insubordinate generals on one hand, and the distant authority of Napoleon on the other. They found themselves between a disobedience that upset all their plans, and a will that, despite the distance that separated them, paralysed them without guiding them. Talavera summed up this sad state of affairs.[11]

The second is highlighted by Napoleon himself, who wrote to Victor that he had 'seen with sadness that the attack was made piecemeal instead of concentrated'.[12] It is true that the main attack was meant to be a general one across the whole front, but it actually turned out to be a series of partial attacks. Although coming close to success in the centre, these illustrated a lack of coordination and synergy that a single, effective commander would have been able to assert. Overwhelming force was not concentrated at the critical point and even when the French were successful in the centre, they were unable to apply the *coup de grâce*. The attacks on the other points of the line, apart from being uncoordinated, had committed virtually the whole army, leaving insufficient reserves available to exploit a success. In most battles there is a critical point at which timely intervention by one commander-in-chief or the other will decide the battle. At Talavera, while Joseph hesitated to commit his own reserve, Wellesley (by this time lacking a credible reserve of his own) weakened the critical point of his line (the Medellin) in order to reinforce the point in his line where the French had apparently penetrated. The heroic resistance of Mackenzie's brigade, and the timely commitment of the 1/48th, decided the battle.

Joseph's unsuitability as a commander-in-chief will already be obvious. As long as his subordinate generals felt they could undermine his authority and bully him into a particular course of action, it was inevitable that the failure of the whole command team to pull in the same direction and with a unity of purpose would ultimately lead to their downfall. Victor, who was considered an impetuous commander, clearly understood what Napoleon's intent would have been, had he been in command: a coordinated and overwhelming effort to destroy the British army. This was inevitably going to bring him into conflict with Joseph, who, with Jourdan's council, was a far more timid commander, who preferred to achieve his aim, the defeat of the allied advance on Madrid, by the certainty of Soult's manoeuvre on their line of communications rather than the uncertainty of a bloody battle. Even French commentators are clear on the differences between the two: Guy de Beler states, 'Victor and Jourdan; the second erring on the side of prudence, the first by an excess of daring and indiscipline.'[13] With such a contrast in the views of his two key subordinates it is little surprise that Joseph appears indecisive.

Strongly posted as the Spanish were, the French chose not to send forward even a reconnaissance in force to explore just how strong the position was. This must be considered a mistake given the unprovoked rout of the night before, which should have been interpreted as a show of rocky Spanish morale. A reconnaissance in force could well have shown the Spanish army as the weak link in the allied position and ripe for an attack which, if successful, would have seriously compromised the British position and would, in all probability, have forced them into a risky withdrawal.

Joseph was quick to blame the impetuous Victor for the failure, writing to the Marshal: 'The plateau of Talavera was poorly attacked by you, three times: on the evening of the 27th, and on the morning of the 28th with too few forces. On the 28th, I ordered you to attack with three brigades at once, while the three other brigades remained in reserve; it was not done.'[14] Joseph concluded his long letter of reproaches by announcing that he had requested that the Emperor recall him to France. However, in a letter dated 13 December 1809, the Emperor ordered Berthier to write to Victor that he did 'not hold a grudge against him for his conduct at Talavera', and 'that otherwise I know his talents and his ability in war … and that I hope that he will always justify the favourable opinion that I have of him'.[15]

The Spanish Perspective

The Spanish did not see much fighting, but this is hardly cause for censure. Despite the poor performance of some of their troops the night before the battle, they performed creditably enough in the little fighting they were involved in; indeed, the charge of the Regimiento del Rey was described as the most creditable act of the Spanish cavalry in the whole of the war. Although there was clearly an atmosphere of dislike and distrust between the two allied armies, one British soldier was moved to admit: 'A body of Spanish artillery on the left was excellently served; and their cavalry made a gallant charge, which was entirely successful.'[16]

If they played little enough part in the fighting, however, they performed a vital role in securing the right flank of the British army, whose position on the Medellin would have been untenable with that flank in the air. Wellesley would certainly not have been able to face the French alone at Talavera, as the frontage of the position was too great for his small army. Instead he would have been forced to find another position with a narrower frontage, or to have given up the advance on Madrid altogether. We must also not overlook the reinforcements that Cuesta sent to Wellesley at his request, and the lack of hesitation with which they were dispatched. The artillery played a creditable role in repulsing Leval's attacks on the Pajar and Ruffin's in the northern valley, and Bassecourt's and Albuquerque's divisions played a vital, if largely static, role in refusing the British left flank. All in all, although the Spanish cannot claim to have decided the battle they were certainly instrumental in winning it.

Summary
We must conclude that if the battle was a British success, then the campaign was clearly a failure. The reasons for this are only partially to do with what happened at Talavera and the allied incapacity to follow up the victory. We must also look to the incompetence and disobedience of orders on the part of Venegas, a failure of logistics and, finally, Soult's manoeuvre on Plasencia.

Venegas's failure to deny Sébastiani the opportunity to join Joseph against Wellesley, and, once he had let him slip away, his failure to press strongly on Madrid with the overwhelming superiority he enjoyed ensured that Joseph was able to concentrate a force sufficiently strong to successfully block the allied advance at Talavera. With hindsight it is easy to feel that Wellesley and Cuesta were too quick to predicate their plan with such reliance on someone who had already displayed what was at best a mediocre fitness for high command. However, a convincing victory at Talavera would have made reliance on Venegas irrelevant.

Most British historians give the failure of the Central Junta to feed his men as the most compelling reason for Wellesley's refusal to go further. He later wrote, 'We are dying of hunger ... having no provisions, no stores, no means of transport; being overloaded with sick; the horses of the cavalry being scarcely able to march, or those of the artillery to draw guns; and the Officers and soldiers being worn down by want of food, and privations of every description.'[17] However, despite the difficulties of feeding his men, an advance on Madrid against a defeated and demoralized enemy offered not only the prospect of a successful campaign but also the resources of the capital and its surrounding area. These would most surely have been available earlier than the month it took Wellesley to get back Badajoz.

While the supply situation and the exhaustion of his troops no doubt contributed to Wellesley's decision not to pursue the French, the defence of

Marshal Soult was Wellesley's most implacable and enduring opponent in the Peninsula. There can be no doubt that it was his march on the British communications, and not the supply situation, that forced Wellesley to retreat towards Portugal rather than continue the march on Madrid.

Portugal was always his stated priority. While Napoleon would certainly have pursued a defeated enemy and occupied his capital, Wellesley was determined to maintain a secure base in Portugal and see to the French later. Although Soult failed to threaten the British lines of communication early enough to force Wellesley to retreat before Talavera was fought, as Joseph had hoped, his arrival in the allied rear was still the decisive factor in convincing Wellesley that he should ensure the security of Portugal before the seizing of Madrid. We can only speculate on what Soult would have done, and what Joseph would have ordered him to do, if Wellesley had chosen to march on Madrid.

Thus ended Wellesley's first venture into Spain and the campaign of Talavera. Although he had not achieved his aim he had learnt a number of hard lessons that were all to shape his future operations.

Firstly, Wellesley had a clear idea of the capabilities of the Spanish armies and the incompetence of their commanders. Although this may appear a harsh judgement, we have already examined the reasons for it. Until something could be done to improve their training and discipline, he now knew he could not rely on them. Secondly, he understood he must never rely on anyone but himself to ensure that his army was fed. In later years he never moved without a heavy supply train and was pitiless in driving his commissariat. Thirdly, he realized that his army was still not as professional as it needed to be. The failures and negligence of his troops had exposed his army to heavy losses: the surprise at Casa Salinas, the lack of preparedness for the night attack, the loss of control

Wellesley was to learn many lessons from his hard-fought victory at Talavera, and these were reflected in the tactics he used in many of his later, more famous, victories.

of the counter-attack in the centre of the line and the charge of the 23rd Light Dragoons were all symptoms of this.

Wellesley also saw that refinements were needed to his tactical system. To protect his infantry from the superior French artillery, and to confuse their attacks, he was careful to put as much of his line as possible on a reverse slope position in a way he was unable to do at Talavera. He also strengthened his light infantry screen to ensure that his troops would not be surprised and that they countered the effectiveness of his adversary's skirmishers. Finally, although the only evidence is the fact that it did not happen again, he ensured that the undoubted decisiveness of the charge that followed the volleys of musketry was not lost through a lack of control of the troops that took part in it, and that they were recalled to the line when the French had been broken. Unhappily for him he was not as successful in this with his cavalry as he was with his infantry.

The French should also have learnt some valuable lessons, and it seems strange to have to conclude that some of them, at least, did not. Although the French soldiers learnt to respect their British counterparts, many of their commanders appear to have ignored the lessons taught to them at this battle. Despite their success with attacks in column throughout the rest of Europe, they did not appreciate that in the British they had found an adversary who would not be intimidated by such imposing formations and whose firepower was sufficient to bring them to a halt. They did not learn that these types of attack would not only fail, and fail consistently, but would also cost them heavy casualties.

Although many French marshals learnt the folly of frontal attacks across ground of British choosing, they did not attempt to adjust their tactics and develop ways of countering the British system. Indeed they do not seem to have carried out any post-mortem on any of their repeated failures against the British, and it is surprising that there is little or no evidence of the use of *l'ordre mixte* or some other tactical innovation in subsequent battles. Instead, one French commander after another, apparently dismissive of his colleagues' failure to beat the British, and confident that his own brilliance would reverse the trend, used the same tactics with the same results.

Despite the heavy losses, Talavera vindicated Wellesley's tactics and the growing reputation of the British soldier for steadiness and high morale. The further development of his tactical principles would ensure that Wellesley would retire undefeated, and that the 'redcoats' would increasingly consider themselves the superior of their French counterparts. This moral ascendancy had a considerable influence over their future meetings and reversed a trend that the French had established in the rest of Europe.

In recognition of his success, Wellesley was made captain general in the Spanish army by a grateful Central Junta, and on 12 September he heard that he had been created Viscount Wellington by the British government. On the 16th he concluded a letter, 'This is the first time I have signed my new name.'[18]

Cuesta, who no doubt claimed some credit for the victory, was not so lucky. Soon after the battle, Wellesley's brother, in his recent appointment as British 'ambassador-extraordinary' to the Central Junta, was appealing to this body to remove him from command. There can be no doubt that this was as a result of his brother's lengthy correspondence describing the frustrations and lack of cooperation that he had experienced in dealing with his reluctant ally. However, before this request was fully considered, and perhaps in anticipation of its result, Cuesta offered his resignation. In the weeks following the battle his health had deteriorated to the point that he suffered a stroke on the night of 12/13 August that left him without the use of one of his legs. He was appointed as governor of the Balearic Islands and departed with nothing more than a flattering letter from the Central Junta. Regrettably his successor, his former second in command, General Eguia, proved every bit as incompetent and uncooperative as Cuesta had been, and the British army found itself no better served than before.

Chapter Eleven

A Tour of the Battlefield

Talavera de la Reina, to give the town its full name, is situated in the attractive Tagus valley 70 miles (113km) to the south-west of Madrid. It is quite a large town that had expanded beyond its ancient walls long before 1809. It is probably best known for its distinctive, elaborately decorated ceramics, but my lasting impression will be of a very busy town characterized by its urban sprawl, large red-brick apartment blocks and light industry, all appearing to lack any vestige of town planning.

Although essentially a modern town lacking much historical character, the maze of small streets and its distinctly Spanish 'feel' do have a certain attraction. As it formed the anchor of the allied right, the town does have an important connection to the battle, and some exploration of its streets offers a relevant and interesting contrast to the time spent on the rest of the battlefield.

Getting There

In these days of cheap flights a trip to Talavera really doesn't need to be too expensive. Although many people might choose to combine it with a visit to other Peninsula battlefields, it can just as easily be visited over a long weekend.

All the budget airlines have flights to Madrid from across the UK. Of course, booking well ahead will secure the best deals. Once in Madrid, time may be put aside to visit the Museo del Ejército (Museum of the Army) in Méndez Núñez near the Retiro Park. The museum is situated in a beautiful former royal apartment and is full of interesting exhibits. Regrettably it does not have a very comprehensive Peninsular War section and has little to offer on any of the battles in which the British participated. It concentrates, perhaps unsurprisingly, on Bailén and the sieges of Zaragoza and Gerona, but also has an excellent collection of Spanish uniforms. The library and archives are accessible with prior written application to Museo del Ejército, C/. Méndez Núñez 1, 28014 Madrid. The staff are very friendly and helpful, and many speak good English. The museum is open from 10.00 am to 2.00 pm from Tuesday to Sunday, and entry costs only €1.

From Madrid it is a painless journey to Talavera whichever way you choose to get there. It lies on the main rail line from Madrid to Badajoz, giving a choice of between six and eight trains a day from Atocha station. The other option is to hire a car, and this is as easy in Madrid as in any other big city. Spain has a well-developed motorway system, and once again Talavera lies on the main route (A5/E90) from Madrid to Badajoz. Spanish motorways also have the advantage of not being anywhere near as busy as they are in the UK. The journey from Madrid airport takes about an hour (but beware the rush hour!).

Talavera could hardly be described as a tourist hotspot, but like any busy town there are a variety of modern hotels to suit any pocket. These can be perused on the Talavera town website at www.talaveradelareina.com. Most have opened recently and offer a complete range of comforts.

Preparation

Whether you choose to get around the battlefield on foot or by car, a detailed map of the area is a must. The Mapa Topográfico Nacional de España produce both the 1 cm to the kilometre (1:50,000) and the more detailed 2 cm to the kilometre (1:25,000) maps. I would strongly recommend the latter. There is a standing joke in the British army that says that every battle is fought at the join of four separate map sheets, and regrettably Talavera is no exception. For comprehensive coverage of the battlefield and immediate vicinity, the 1:50,000 sheets required are 16–25 (Talavera de la Reina), 16–24 (Navamorcuende), 15–24 (Navalcán) and 15–25 (Calera y Chozas). In 1:25,000 you will require 601-IV (Mejorada), 602-III (Cervera de los Montes), 626-II (Velada) and 627-I (Talavera de la Reina). For the less dedicated or affluent the Talavera map in each series covers the core of the battlefield, including the town itself, and is adequate in order to walk the whole area of the fighting. These maps can be ordered from any good map shop or online (try www.themapshop.co.uk). I would also recommend that you take a copy of an old map (such as that in Oman's *History*) showing the deployment of the two sides, as this will greatly aid you in identifying the extent of each line. I found it very useful and interesting to transpose the deployment shown on Oman's map onto my modern map.

Whatever the time of year, a pair of sturdy walking shoes is also vital and, if travelling on foot, a packed lunch and liquid refreshment should also be carried, as neither is available on the routes we shall explore.

The Battlefield in General

Despite the best efforts of mankind, there is still plenty of interest to visit on the battlefield. However, that is not to say that much of the terrain over which the battle was fought does not bear modern scars. Of course the town itself has grown considerably in the last 200 years, but luckily for the visitor this expansion has tended to be along the main arterial routes that go to the east and west rather than towards the battlefield that lies to the north.

Inside the town there are two sites related to the battle that are worth visiting. The first is the Basílica de Nuestra Señora del Prado. This church, now submerged in the built-up area but situated in a pleasant park next to the bullring, was well outside the eastern edge of the town in 1809 and was incorporated into the first Spanish line. Sergeant Nicol of the 1st Battalion of Detachments reports that the Spanish 'planted their heavy cannon in front of a chapel at our right'.[1] It is also worth visiting the impressive old town walls. Although redundant at the time of the battle, they would still have been a considerable obstacle to the French if they had chosen to storm the town. They were manned by the Spanish third line. It is reassuring to see that these truly impressive walls, clearly long neglected, are now being restored. An hour walking around their perimeter is well worth the effort if the time is available. A large-scale map of the town is available free from the Tourist Information Office (e-mail: infotur@aytotalaveradelareina.es).

The railway marks the northern extent of the town. It is only when you cross this that you can really appreciate the lie of the land across which the battle was fought. For the first mile or so along the allied line the ground is virtually flat. All the olive groves and vineyards that are mentioned by the first-hand accounts of the battle have unfortunately been cleared, and you have to travel

Most of Talavera's impressive old walls remain. This photograph shows part of the wall in the east of the town that was manned by Spanish troops to help anchor the allied right.

well out of town to see and get a feel for how these would have affected the battle (for those with a car, a journey along the road towards Toledo will enable you to do this). This area of the battlefield is now arable farmland with a large scattering of farms and villas. The Portiña brook still appears to run along its original course, although it is now contained between two artificially built up banks, which I presume is to prevent flooding. Even so its path shows what little cover was available to Campbell's and Sherbrooke's divisions who occupied this part of the line.

Some recent visitors to the battlefield claim not to have been able to locate the Pajar de Vergara. However, there is a distinctive rise exactly where it is shown on most maps of the battle, even if it is not as elevated as it is sometimes portrayed and rather camouflaged beneath an orchard and farm buildings. Some confusion might arise from the fact that it cannot be identified on a modern map because of the contour interval being 10 metres; it is certainly not that high and is now topped by a large farmhouse. Interestingly, the slope is much steeper on the British side and drops more gradually towards the French lines.

The southern slope of the Cerro de Medellin rises quite gently at first, and it is here that we meet the Madrid to Badajoz motorway that regrettably cuts straight through the battlefield. However, I must say that, despite the difficulties it presents in criss-crossing the battlefield, its aesthetic intrusion is not too great.

While the slope up to the summit of the Medellin begins to get steeper, our attention moves further to the east where the British line ran along the banks of the Portiña. Here it is the precipitous banks of this otherwise rather insignificant stream that catch our attention. Though it is difficult to be sure of how the motorway construction and other works may have altered the depth and steepness of the banks, they cannot have made a substantial difference away from the immediate vicinity of the motorway.

The area of the Medellin and the Cerro de Cascajal is probably the least affected by the passage of time. Despite the large, but not modern, farm on the Cascajal, the lie of the land is virtually unchanged and is the most atmospheric and imposing part of the battlefield. The most significant piece of terrain on the British side is that which is now capped by an underground reservoir. This is a small ridge-line, the end of which, unlike the Medellin itself which lies 550 yards (500m) back from the Portiña, really does dominate the approaches from the Cascajal. Once again the contour interval is too great to identify how important this piece of terrain is by examining a map, and it is only when there in person that this can be fully understood. It is surprising that neither contemporary, nor near contemporary, maps of the battlefield really identify it, merely showing the ground dropping away from the summit of the Medellin to the Portiña. It was on this piece of high ground that the British line was positioned. The absence of this key terrain on many maps of the battle just goes to prove that it is impossible to really understand a battle without visiting the ground on which it was fought.

It is the shallow valley to the north of the Medellin that has most suffered by the hand of man. A fair proportion of the valley now lies under water thanks to the dam that has been built between the Medellin and Cascajal. The resultant reservoir has covered the ground over which the 23rd Light Dragoons charged, the ravine at which they came to grief, the Valdefuentes farm which marked the limit of the French advance in this valley, and the ground across which they moved.

Beyond the reservoir are the slopes that rise to the Sierra de Segurilla. It is here that Bassecourt's Spanish light infantry was deployed. It is hard to get a real feel for this ground when observing from the Medellin or Cascajal heights, but closer inspection reveals them to be very rocky and hard going, if not particularly steep. This is ideal defensive ground for light infantry, and it would have been a considerable undertaking for Ruffin's men to dislodge the Spanish troops from this difficult terrain.

The Ground in Detail: A Recommended Tour
In this section I have tried to outline a tour of the battlefield that takes in all its most interesting areas, given the impact of modern development, and to place the visitor at the points on the battlefield that witnessed the most important and dramatic events. This tour could be completed on foot on a day's excursion by car or train from Madrid. If using a car to move around the key points, or with more than one day to visit the battlefield, other recommended sites can be visited, as discussed in the next section. If the recommended tour is done on foot then the route is approximately 7 miles (11km) starting at, and returning to, Talavera station. Although I have endeavoured to provide some comprehensive sketch maps I do recommend (again!) that visitors acquire the maps detailed earlier. Do not attempt to navigate by old battlefield maps, as not only do many give a wildly inaccurate impression of the geography of the battlefield, but the many modern routes and buildings are necessarily unmarked.

Whether on foot or in a car, the tour best starts by leaving Talavera in the north following the signs for the CM 9512 to Mejorada and Segurilla. This road crosses the railway over a bridge a few hundred yards to the west of the railway station, and then takes a left turn at the roundabout just beyond the bridge. Stop Site 1 is about 875 yards (800m) up this road where a prominent track bears to the right (signposted Vivero).

Stop Site 1
As this is the first stop on our tour it is important to get our orientation. This is best done by looking at the map opposite, where I have attempted to superimpose the two sides' deployment over a modern sketch map. Here you

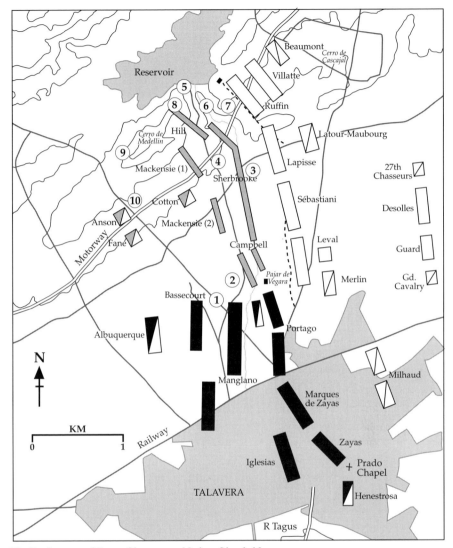

The Deployment of Forces Shown on a Modern Sketch Map.

are standing just behind the extreme left of the Spanish line. It is striking how flat the ground is, and it is difficult to see how this could have suggested itself as a potential defensive position. Of course this was the weak point of the line: the strength lies in the anchor of the right on the River Tagus and the town, and on the Cerro de Medellin on the left. The Medellin is clearly visible from here and it can be seen how its longer slopes face north-west and south-east rather than towards the French advance that came from the east.

In 1809 the ground we are now standing on was covered in olive groves and vineyards, and it is interesting to speculate on the true effect these would have had on observation and manoeuvre. A look at their modern equivalents can certainly help us, though modern farming methods have certainly made them more orderly and better maintained than 200 years ago. Most modern groves have bare soil beneath the trees that is kept clear of all grass and undergrowth, no doubt making it easier to collect a higher proportion of the crop. In 1809 it is likely that there was grass below the trees, but other undergrowth would have been cleared. All this would have ensured that apart from the trees themselves there would have been little obstacle to the movement of a reasonably loose but still formed and controlled column. Given that the French were now experienced in fighting over the more rugged terrain of Spain, they would have been well used to moving and fighting in these looser formations. This is another example of when movement in column would certainly be easier to keep in order than line, and events in the battle seem to support this.

Far more of a problem than movement through an olive grove would be observation, and this was an issue for both sides. Although the trees are generally quite widely spaced, observation is severely hampered. Depending on the maturity of the trees and the distance between them, visibility can range from 25 to 200 yards. Unless looking down a line between neatly planted trees

Virtually the whole front of the Spanish army was covered by olive groves, but this photograph shows the only one that remains. It illustrates how observation and fields of fire were affected, and how loose the French columns must have been to move through them.

(which must have been more unusual then than it is now), I would guess that the average field of observation was no more than 100 yards. Thus for the allies the vigilance of their light troops deployed forward of the main line was vital to their security, and we have seen how the British at least failed in this duty more than once.

Perhaps the greatest advantage the olive groves offered both sides was the unlikelihood of troops being tempted to open fire too early and wasting their fire, a bad habit among even experienced troops. Both sides faced the fear caused by the uncertainty of what lay beyond their limited vision, and we must not underestimate how much impact this could have had on their morale. It would have inevitably caused some hesitation in an advance and caution among the troops. It would also have made it difficult for officers to decide when they should make any deployments. It is highly likely that officers would have been sent forward with the light troops to see the lie of the land and to identify the enemy line so that information could be sent back to the commanders of the main body. We have also seen how the olive groves impacted on the deployment of artillery, and in particular the difficulties the French faced trying to support Leval's advance and their inability to turn the limbers quickly, which resulted in their being captured.

Unlike in France where they cover considerable areas, the local vineyards are small and clearly of a size that would produce only sufficient wine for the use of the family on whose land they lie, rather than being a cash crop. Those that remain in the area beyond the present-day battlefield consist of low, well-spaced bushes that would provide no obstacle to either movement or observation.

We now proceed up the track towards the north about 400 yards (365m). On the left is the Villa Christina: this is Stop Site 2.

Stop Site 2
If we look to the right we will be able to identify the Pajar de Vergara, on which the unfinished earthwork, or redoubt, was located. In fact we get a better impression of its elevation from this side than from the French perspective, from which the slope is actually quite gentle. Oman visited the battlefield in 1903 when he described it as 'a low knoll twenty feet high, now crowned by a large farmhouse, which occupies the site of the old battery'.[2] This farmhouse still stands.

British artillery was not routinely protected by earthworks on the battlefield, but as the Pajar was the only physical feature that offered a small advantage to the defenders it could not be ignored, and even a small amount of extra work could enhance it. Its position also offered the British something on which to anchor their right flank, given the lack of confidence in their Spanish allies. It would also allow them to improve their field of fire that was otherwise obstructed by the olive groves; we are told that they could not see more than 200 yards (180m).

This photo shows the terrain at about the centre of the British line looking east towards the French line. It was across this ground that the crisis of the battle was fought out. It is absolutely flat, and in 1809

Perhaps the greatest value of the bank that was thrown up here was the protection it offered to the gun crews from skirmisher fire. While grapeshot fired at such close range would have been devastating against formed troops, as the two battalions of the 4th Baden Regiment found to their cost, it is possible that the olive trees would have allowed the Baden skirmishers to get sufficiently close to cause potentially significant casualties among the gun crews. Even a low earth-bank would have offered a considerable amount of cover, and peace of mind, to the crews who would have otherwise been completely unprotected.

The Portiña runs between us and the Pajar, marked by the small bank that runs along the far side of the field in front of us. Here we are standing where Kemmis's brigade (1/40th, 97th and 2nd Detachments) was located, no doubt to provide some security for the guns on the Pajar. It was always a tricky decision for commanders with this mission as to where to position their troops, as the guns often attracted a considerable amount of artillery fire, and this would often cause considerable casualties among their guard force. From where Kemmis was positioned it is likely that the aim was also to provide an extra bit of depth on what is the extreme right of the British line. Just to the left of the Pajar is where the British line crossed the Portiña brook.

We now carry on up the track that runs parallel to and about 220 yards (200m) behind the British line that here stood just this side of the Portiña. We are crossing the ground where the crisis of the battle was played out. After repulsing the attack of Sébastiani's division, H. Campbell's brigade (1/2nd and 1/3rd Guards), Cameron's (1/61st and 2/83rd) and Langwerth's brigade (1st and 2nd KGL) all pursued the retreating French too far and were counter-

it was covered in long, parched grass. The trees immediately across the field in the foreground mark the line of the Portiña Brook.

attacked and broken by the French reserves. They rushed back towards their own lines, and it was only the steadiness of Mackenzie's brigade (2/24th, 2/31st and 1/45th) and the timely intervention of the 1/48th sent down from the Medellin by Wellesley himself that averted a catastrophe for the British.

After about 850–900 yards (775–825m) we reach a tarmac road. Before starting to slowly ascend towards the Medellin we will turn right along the road that runs alongside a small canal. (Note that this is a service road for the canal and there is no entry to routine traffic.) After about 400 yards (365m), just after we have crossed the Portiña, we come to Stop Site 3.

Stop Site 3

We can now look down the right of the British line along the path of the Portiña. We are just forward of the junction of Cameron's and H. Campbell's brigades who stood behind it. We can see how little cover was available and how flat the ground is. This part of the line was covered in long grass that must have been parched and brown at the height of summer. There were no olive groves here and, apart from the modern cultivation, it probably looks little different now than it did 200 years ago. Off to the west is the position of Cotton's light cavalry brigade (14th and 16th Light Dragoons), which was in a position to support the line on this flat ground. One wonders why they took such little part in both the initial pursuit after the repulse of the main French attack here, and particularly against the French counter-attack after the Guards themselves had been thrown back after their own pursuit of the French got out of hand. No account of the battle adequately explains this.

A view from the French centre-left. The highest point is the Medellin; it is no surprise that Wellesley could see the whole of the British and French lines from the summit. It appears that the view from the top was so dominating that there is no reference to his ever leaving that single point – quite unusual for a commander who earned a reputation for always being at the critical point on a battlefield. It was across the flat ground that the main French attack came (from right to left) and across which the outcome of the battle was decided.

We must now retrace our steps to the crossroads and turn right towards the Medellin. Immediately on our left is a small olive grove which can at least give us a feel for what was present on a much greater scale across the flat ground that constituted the right of the British line, and how movement and observation might have been affected. We are now about halfway along the British line, and it is only here that the ground starts to rise to any appreciable extent. As you climb you will pass a fenced water-company facility on your right. Just past this, and before you reach the motorway, turn right onto the faint track that takes you across some waste ground. If you are travelling by car it is recommended that you park it just off the road. Follow the track through the scrub to where you meet the steep banks of the Portiña. This is Stop Site 4.

Stop Site 4
We are now standing in the King's German Legion's portion of the line. By my rough estimation the motorway runs about where the brigades of Löw (5th and 7th Line KGL) and Langwerth (1st and 2nd Line KGL) met. We are well placed to see how steep the banks were here, and it is not difficult to

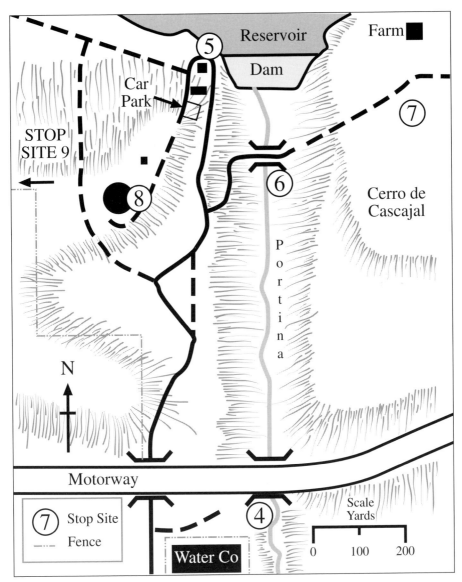

The Northern End of the Battlefield.

sympathize with the French soldiers of Lapisse's division who had to struggle up these banks in order to close with the British line. The dense brush that now covers the area does not get a mention in the eyewitness accounts of the battle, and we must therefore presume that the visibility was much better then than it is now. The more surefooted may wish to move down for a close look at the Portiña. Although its flow can now be controlled by the dam, we do know that on the day of battle it was described as 'a small rivulet, dry in many places, but where there were pools, black ugly snakes were plentiful'.[3] This pretty well describes the stream as it is now, although I haven't seen any snakes.

It is difficult to be sure how close to the edge of the Portiña's steep banks the KGL battalions would have been deployed. There was clearly some advantage to standing from 50 to 100 yards (45–90m) back from the edge and firing a devastating volley on the French as they came over the lip in a certain amount of disorder, having just struggled up the bank. Such a volley, followed up by a bayonet charge, would inevitably have pushed the attackers back into the ravine. The other alternative was to stand on the edge and fire down on the attacking troops as they struggled up the steep slope. The fact that the KGL was surprised by the night attack of the 9ème légère supports the view that it was indeed positioned some distance from the edge.

Follow our route back to the road, which now becomes a gravel track, and turn towards the motorway. Before dropping down look up and slightly left for a good view of the summit of the Medellin, now marked by a rather impressive villa, where Wellesley had his command post. Even from here it is evident what a dominating position this was.

Proceed under the motorway. On the far side we continue along the line of the KGL, and it is here that I believe the French night attack fell. This is where Löw's brigade was deployed, and it can be seen that the banks of the Portiña are not quite so steep here. Oman puts this down to luck, but the French had plenty of time to identify the best point of attack before it got dark. It was upon Löw's troops that the main weight of the 9ème légère fell, in particular the 7th KGL, who were broken with the loss of 150 men, half of them prisoners. Langwerth's brigade to the south was also pushed back. From this position the French then swung slightly right and headed for the summit of the Medellin, brushing with Donkin's brigade, which was deployed further back in support of the German brigades. From here we can see to what extent they had penetrated the British line when they temporarily occupied the Medellin before General Hill's counter-attack pushed them back again.

As you reach a small rise about 300 yards (275m) from the motorway you will see before you a prominent ridge-line that runs down from the summit of the Medellin surmounted by a red-brick, flat-roofed building. This ridge and the height at its eastern end are given no mention in any accounts of the battle or shown on any old maps, and yet from here it is clear how important a post this must have been. There is little doubt in my mind that it was across this height that the main British line stood. Oman's map does not show this feature and places the British line further back, protecting the Medellin, which produces an unlikely gap between it and the KGL brigades.

We now move on along the track that from Oman's map appears to follow pretty much the same line as in 1809. As we crest the next rise 200 yards (180m) on we see over on our right a prominent farm standing on a plateau. Although this farm did not exist 200 years ago, it neatly marks the top of the Cerro de

Cascajal, the main French position during the battle. A hundred yards (90m) further on we come to a Y junction. Follow the track to the left; we are now travelling across the lower slopes of the Medellin up which the French advanced on the morning of 28 July, only to be thrown back down again after a close-range musket duel. To our right is the modern Portiña dam. Follow the track to the western edge of the dam; this is Stop Site 5. If you are in a car follow the track round the hairpin bend and park in the small car-park on the left and then walk back to the Stop Site.

Stop Site 5

From here we have a good view across the reservoir to the north. How sad that the ground over which the action was fought here is now under water! Ruffin's division, supported by a brigade (Cassagne's 27ème légère and 63ème de ligne) from Villatte's division, started its attack from the north of the Cascajal, which is over our right shoulder. They advanced down the line of the valley across our front, with Ruffin to the north and Cassagne's brigade closest to where we stand. Merlin's cavalry (10ème and 23ème Chasseurs à Cheval, Polish Vistula Legion Lancers and Westphalian Chevaux-Légers) supported the infantry. To do this they would normally march at least 400 yards (365m) behind them. The gap would have ensured that if the infantry broke or became disordered, this would not have communicated itself to the supports. They would then have had the time and space to deliver an effective counter-charge.

At the base of the Medellin to our left was the farm of Valdefuentes, which also now regrettably lies submerged. It was as the French infantry reached this point that they were charged by Anson's cavalry brigade (23rd Light Dragoons and 1st KGL Hussars). Forced into square by the British charge, the French suffered heavy casualties from the British artillery on the Medellin. Cassagne's brigade, who took no other part in any of the fighting, lost over 200 men during this time. The 23rd Light Dragoons continued their charge past the French infantry, and the remaining 160 or so charged on against the 1,200 men of Merlin. It is hard to understand what they thought they could achieve against such superior numbers and it is no surprise that so few were able to return to their own lines. Some French sources claim that the remnants of the 23rd were pursued as far as the Alberche river before they were finally killed or captured. Colonel Elley, who was one of the few to escape, swung north onto the slopes of the Sierra de Segurilla and then made his way back through the Spanish troops of Bassecourt.

The rocky slopes of the Sierra de Segurilla that were occupied by Bassecourt have already been described. These can be seen rising on the far side of the reservoir. They would have taken Ruffin's troops a considerable time to clear of Spanish infantry, and it is doubtful if he could have spared a large enough force to be sure of achieving this. During the early years of the war the Spanish had shown themselves capable of a stubborn and ferocious defence of a strong

A spectacular view of the northern valley and Medellin from the heights of the Sierra de Segurilla (looking south). The dam can be seen to the left with the patch of clear ground just beyond it marking the Cascajal. On the right can be seen the peak of the Medellin (with the town of Talavera beyond it).

position. By the time Ruffin's attack was launched on the 28th the crisis in the British centre had been averted, and for the French, the battle could be saved only by quick and decisive action. As it happened, Ruffin did not have the time, the force or the determination to turn defeat into victory. To be fair, the tactical situation he faced was hardly favourable: the British were still securely ensconced on the Medellin and the troops there had not been in action since early morning, apart from having to endure almost continuous artillery fire. To his front remained two brigades of fresh British heavy cavalry and the complete Spanish cavalry division of the Duke of Albuquerque. On his right, occupying the high and rocky slopes of the Sierra de Segurilla, was Bassecourt's light infantry. Finally, there was the Spanish and British artillery on the Medellin which had a wide field of fire and had already caused considerable casualties to his exposed columns and squares. Bearing in mind that Ruffin's division had conducted both the night attack and the first attack of the morning, we must doubt their commitment, given the heavy casualties they had sustained, as well as the fact that they must have been pretty exhausted. Perhaps the French general can be forgiven for feeling he had been given 'mission impossible'. Early in the morning of the 28th, when there were no allied troops in the valley and less artillery on the Medellin, there might have been a chance of success, but the opportunity had slipped by.

Unfortunately it is not possible to make out the concrete reservoir that marks the British front line, but it lies about two-thirds of the way along the ridge that runs down to the left from the Medellin. Anson's cavalry charge started on the right of the photo and hit the French attack just before the line of the dam.

We now make our way back towards the Y junction that we passed earlier and turn left. The more adventurous might want to cut the corner off and get a feel for just how difficult the slope is. Follow the track down to Stop Site 6, which is on the bridge over the Portiña.

Stop Site 6

We have already heard how the Portiña looked on the day of the battle, and although the dam now controls its level the old description still seems to fit it rather well. But here we are more interested in the slopes that meet it on each side. We note that on the French side the slope is actually quite gradual compared to the British side, and far less of an obstacle. These will have changed little in the intervening years, and although contemporary descriptions tell of scattered scrub, I feel sure the undergrowth was not as dense then as it is now.

At 5.00 am on 28 July a heavy artillery barrage heralded the first French attack, which was launched across this ground by Ruffin's division. It is strange that Victor, whose corps consisted of three divisions, should choose the same one with which he had attacked the night before. These troops must have been particularly tired and perhaps also a little demoralized after their failure, however close a call it had turned out to be. We are standing in the path of the three battalions of the 24ème de ligne that formed the centre of the attack. On the French right, attacking the extreme left of the British line on the Medellin was the 9ème légère, and on their left the 96ème de ligne. After a furious firefight the British line charged and sent the French columns tumbling back down the hill. Some of the pursuing redcoats actually crossed onto the French side of the Portiña before coming under fire from the French reserves and retiring back to their own lines. This attack was over by 8.30 am, and this sector of the battlefield saw no further fighting.

We will now follow the track up onto the Cerro de Cascajal to a point level with the large farmhouse. This is Stop Site 7.

Stop Site 7

The maximum effective range of artillery at this time was considered to be between about 1,200 and 1,800 yards (1,100–1,650m), depending on calibre. However, given the difficulties of accurately identifying targets at this range, it was rarely deployed much more than 1,000 yards (915m) from the enemy line. It is therefore a fair estimate to say that we are standing more or less on the line where the powerful French artillery deployed. This would have put the entire British line opposite well within range. Although apparently very exposed and dominated by the higher ground on the British side of the Portiña, the British tactic of concentrating their own fire against infantry and the fact that they were considerably outgunned did not make this a particularly risky position for the French gunners. In fact the level ground offered them a position far more suitable for the deployment of artillery than the steep slopes of the Medellin did for their British counterparts. Because of its ideal location the majority of Victor's artillery was deployed here; he had forty-eight guns within his corps in six batteries each of eight guns. Pieces were generally placed ten to twenty paces apart, so it is quite possible that the line of guns ran from one side of the

We are standing at Stop Site 7 on the Cerro de Cascajal, approximately where the French artillery was lined up. This spot offers a perfect view of where the British line stood on the Cerro de Medellin (looking south-west). On the right, the reservoir covers the shallow northern valley with the Sierra de Segurilla rising beyond. In the centre the ground drops down gently from where we stand to the Portiña Brook.

plateau to the other, especially as the interval between the guns was likely to be at the greater end because of the need for the advancing infantry to pass through them as they moved forward to the attack. Some French infantry would have been nearby to ensure the security of the guns, but the majority of the assault columns would have waited much further back where they were not needlessly exposed to British artillery fire.

As this is the best view of the British line from the French perspective, it is quite likely that Joseph, Jourdan and Victor debated the advantages and disadvantages of continuing the battle from near this point. Indeed, Victor probably spent most of the battle in this area as he coordinated the attacks of his corps. As the high point of the French position it also gives reasonable views to the south, where Talavera can be clearly seen in the distance.

Looking at the imposing heights of the Medellin it is easy to understand the reluctance of Joseph and Jourdan to attack them head-on; the advantage to approaching them from either flank is so overwhelming it merely exposes Victor's arrogance and folly in believing they could be taken by attacking straight up the slope. On the morning of 28 July, this approach could have been justified only if the force that carried it out was merely trying to fix the British line in position while another force attacked from the northern valley, which was not occupied by any allied force at this time.

Those who have plenty of time may wish to follow the French line to the south along the Cascajal and down towards the motorway running parallel to the Portiña. By using the very large pipe that takes the stream under the motorway you can avoid being stopped by its carriageway. This is no problem unless there has been recent heavy rain, as the Portiña is little more than a trickle and the pipe is wide enough not to have to put your feet in the water. This trip is particularly useful to get a real feel for how much of an obstacle the Portiña banks are. Certainly it is to the credit of the 9ème légère that they

Slightly left of centre, on the skyline, is the peak of the Medellin from where Wellesley commanded. Just in front of it, though separated by 550 yards (500m), the square building sits on the small ridgeline that marks the British front line.

negotiated these banks at night and saw off Löw's KGL brigade on the far side
before setting off towards the right and the summit of the Medellin. My
feeling is that they must have crossed just to the north of the motorway and
then followed the ridge-line that leads up to the Medellin itself. It is no
coincidence that the banks here are not quite as steep as they are to the north
or south. The French commanders had plenty of daylight to identify the best
route across, and once that had been achieved the heights would have been
silhouetted against all but the darkest sky. As the battle was fought at the height
of summer it is hard to believe it was so dark that the distinctive heights of the
Medellin could not be made out from such a short distance.

It is now time to retrace our steps back across the Portiña to the British side
across the bridge near the dam. Follow the track back past Stop Site 5 and
round the hairpin bend to the small car park. Carry on up the slope until you
find yourself next to the underground concrete reservoir where you have an
excellent view to the east and can look down on the Cerro de Cascajal.
Climbing up onto the roof of the reservoir itself offers an even better view for
the more athletic (there is a need to negotiate a balustrade in order to do this).
This is Stop Site 8.

Stop Site 8

From this point we have a good view of the French position on the Cascajal
and over the whole of the battlefield to the south. Sitting here on the ground
just reinforces how very difficult it is to get a real feel for the lie of the land
on this part of the battlefield by looking at any of the old maps published
after the battle. Note that the summit of the Medellin lies about 500 yards
(450m) to our rear. That is where Wellesley appears to have spent most of

*A fine view of the Cascajal from Stop Site 8 (the British front line). The dam can just be seen on the
left and the motorway on the right. The farm on the left marks the highpoint of the plateau, and it was
across the open ground that the French guns were deployed. The French columns would have formed up*

the battle. Of course the villa was not there then, and it is a shame that its presence denies us the ability to view the battlefield through the British commander's eyes. From such a vantage point it is easy to imagine how he was able to anticipate every move that the French made. On the evidence of his own visit, Oman relates, 'every one of Villatte's battalions must have been counted by Wellesley, who could also mark every man along the whole French front, even to and among the olive groves occupied by Leval's Germans'.[4]

It is difficult to be absolutely sure of where the British line was deployed on this part of the battlefield, though most old maps of the site are in general agreement. It seems that Stewart's brigade (29th, 48th and 1st Detachments) lay just a little further back towards the Medellin from where we are now situated. It is easy to see the difficulty of finding a reverse slope position where the line would be protected from the powerful French artillery opposite, and of finding suitable ground for cannon. Given the lack of flat ground and the room taken up by a six-gun battery, it is not surprising that Rettberg's battery was actually split into two half-batteries. Also note the re-entrant and small ridge-line to the south that lead up towards the summit; either would have made a convenient approach for the night attack by the French, and as no one disputes the fact that they actually occupied the highest point we can see to what extent the British line had been penetrated.

From this point it is hard to imagine looking down on the long line of French guns that ran along the Cascajal plateau (and harder still to imagine what is was like to lie on relatively open terrain while they tried to kill you!). The ground then was virtually completely open with few, if any, of the small trees and bushes that now cover the area. Looking down towards the Portiña it is also

beyond the guns, out of range of the British artillery. It was across this ground that Victor's corps attacked on the morning of 28 July.

A view of the peak of the Medellin looking back (west) from Stop Site 8. From here it can be seen what a dominating position it was and how hard a climb for the French infantry. Contemporary accounts suggest that the area was not so covered in scrub as it is today.

hard to believe that the French attacked straight up this slope in the early morning of 28 July, and one cannot help but pity the poor French soldiers who toiled up such a steep slope to their deaths. As you walk around this imposing battlefield I defy you to resist the temptation to look around on the ground for a musket ball or other relic from the battle!

From Stop Site 8 follow one of the many paths that lead through the scrub towards the summit of the Medellin. Once you hit the fence that surrounds it, follow it round to the right so that you find yourself being led along the line of the valley with the Medellin on your left. From this path you will get frequent panoramic views of the northern valley, reservoir and the Sierra de Segurilla beyond. After a walk of 600–700 yards (540–640m) you will find yourself on a small rise with the old battlefield monument directly above you on the ridge-line. This is Stop Site 9.

Stop Site 9

From here we have an outstanding view across the northern valley and in particular the route along which Anson's light cavalry brigade charged. During my own visits, and despite the time warp, I could not help thinking of the 'Valley of Death' of later years. The ground does not seem to have changed much, with most of it covered in the long grass described by contemporary accounts. The brigade's start point was approximately level with our current location, giving them about 500 yards (450m) to cover. One can imagine what a grandstand view Wellesley and the others on the Medellin would have had of the charge, and one cannot but wonder how they were unable to see the ravine that broke the cohesion, if not the determination, of the 23rd Light Dragoons. We have already discussed the real impact the ravine had on the charge, but what a pity that the reservoir now covers the critical point. When Oman visited the battlefield, the ravine could still be seen:

> In its upper part, where the German regiment met it, the obstacle is practically unchanged. But nearer to the farm of Valdefuentes it has almost disappeared, owing to the extension of cultivation. There is only a four foot drop from a field to a piece of rough ground full of reeds and bent-grass, where the soil is a little marshy in April.[5]

We continue our way along the track for another 400 yards (365m), where we will reach a tarmac road. We must now turn to the left and very carefully follow the road for 200 yards (180m) until we can turn into the parking area that marks the modern battlefield memorial. This road is neither particularly busy nor narrow, but the traffic does move quickly and it follows a long blind corner for the oncoming traffic. Particular care should be taken if using this route as there is no pavement, and if this is a concern the memorial should be visited by car.

The old monument. This now stands rather forlornly on the rear slopes of the Medellin having presumably been moved from the peak when the modern villa was built. There is no inscription and it stands on private land.

Stop Site 10

The modern concrete memorial is not particularly pleasing on the eye but is certainly imposing. Although well back from the front line on the Medellin, it still offers a commanding view of the central and southern parts of the battlefield. Inscribed on each of the three 'wings' are the orders of battle of each of the three armies, listing all the regiments and formations present at the battle (although one or two regiments have been omitted, most notably the 97th Foot and 23rd Light Dragoons). Next to the memorial is a very interesting map of the battle made out of tiles in the Talavera style, although regrettably there is no other reference to or account of the events that happened here nearly 200 years ago. The area is also rather poorly maintained.

As a final point of interest, an old and very decrepit farm complex dominates the entrance to the parking area. This area fits perfectly with the description of where the British baggage and field dressing station was located in relation to the line of battle, and the location appears on several old maps I have seen. I cannot help but think that this farm was there in 1809. In his book *Wellington's Doctors*, Dr Martin Howard locates the Talavera dressing station, 'concealed behind the Cerro de Medellin hill in the centre of the British position about

The modern monument stands next to the motorway (foreground) and about 550 yards (500m) behind the British front line. It has a fine view over the south of the battlefield towards the town of Talavera.

700 yards behind the most advanced troops',[6] and Sergeant Nicol of the 1st Battalion of Detachments describes how after being wounded he hobbled back to a 'large white house where many wounded men were waiting to be dressed'.[7] As well as being 700 yards (640m) behind the front line, this derelict farm would certainly have made an excellent location, easy to find and providing shelter and possibly water and straw for the wounded.

This completes our tour, and all that remains is to take the long, straight road back to town. If you have a good map and the time you could always take a less direct route back through the centre of the battlefield, perhaps looking at it from the French perspective. There are many tracks that are not marked on the maps that can be explored, and this can be very rewarding.

Other Sites to Visit

A visit to the Prado Chapel and a walk around the old walls of Talavera have already been recommended but not included in the detailed tour of the battlefield. If the visitor has travelled by train, and is thus stranded by the lack of a car, then this is an ideal opportunity to explore the town. Those with their own means of transport may use this freedom to explore some interesting sites beyond the boundaries of the battlefield.

The first of these might be the River Alberche. This is best viewed from where the main road from Talavera heading for Madrid and Toledo crosses it a little over 3 miles (5km) from the centre of town. Just before the bridge is a small road that goes to the left. By taking this left and then turning down a track to the right soon afterwards the visitor reaches the river. The old, derelict bridge lies parallel to its modern equivalent and appears to mark where the original wooden bridge once stood. Some impressive concrete pillboxes dating from the Spanish Civil War protect the modern bridge.

Like the Portiña, a dam further upstream now controls the flow of the Alberche. However, there is still plenty of evidence as to how the river once looked. We know that, in summer at least, the river was fordable in many places and therefore in itself little or no obstacle to infantry and cavalry. This inevitably reduced its value as an obstacle behind which to site a defensive position. Oman

The Casa de Salinas (now named 'Las Torres').

describes it as being lined with 'underwood', which masked it from view, and notes that the eastern bank was covered in thickets. On 22 July, Victor took position on 'a range of heights, about 800 yards behind the Alberche'.[8] These 'heights' are not apparent, and I feel Oman is describing what is actually a very gradual slope leading up from the river. It is hard to envisage this as the 'formidable' position he describes.[9] Wellesley was certainly not impressed and was keen to attack Victor on 23 July, only for Cuesta to frustrate his plans.

The other site that is worth a visit is the Casa de Salinas. Not marked by name on our modern maps and its general area now scattered with many more farms and villas, it is no surprise that it is hard to find. Older maps give us a general area in which to look, but without an accurate scale or modern roads and tracks marked it is still difficult to pinpoint. A 'ruined house'[10] in 1809, Casa de Salinas is now a very desirable residence that has been renamed 'Las Torres' and is marked as such on the map. It can be found at grid reference 491286 (on either scale map). It is an impressive building which retains the twin towers from one of which Wellesley narrowly escaped capture when the French launched their surprise attack on the 27th. Please respect the privacy of the present owners.

Despite the intervention over the years of modern man, the battlefield of Talavera is well worth a trip. The key terrain of the Medellin and Cascajal is mostly common ground across which you are free to explore, and still offers a fascinating glimpse of what the ground looked like, and perhaps even a hint of what it must have been like to have stood there nearly 200 years ago. Enjoy your visit!

Annex A

The British Infantry Regiments at Talavera

1809	1815	1881	2005
2nd Guards	Coldstream Guards	Coldstream Guards	Coldstream Guards
3rd Guards	3rd Guards	Scots Guards	Scots Guards
3rd Foot	3rd East Kent Regt	Buffs (East Kent Regt)	Princess of Wales's Royal Regt
7th Fusiliers	7th (Royal Fusiliers) Regt	Royal Fusiliers (City of London Regt)	Royal Regiment of Fusiliers
24th Foot	24th (Warwickshire) Regt	South Wales Borderers	Royal Regiment of Wales
29th Foot	29th (Worcestershire) Regt	Worcestershire Regt	Worcestershire and Sherwood Foresters Regt
31st Foot	31st (Huntingdonshire) Regt	East Surrey Regt	Princess of Wales's Royal Regt
40th Foot	40th (2nd Somerset) Regt	Prince of Wales's Volunteers (South Lancashire Regt)	Queen's Lancashire Regt
45th Foot	45th (Nottinghamshire) Regt	Sherwood Foresters Regt	Worcestershire and Sherwood Foresters Regt
48th Foot	48th (Northamptonshire) Regt	Northamptonshire Regiment	Royal Anglian Regt
53rd Foot	53rd (Shropshire) Regt	King's Shropshire Light Infantry	Light Infantry
60th Foot	60th (Royal American) Regt	King's Royal Rifle Corps	Royal Green Jackets
61st Foot	61st (South Gloucestershire) Regt	Gloucestershire Regt	Royal Gloucestershire, Berkshire and Wiltshire Regt
66th Foot	66th (Berkshire) Regt	Princess Charlotte of Wales's (Royal Berkshire Regt)	Royal Gloucestershire, Berkshire and Wiltshire Regt
83rd Foot	83rd Foot	Royal Irish Rifles	Royal Irish Regt
87th Foot	87th (Prince of Wales's Own Irish) Regt	Princess Victoria's (Royal Irish Fusiliers)	Royal Irish Regt
88th Foot	88th (Connaught Rangers) Regt	Connaught Rangers	[Disbanded in 1922]
97th Foot	97th (Queen's Own) Regt	Queen's Own Royal West Kent Regt	Princess of Wales's Royal Regt

Annex B

The British Army at Talavera, as at 25 July 1809

Cavalry Division (Lieutenant General Payne)
Fane's Brigade
3rd Dragoon Guards	525
4th Dragoons	545

Anson's Brigade
23rd Light Dragoons	459
1st Light Dragoons KGL	451

Cotton's Brigade
14th Light Dragoons	464
16th Light Dragoons	525
Cavalry total:	2,969

1st Infantry Division (Lieutenant General Sherbrooke)
H. Campbell's Brigade
1/Coldstream Guards	970
1/3rd Guards	1,019
Company 5/60th	56

Langwerth's Brigade
1st Line Bn KGL	604
2nd Line Bn KGL	678
Light Coy/Light Bn KGL	106

Cameron's Brigade
1/61st Foot	778
2/83rd Foot	535
Company 5/60th	51

Von Löw's Brigade
5th Line Bn KGL	610
7th Line Bn KGL	557
1st Division total:	5,964

2nd Infantry Division (Major General Hill)
Tilson's Brigade
1/3rd Foot	746
2/48th Foot	567

2/66th Foot	526
Company 5/60th	52

R. Stewart's Brigade

1/29th Foot	598
1/48th Foot	807
1st Bn Detachments	609
2nd Division total:	3,905

3rd Infantry Division (Major General Mackenzie)
Mackenzie's Brigade

2/24th Foot	787
2/31st Foot	733
1/45th Foot	756

Donkin's Brigade

2/87th Foot	599
1/88th Foot	599
5/60th Foot (5 coys)	273
3rd Division total:	3,747

4th Infantry Division (Brig A. Campbell)
A. Campbell's Brigade

2/7th Foot	431
2/53rd Foot	537
Company 5/60th	64

Kemmis's Brigade

1/40th Foot	745
97th Foot	502
2nd Bn Detachments	625
Company 5/60th Foot	56
4th Division total:	2,960

Artillery
3 British batteries (681)
Lawson's (6 × 3-pounders)
Sillery's (5 × 6-pounders, 1 × howitzer)
Eliott's (5 × 6-pounders, 1 × howitzer)

2 KGL Batteries (330)
Rettberg's (5 × heavy 6-pounders, 1 × howitzer)
Heyse's (5 × heavy 6-pounders, 1 × howitzer)

Engineers
22

British army total:	**20,578**

Annex C
The Spanish Army of Extremadura

Infantry
Vanguard (Brigadier General Zayas)
2nd Volunteers of Catalonia
2nd Bn Cazadores de Barbastro
Cazadores de Campo-Mayor (1 bn)
Cazadores de Valencia y Albuquerque (1 bn)
2nd Battalion Voluntarios de Valencia

1st Division (Major General Marques de Zayas)
Cantabria Infantry Regiment (3 bns)
Granaderos Provinciales (1 bn)
Canarias Infantry Regiment (1 bn)
Tiradores de Mérida (1 bn)
Provincial de Truxillo (1 bn)

2nd Division (Major General Iglesias)
2nd Majorca Infantry Regiment (1 bn)
Velez-Malaga Infantry Regiment (3 bns)
Osuna Infantry Regiment (2 bns)
Voluntarios Estrangeros (1 bn)
Provincial de Burgos (1 bn)

3rd Division (Major General de Portago)
Badajoz Infantry Regiment (2 bns)
2nd Antequera Infantry Regiment (1 bn)
Imperial de Toledo (1 bn)
Provincial de Badajoz (1 bn)
Provincial de Guadix (1 bn)

4th Division (Major General Manglano)
Irlanda Infantry Regiment (2 bns)
Jaen Infantry Regiment (2 bns)
3rd Seville Infantry Regiment (1 bn)
1st Bn Leales de Fernando VII (1 bn)
2nd Volunteers of Madrid (1 bn)
Voluntarios de la Corona (1 bn)

5th Division (Major General Bassecourt)
Real Marina, 1st Infantry Regiment (2 bns)
3rd Bn Africa Infantry Regiment
Murcia Infantry Regiment (2 bns)
1st Battalion Reyna Infantry Regiment
Provincial de Siguenza (1 bn)

Cavalry
1st Division (Lieutenant General de Henestrosa)
Rey Cavalry Regiment
Calatrava Cavalry Regiment
Voluntarios de España
Imperial de Toledo
Cazadores de Seville
Reyna Cavalry Regiment
Villaviciosa Cavalry Regiment
Cazadores de Madrid

2nd Division (Lieutenant General Duque de Albuquerque)
Carabineros Reals (1 sqn)
Infante Cavalry Regiment
Alcantara Cavalry Regiment
Pavia Cavalry Regiment
1st Hussars of Extremadura
2nd Hussars of Extremadura

Artillery
30 guns

Total:
41 Infantry Battalions	26,000
2 Cavalry Divisions	6,000
Artillery	800

The French Army at Talavera

I Corps (Marshal Victor)
1st Division (Général de division Ruffin – 5,286)
Brigade (Général de brigade)
9ème légère (3 bns)
24ème de ligne (3 bns)

Brigade (Général de brigade Barrois)
96ème de ligne (3 bns)

2nd Division (Général de division Lapisse – 6,862)
Brigade (Général de brigade Laplannes)
16ème légère (3 bns)
45ème de ligne (3 bns)

Brigade (Général de brigade Solignac)
94ème de ligne (3 bns)
95ème de ligne (3 bns)

3rd Division (Général de division Villatte – 6,135)
Brigade (Général de brigade Cassagne)
27ème légère (3 bns)
63ème de ligne (3 bns)

Brigade (Général de brigade Puthod)
94ème de ligne (3 bns)
95ème de ligne (3 bns)

Corps Cavalry (Général de brigade Beaumont – 980)
2ème Hussars
5ème Chasseurs à cheval

Corps Artillery
48 guns

IV Corps (Général de division Sébastiani)
1st Division (Général de division Sébastiani – 8,118)
Brigade (Général de brigade Rey)
28ème de ligne (3 bns)
32ème de ligne (3 bns)

Brigade (Général de brigade Liger-Belair)
58ème de ligne (3 bns)
75ème de ligne (3 bns)

2nd Division* (Général de division Valance – 1,600)
4th Polish Regt (2 bns)

3rd Division (Général de division Leval – 4,537)
Brigade (Oberst von Porbeck)
2nd Nassau Regt (2 bns)
4th Baden Regt (2 bns)
Baden Foot Bty (8 × 6-pounders)

Brigade (Général de brigade Chassé)
2nd Dutch Regt (2 bns)
3rd Dutch Horse Bty (6 × 6-pounders)

Brigade (Général de brigade Grandjean)
Hesse-Darmstadt Gross und Erbprinz Regt (2 bns)
Frankfurt Bn

Corps Cavalry (Général de brigade Merlin – 1,188)
Brigade (Général de brigade Strolz)
10ème Chasseurs à Cheval
26ème Chasseurs à Cheval

Brigade (Général de brigade Ormancy)
Polish Chevaux-Léger-lancier Regt
Westphalian Chevaux-Léger Regt

Corps Artillery
30 guns

1st Dragoon Division (Général de division Latour-Maubourg – 3,279)
1er Dragoon Regt
2ème Dragoon Regt
4ème Dragoon Regt
9ème Dragoon Regt
14ème Dragoon Regt
26ème Dragoon Regt

2nd Dragoon Division (Général de division Milhaud – 2,356)
5ème Dragoon Regt
12ème Dragoon Regt
16ème Dragoon Regt
20ème Dragoon Regt
21ème Dragoon Regt
3rd Dutch Hussar Regt

Reserve (King Joseph)
Brigade (Général de division Dessolles – 3,337)
12ème légère (3 bns)
51ème de ligne (3 bns)

Guard Infantry (1,800)
Guard Grenadier Regt (2 bns)
Guard Tirailleur Regt (2 bns)

Guard Cavalry (350)
Guard Chevau-Léger Regt

Cavalry (350)
27ème Chasseur à Cheval Regt

* The other two regiments of Poles that made up the 2nd Division, IV Corps, remained under command of Valance and were left to cover the Army of La Mancha.

British Losses on 27 July

Regiments	In the combat of Casa de Salinas						
	Killed		Wounded		Missing		Total
	Officers	Men	Officers	Men	Officers	Men	
Cavalry							
14th Light Dragoons	–	–	–	1	–	–	1
1st Light Dragoons KGL	–	2	1	1	–	–	4
3rd Division							
Mackenzie's Brigade							
2/24th Foot	–	1	1	6	–	1	9
2/31st Foot	1	23	5	88	–	2	119
1/45th Foot	–	4	1	13	–	7	25
Donkin's Brigade							
5/60th	–	3	1	4	–	19	27
2/87th	1	26	10	127	–	34	198
1/88th	2	7	–	25	–	30	64
Total	4	66	19	265	–	93	447

Regiments	In the French night attack						
	Killed		Wounded		Missing		Total
	Officers	Men	Officers	Men	Officers	Men	
Cavalry							
Staff	1	–	–	–	–	–	1
1st Division							
Cameron's Brigade							
1st Coldstream Guards	1	–	–	2	–	–	3
Langwerth's Brigade							
1st Line Bn KGL	–	2	–	7	–	–	9
2nd Line Bn KGL	–	–	–	3	–	–	3
Lt Coys, Lt Bn KGL	–	4	2	25	–	5	36
Von Löw's Brigade							
5th Line Bn KGL	–	6	–	34	–	11	51
7th Line Bn KGL	–	19	1	49	–	77	146
2nd Division							
Tilson's Brigade							
2/48th Foot	–	–	–	3	–	–	3
R. Stewart's Brigade							
1/29th Foot	–	10	1	43	–	1	55
1/48th Foot	–	–	–	8	–	–	8
1st Bn Detachments	1	14	–	40	2	13	70
Artillery	–	–	–	2	–	–	2
Engineers	–	–	1	–	–	–	1
Total	3	58	6	219	2	107	395

British Losses on 28 July

Regiments	Killed		Wounded		Missing		Total
	Officers	Men	Officers	Men	Officers	Men	
Staff	4	–	9	–	–	–	13
Cavalry							
Fane's Brigade							
3rd Dragoon Guards	–	–	1	1	–	1	3
4th Dragoons	–	3	–	9	–	–	12
Cotton's Brigade							
14th Light Dragoons	–	3	6	6	–	–	15
16th Light Dragoons	–	6	1	5	–	2	14
Anson's Brigade							
1st Light Dragoons KGL	–	1	2	32	–	2	37
23rd Light Dragoons	2	47	4	46	3	105	207
Subtotal							*301*
Infantry							
1st Division							
H. Campbell's Brigade							
1/2nd Guards	1	33	8	251	–	–	293
1/3rd Guards	5	49	6	261	–	1	322
Subtotal							*615*
Cameron's Brigade							
1/61st Foot	3	43	10	193	–	16	265
2/83rd Foot	4	38	11	202	–	28	283
Subtotal							*548*
Langwerth's Brigade							
1st Line Bn KGL	2	37	10	241	–	1	291
2nd Line Bn KGL	–	61	14	288	–	24	387
Lt Coys, Lt Bn KGL	–	6	–	37	–	–	43
Subtotal							*721*
Von Löw's Brigade							
5th Line Bn KGL	3	27	6	118	–	101	255
7th Line Bn KGL	–	17	4	35	–	54	110
Subtotal							*365*

Regiments	Killed		Wounded		Missing		Total
	Officers	**Men**	**Officers**	**Men**	**Officers**	**Men**	
2nd Division							
Tilson's Brigade							
1/3rd Foot	–	26	2	107	–	7	142
2/48th Foot	–	12	2	53	1	–	68
2/66th Foot	–	16	11	88	–	11	126
Subtotal							*336*
R. Stewart's Brigade							
1/29th Foot	–	26	6	98	–	2	132
1st Bn Detachments	–	26	9	166	–	2	203
1/48th Foot	–	22	10	135	–	1	168
Subtotal							*503*
3rd Division							
Mackenzie's Brigade							
2/24th Foot	–	44	10	268	–	21	343
2/31st Foot	–	21	3	102	–	5	131
1/45th Foot	–	9	2	134	1	12	158
Subtotal							*632*
Donkin's Brigade							
5/60th	–	7	6	25	–	12	50*
2/87th Foot	–	9	3	43	–	5	60
1/88th	1	12	3	69	–	–	85
Subtotal							*195*
4th Division							
A. Campbell's Brigade							
2/7th Foot	1	6	3	54	–	1	65
2/53rd Foot	–	6	2	30	–	1	39
Subtotal							*104*
Kemmis's Brigade							
1/40th Foot	–	7	1	49	–	1	58
1/97th Foot	–	6	–	25	1	21	53
2nd Bn Detachments	–	7	–	13	–	1	21
Subtotal							*132*
Artillery							
British	1	7	3	21	–	–	32
KGL	–	3	–	30	–	1	34
Subtotal							*66*
Engineers	–	–	1	–	–	–	1
Staff corps	–	–	2	–	–	–	2
Total	**27**	**643**	**171**	**3235**	**6**	**439**	**4521**

* Casualties for the 5/60th include those sustained by the whole battalion, including those in the companies attached to the other brigades.

Annex G
French Losses on 27–28 July*

Regiments	Killed		Wounded		Missing		Total
	Officers	Men	Officers	Men	Officers	Men	
I Corps							
État-Major	–	–	1	–	–	–	1
1st Division							
9ème légère	3	35	14	340	–	65	457
24ème de ligne	1	92	17	456	1	–	567
96ème de ligne	3	36	19	548	–	–	606
État-Major	–	–	2	–	–	–	2
Subtotal							*1632*
2nd Division							
16ème légère	8	49	8	342	–	–	407
8ème de ligne	3	41	17	376	–	–	437
45ème de ligne	3	43	12	328	–	2	388
54ème de ligne	2	54	14	462	–	–	532
État-Major	–	–	3	–	–	–	3
Subtotal							*1767*
3rd Division							
27ème légère	1	25	4	159	–	–	189
63ème de ligne	–	2	2	36	–	–	40
94ème légère	1	20	1	123	–	–	145
95ème de ligne	–	–	–	27	–	–	27
Subtotal							*401*
Corps Cavalry							
2ème Hussars	–	3	2	11	–	–	16
5ème Chasseurs	–	1	3	19	–	–	23
Subtotal							*39*
Artillery and Engineers	1	9	1	53	–	–	64

Regiments	Killed		Wounded		Missing		Total
	Officers	Men	Officers	Men	Officers	Men	
IV Corps							
1st Division	13	187	67	1852	–	61	2180
2nd Division (2 bns 4th Polish Regt only)	–	3	–	37	–	–	40
3rd Division	6	97	24	803	–	77	1007
Subtotal							*3227*
Cavalry divisions							
1st Div of Dragoons (Latour-Maubourg)	–	13	9	61	–	–	83
2nd Div of Dragoons (Milhaud)	–	–	–	3	–	–	3
Milhaud's Arty	–	–	–	3	–	–	3
Light Cavalry Div (Merlin)	–	6	–	42	–	–	48
Subtotal							*137*
Total	**45**	**716**	**220**	**6081**	**1**	**205**	**7268**

* The French returns for Talavera cover the casualties sustained over the two days of fighting so it is impossible to be precise about the breakdown for each day.

Notes

Chapter One. Wellesley Returns to the Peninsula

1. Marshal Victor to Marshal Jourdan, Torremocha, 24 May 1809, quoted in Oman, Sir Charles, *A History of the Peninsular War* (Oxford: Clarendon, 1902–30), vol. I, pp. 443–4.
2. Wellesley to Frere, Abrantes, 13 June 1809. Wellington, Arthur Wellesley, 1st Duke of, *Dispatches of Field Marshal the Duke of Wellington, during His Various Campaigns in India, Denmark, Portugal, Spain, the Low Countries, and France from 1799 to 1818*, ed. Lieutenant Colonel Gurwood, 13 vols (London: John Murray, 1837–9), vol. IV, p. 422 [hereafter, WD].

Chapter Two. The Armies

1. Munster, Earl of, Colonel Fitzclarence, *Talavera Campaign*, Napoleonic Archive (repr. F.S.P. Books), p. 29.
2. Atkinson, C. T., *The South Wales Borderers 24th Foot, 1689–1937* (Cambridge: University Press, 1937), p. 197.
3. Ibid.
4. Stewart to Castlereagh, 15 June 1809, quoted in Fortescue, J. W., *A History of the British Army*, 2nd edn, 13 vols (London: Macmillan, 1935), vol. VII, p. 234.
5. Rigaud, Major General G., *Celer et Audaux: A Sketch of the Services of the Fifth Battalion Sixtieth Regiment (Rifles) during the Twenty Years of Their Existence* (repr. Cambridge: Ken Trotman, 2002), p. 69.
6. Quoted in Rogers, Colonel H. C. B., *Wellington's Army* (London: Ian Allan, 1979), p. 51.
7. Ibid., p. 50.
8. Dundas, D., *Instructions and Regulations for the Movements of the Cavalry* (London, 1796).
9. Tomkinson, Lieutenant Colonel C., *Diary of a Cavalry Officer in the Peninsular and Waterloo Campaigns, 1809–1815* (repr. London: Frederick Muller, 1971), p. 136.
10. Ibid., p. 135.
11. WD, vol. II, p. 112.
12. Stanhope, P. H, 5th Earl, *Notes of Conversations with the Duke of Wellington, 1831–1851* (London: John Murray, 1888), p. 149.
13. Ibid., p. 220.
14. Leslie, Major J. H., *The Services of the Royal Regiment of Artillery in the Peninsular War* (repr. Cambridge: Ken Trotman, 2003), p. 99.
15. Lieutenant Colonel Robe to Lieutenant General Burrard, 1 November 1808, quoted in ibid., p. 77.
16. Londonderry, C. W. Vane, Marquess, *Story of the Peninsular War* (repr. London: Empiricus, 2002), p. 164.
17. WD, vol. IV, p. 513.
18. Wellesley to Secretary of State, Merida, 25 August 1809, WD, vol. V, p. 84.
19. Wellesley to Castlereagh, 1 August 1809, WD, vol. IV, p. 553.
20. Public Records Office, quoted in R. Chartrand and W. Younghusband, *Spanish Army of the Napoleonic Wars*, vol. II, *1808–1812*, Men-at-Arms Series (Oxford: Osprey, 1999), p. 6.
21. Quoted in Elting, Colonel J. R., *Swords around a Throne: Napoleon's Grande Armée* (London: Weidenfeld & Nicholson, 1989), p. 511.
22. Colin, Commandant J., *The Transformations of War* (London: Hugh Rees, 1912), p. 351.
23. Surtees, W., *Twenty-Five Years in the Rifle Brigade* ([1833]; repr. London: Muller, 1973), p. 109.
24. Londonderry, op. cit., p. 165.
25. Rocca, A. J. M. de, *Memoirs of the War of the French in Spain* (London: John Murray, 1815), p. 90.
26. Ibid., p. 92.
27. Stanhope, op. cit., p. 9.
28. Oman, *History of the Peninsular War*, vol. II, p. 36.
29. Brandt, H. von., *In the Legions of Napoleon*, trans. Jonathon North (London: Greenhill, 1999), p. 80.
30. Ibid., p. 81.
31. Elting, op. cit., p. 390.
32. Stanhope, op. cit., p. 94.

Chapter Three. The Commanders

1. Glover, M., *Wellington as a Military Commander* (London: Penguin, 1968), p. 33.
2. Ibid., p. 47.
3. WD, vol. IV, pp. 261–3.
4. Oman, *History of the Peninsular Wars*, vol. II, p. 303.
5. Wellesley to a Royal Commission, quoted in ibid., p. 303.
6. Grattan, W., *Adventures with the Connaught Rangers, 1809–1814*, Second Series (London: Colburn, 1853), p. 50.
7. Oman, op. cit., vol. II, p. 310.
8. Ibid., vol. I, p. 68.
9. Londonderry, op. cit., p. 164.
10. Stothert, W., *A Narrative of the Principal Events of the Campaigns of 1809, 1810 & 1811 in Spain and Portugal* (repr. Cambridge: Ken Trotman, 1997), pp. 76–7.
11. Oman, op. cit., vol. II, p. 157.
12. Ibid., vol. II, pp. 466–7.
13. Stanhope, op. cit., p. 46.
14. Ross, M., *The Reluctant King: Joseph Bonaparte, King of the Two Sicilies and Spain* (London: Sidgwick and Jackson, 1976), p. 17.
15. Quoted in Gates, D., *The Spanish Ulcer: A History of the Peninsular War* (London: Guild, 1986), p. 38.

16. Ross, op. cit., p. 163.
17. Ibid., p. 165.
18. Quoted in Young, Brigadier P., *Napoleon's Marshals* (London: Osprey, 1973), p. 53.

Chapter Four. Tactics
1. Quoted in Oman, *History of the Peninsular War*, vol. II, p. 300.
2. Ibid., vol. I, p. 120.
3. Girod de l'Ain, Général Baron J. M. F., *Dix ans des mes souvenirs militaires de 1805 à 1815* (Paris: Dumaine, 1873), p. 111.
4. Quoted in Oman, Sir Charles, *Wellington's Army, 1809–1814* (London: Edward Arnold, 1912), p. 79.
5. Munster, op. cit., pp. 20–21.

Chapter Five. Plans
1. Wellesley to O'Donoju, Plasencia, 16 July 1809, WD, vol. IV, p. 515.
2. Joseph to Napoleon, Almago, 2 July 1809, quoted in Oman, *History of the Peninsular War*, vol. II, p. 456.
3. Londonderry, op. cit., p. 167.
4. Munster, op. cit., p. 26.
5. Londonderry, op. cit., p. 167.
6. Stothert, op. cit., p. 80.
7. Stanhope, op. cit., p. 46.
8. Napier, Colonel W. F. P., *History of the War in the Peninsula and in the South of France from the year 1807 to the year 1814*, 6 vols, Chandos Classics (London: Warne, 1890), vol. II, p. 165.

Chapter Six. 27 July 1809
1. Cunliffe, M., *The Royal Irish Fusiliers, 1793–1950* (London: Oxford University Press, 1952), p. 78.
2. Schaumann, A. L. F., *On the Road with Wellington: The Diary of a War Commissary* (repr. London: Greenhill, 1999), p. 184.
3. Dalbiac, Colonel P. H., *History of the 45th 1st Nottinghamshire Regiment (Sherwood Foresters)* (London: Swann Sonnenschein, 1902), p. 58.
4. Fortescue, op. cit., vol. VII, p. 227.
5. Pearse, Colonel H. W., *History of the 31st Foot (Huntingdonshire Regiment) and the 70th Foot (Surrey Regiment): Subsequently the 1st and 2nd Battalions the East Surrey Regiment*, 2 vols (London: Spottiswoode, Ballantyne, 1916), p. 106.
6. Girod de l'Ain, op. cit., p. 139.
7. Dalbiac, op. cit., p. 58.
8. Wellesley to Castlereagh, Merida, 25 August 1809, WD, vol. II, p. 514.
9. Leach, Lieutenant Colonel J., *Rough Sketches of the Life of an Old Soldier during Service in the West Indies, at the Siege of Copenhagen in 1807, in the Peninsula and the South of France in the Campaigns from 1808 to 1814 with the Light Division, in the Netherlands in 1815 including the Battles of Quatre Bras and Waterloo* (London: Longman, 1831), p. 514.
10. Quoted in Fletcher, I., *Voices from the Peninsula: Eyewitness Accounts by Soldiers of Wellington's Army, 1808–1814* (London: Greenhill, 2001), p. 52.
11. Wellesley to O'Donoju, Cazalegas, 25 July 1809, WD, vol. IV, p. 530.
12. Wellesley to Castlereagh, Talavera, 29 July 1809, ibid., p. 533.
13. Ibid.
14. Quoted in Fletcher, op. cit., p. 46.
15. Fortescue, op. cit., vol. VII, p. 225.
16. Dalbiac, op. cit., p. 60.
17. Ibid., p. 59.
18. Quoted in Fletcher, op. cit., p. 46.
19. Wellesley to Castlereagh, Talavera, 29 July 1809, WD, vol. IV, p. 533.
20. Beamish, Major N. L., *History of the King's German Legion* (London: Boone, 1832–7), vol. I, p. 207.
21. Oman, *History of the Peninsular War*, vol. II, p. 519.
22. Nicol, Sergeant, 'The Gordon Highlanders in Spain', in Macbride, M., *With Napoleon at Waterloo, and Other Unpublished Documents of the Waterloo and Peninsular Campaigns* (London: Francis Griffiths, 1911), p. 98.
23. Ibid.
24. Ibid.
25. Beamish, op. cit., p. 208.
26. Munster, op. cit., p. 30. There is particular uncertainty in my mind about the role played by Donkin's brigade during this night attack. The majority of commentators do not mention it as coming into action at all, and even some of the regimental histories are rather vague about where it was and whether it engaged the 9ème légère. This may well be as a result of there being no concrete evidence, and because the official casualty returns do not record any casualties to the brigade in the figures given (see Annex E), though there is the chance that the brigade gave a single casualty figure for the whole of the 27th which included the night attack and the fighting at Casa Salinas. One of the small ridges on the Medellin may have shielded Donkin's troops from the French, but I have included their participation on the basis of this quote from the Earl of Munster and the fact that Lieutenant Girod recalls being engaged halfway up the Medellin. However, in the light of conflicting and vague evidence I am far from convinced that they played any part in the repulse of the night attack.
27. Girod de l'Ain, op. cit., p. 140.
28. Hill, Lord, *Letters from the Peninsula*, Napoleonic Archive (repr. F.S.P. Books), p. 7.
29. Ibid.
30. Nicol, op. cit., p. 98.

31. Ibid.
32. Girod de l'Ain, op. cit., p. 141
33. Ibid.
34. Nicol, op. cit., p. 98.
35. Ibid.
36. Quoted in Oman, *History of the Peninsular War*, vol. II, p. 518.
37. Ibid.
38. Everard, Major H., *History of Thomas Farrington's Regiment: The 29th (Worcestershire) Foot, 1694 to 1891* (Worcester: Littlebury, 1891), p. 303.
39. Nicol, op. cit., p. 99.
40. Wellesley to Castlereagh, Talavera, 29 July 1809, WD, vol. IV, p. 534.
41. Ibid., pp. 534–5.
42. Not including any casualties sustained by Donkin's brigade.
43. Quoted in Haythornthwaite, P., *Uniforms of the Peninsular War, 1807–14* (Poole: Blandford, 1978), pp. 171–2.

Chapter Seven. 28 July 1809
1. Nicol, op. cit., p. 99.
2. Unpublished papers of the Châtaux family, quoted in Coustumier, J. le, *Le maréchal Victor* (Paris: Nouveau monde, 2004), p. 110.
3. Londonderry, op. cit., p. 173.
4. Jourdan's memoirs, quoted in M. Glover, *The Peninsular War, 1807–1814: A Concise Military History* (London: David & Charles, 1974), p. 109.
5. Coustumier, op. cit., p. 110.
6. Fortescue, op. cit., vol. VII, pp. 239–40.
7. Munster, op. cit., p. 34.
8. Knight, C. R. B., *Historical Record of the Buffs (East Kent Regiment) 3rd Foot, 1704–1814* (London: Medici Society, 1935), p. 324.
9. Nicol, op. cit., p. 99.
10. Quoted in Oman, *History of the Peninsular War*, vol. II, p. 523.
11. *Historical Record of the 24th Regiment*, quoted in Muir, R., *Tactics and the Experience of Battle in the Age of Napoleon* (London: Yale University Press, 1998), p. 96.
12. Aitchison, J., *An Ensign in the Peninsular War: The Letters of John Aitchison*, ed. W. F. K. Thompson (London: Joseph, 1984), p. 57.
13. Beamish, op. cit., p. 210.
14. Quoted in Oman, *History of the Peninsular War*, vol. II, p. 524.
15. Quoted in Petre, F. L., *The Royal Berkshire Regiment 49th/66th Foot* (Reading: Barracks, 1925), vol. II, p. 200.
16. Quoted in Oman, *History of the Peninsular War*, vol. II, p. 525.
17. Coustumier, op. cit., p. 110.
18. Munster, op. cit., p. 35.
19. Oman, op. cit., vol. II, p. 526.
20. Munster, op. cit., p. 35.

21. Ibid.
22. Dalbiac, op. cit., p. 60.
23. Nicol, op. cit., p. 100.
24. Everard, op. cit., 306.
25. 'Il faudrait renoncer à faire la guerre', quoted in Oman, op. cit., vol. II, p. 528.
26. Fortescue, op. cit., vol. VII, p. 247.

Chapter Eight. The Main Attack
1. Londonderry, op. cit., p. 174.
2. Nicol, op. cit., p. 100.
3. Schaumann, op. cit., p. 185.
4. Jourdan to Berthier (Napoleon's chief of staff), Bargas, 30 July 1809, contained in Wellington, Arthur Wellesley, 1st Duke of, *Supplementary Despatches and Memoranda of Field Marshal Arthur Duke of Wellington*, ed. his son, the Duke of Wellington, 13 vols (London: John Murray, 1857–72), vol. XIII, p. 345.
5. Quoted in Fletcher, op. cit., p. 50.
6. Munster, op. cit., p. 36.
7. Quoted in Fletcher, op. cit., p. 47. Lieutenant Colonel Bingham commanded the 2/53rd at Talavera.
8. Atkinson, op. cit., p. 205.
9. Fletcher, op. cit., p. 50.
10. Ibid.
11. Wylly, Colonel H. C., *History of the 1st and 2nd Battalions the Sherwood Foresters, 45th/95th Foot, 1740–1914* (Frome: for the Regiment, 1929), vol. I, p. 162.
12. Stothert, op. cit., p. 90.
13. General Chambray, quoted in Griffiths, P., *Forward into Battle* (Chichester: Bird, 1981), p. 36.
14. Aitchison, op. cit., pp. 57–8.
15. Quoted in Haythornthwaite, op. cit., p. 172.
16. Aitchison, op. cit., p. 56.
17. Munster, op. cit., p. 36.
18. Quoted in Cocks, E. C., *Intelligence Officer in the Peninsula: Letters and Diaries of Major the Honourable Edward Charles Cocks, 1786–1812*, ed. J. Page (Tunbridge Wells: Spellmount, 1986), pp. 39–40.
19. Hamilton, Sergeant A., *Hamilton's Campaign with Moore and Wellington during the Peninsular War* (repr. Staplehurst: Spellmount, 1998), p. 80.
20. Aitchison, op. cit., p. 56.
21. Ibid., p. 58.
22. Fortescue, op. cit., vol. VII, p. 248.
23. Napier, *History of the War in the Peninsula*, vol. II, p. 177.
24. Munster, op. cit., p. 36.
25. Atkinson, op. cit., p. 206.
26. Aitchison, op. cit., p. 58.
27. Atkinson, op. cit., p. 206.
28. Most early accounts of the battle, even by those who were present, relied extensively on Wellesley's dispatch of 29 July (to Castlereagh) that gave his account of the battle based on the

reports of his brigade commanders. This dispatch states it was the 48th Foot that repulsed the French counter-attack against the Guards. However, the credit for this clearly lies with Mackenzie's brigade, as described here. The reason for this misunderstanding was due to Mackenzie's death: Wellesley was unaware of the actions of this brigade until after his Talavera dispatch had been written. As we shall see, the 48th came to the succour of the KGL, whose position lay between the Medellin (the position of the 48th) and the Guards brigade. Without wishing to belittle the achievements of the 48th, a single battalion could not possibly have covered the front of three brigades (the two of the KGL and the Guards).

29. Officer of the 48th, quoted in Gurney, Lieutenant Colonel R., *History of the Northamptonshire Regiment, 1742–1934* (Aldershot: Gale and Polden, 1935), p. 140.
30. Beamish, op. cit., vol. I, p. 215.
31. Bingham, quoted in Fletcher, op. cit., p. 47.
32. Gurney, op. cit., p. 141.
33. Schaumann, op. cit., p. 188.
34. Cooper, quoted in Fletcher, op. cit., p. 51.
35. Ibid.
36. Nicol, op. cit., p. 100.
37. My emphasis. Munster, op. cit., p. 37.
38. Fortescue, op. cit., vol. VIII, p. 254.
39. Munster, op. cit., p. 37.
40. Schaumann, op. cit., p. 186.
41. Beamish, op. cit., vol. I, p. 213.
42. Schaumann, op. cit., p. 186.
43. Munster, op. cit., p. 37.
44. Hamilton, op. cit., p. 78.
45. Quoted in Aitchison, op. cit., p. 55.
46. Ibid.
47. Quoted in Beamish, op. cit., vol. I, p. 213.
48. Schaumann, op. cit., p. 186.
49. Beamish, op. cit., vol. I, p. 214.
50. Girod de l'Ain, op. cit., pp. 145–6.
51. Napier, *History of the War in the Peninsula*, vol. I, pp. 484–5.
52. Wellington, *Supplementary Despatches*, vol. XIV, p. 718.
53. Hamilton, op. cit., pp. 78–9.
54. Wellesley to Castlereagh, Talavera, 29 July 1809, WD, vol. IV, p. 535.
55. Schaumann, op. cit., p. 186.
56. Wellesley to Castlereagh, Talavera, 29 July 1809, WD, vol. IV, p. 536.
57. General Châtaux, Chief of Staff I Corps, quoted in Coustumier, op. cit., p. 112.

Chapter Nine. Aftermath
1. Schaumann, op. cit., p. 191.
2. Napier, General Sir George, T., *Passages in the Early Military Life*, ed. General W. C. E. Napier

(London: John Murray, 1884), p. 110.
3. Wellesley to the Duke of Richmond, Talavera, 29 July 1809, WD, vol. IV, p. 566.
4. Quoted in Johnson, D., *The French Cavalry, 1792–1815* (London: Belmont, 1989), p. 96.
5. Fletcher, op. cit., p. 52.
6. Quoted in Haythornthwaite, op. cit., p. 174.
7. Wellesley to Castlereagh, Talavera, 1 August 1809, WD, vol. IV, p. 553.
8. Wellesley to Beresford, Talavera, 29 July 1809, ibid., p. 543.
9. Wellesley to Castlereagh, Talavera, 1 August 1809, ibid., p. 553.
10. Wellesley to Marquis Wellesley, Deleytosa, 8 August 1809, ibid., p. 15.

Chapter Ten. An Assessment of the Battle
1. *The Life and Opinions of General Sir Charles Napier, G. C. B.*, 4 vols (London: Murray, 1857), vol. I, p. 126.
2. WD, vol. IV, p. 510.
3. Ibid., p. 536.
4. Ibid.
5. Dalbiac, op. cit., pp. 62–3.
6. Fortescue, op. cit., vol. VII, p. 254.
7. Bourrienne, M. de, *Memoirs of Napoleon Bonaparte* (London: Hutchinson, undated), p. 386.
8. Joseph to Napoleon, quoted in Oman, *History of the Peninsular War*, vol. II, p. 565.
9. Berthier to Jourdan, Paris, 31 August 1809, contained in Wellington, *Supplementary Despatches*, vol. XIII, p. 359.
10. Ibid.
11. Quoted in Coustumier, op. cit., p. 113.
12. Ibid., p. 113.
13. Ibid., p. 112.
14. Ibid., pp. 112–13.
15. Ibid., p. 113.
16. Hamilton, op. cit., p. 81.
17. Wellesley to Marquis Wellesley, Miajadas, 22 August 1809, WD, vol. V, p. 56.
18. Wellesley to John Villiers, 16 September 1809, ibid.

Chapter Eleven. A Tour of the Battlefield
1. Nicol, op. cit., p. 98.
2. Oman, *History of the Peninsular War*, vol. II, p. 557.
3. Cooper, quoted in Fletcher, op. cit., p. 49.
4. Oman, op. cit., vol. II, pp. 557–8.
5. Ibid., p. 558.
6. Howard, M., *Wellington's Doctors: The British Medical Services in the Napoleonic Wars* (Staplehurst: Spellmount, 1999), p. 41.
7. Nicol, op. cit., p. 102.
8. Oman, op. cit., vol. II, pp. 488–9.
9. Ibid., p. 489.
10. Ibid., p. 503.

Select Bibliography

Official Correspondence

Wellesley, Arthur, 1st Duke of Wellington, *Dispatches of Field Marshal the Duke of Wellington, during His Various Campaigns in India, Denmark, Portugal, Spain, the Low Countries, and France from 1799 to 1818*, ed. Lieutenant Colonel Gurwood, 13 vols (London: John Murray, 1837–9).

Wellesley, Arthur, 1st Duke of Wellington, *Supplementary Despatches and Memoranda of Field Marshal Arthur, Duke of Wellington*, ed. his son, the Duke of Wellington, 13 vols (London: John Murray, 1857–72).

Primary Sources

Aitchison, J., *An Ensign in the Peninsular War: The Letters of John Aitchison*, ed. W. F. K. Thompson (London: Joseph, 1984).

Brandt, H. von., *In the Legions of Napoleon*, trans. Jonathon North (London: Greenhill, 1999).

Cocks, E. C., *Intelligence Officer in the Peninsula: Letters and Diaries of Major the Honourable Edward Charles Cocks, 1786–1812*, ed. J. Page (Tunbridge Wells: Spellmount, 1986).

Cooper, J. S., *Rough Notes on Seven Campaigns in Portugal, Spain, France and America, during the Years 1809–15* ([London: Smith, 1869]; repr. Staplehurst: Spellmount, 1996).

Girod de l'Ain, Général Baron J. M. F., *Dix ans des mes souvenirs militaires de 1805 à 1815* (Paris: Dumaine, 1873).

Grattan, W., *Adventures with the Connaught Rangers, 1809–1814*, Second Series (London: Colburn, 1853).

Hamilton, Sergeant A., *Hamilton's Campaign with Moore and Wellington during the Peninsular War* (repr. Staplehurst: Spellmount, 1998).

Hill, Lord, *Letters from the Peninsula*, Napoleonic Archive (repr. F.S.P. Books).

Leach, Lieutenant Colonel J., *Rough Sketches of the Life of an Old Soldier during Service in the West Indies, at the Siege of Copenhagen in 1807, in the Peninsula and the South of France in the Campaigns from 1808 to 1814 with the Light Division, in the Netherlands in 1815 including the Battles of Quatre Bras and Waterloo* (London: Longman, 1831).

Londonderry, C. W. Vane, Marquess, *Story of the Peninsular War* (repr. London: Empiricus, 2002).

Munster, Earl of, Colonel Fitzclarence, *Talavera Campaign*, Napoleonic Archive (repr. F.S.P. Books).

Napier, General Sir George. T., *Passages in the Early Military Life*, ed. General W. C. E. Napier (London: John Murray, 1884).

Nicol, Sergeant, 'The Gordon Highlanders in Spain', in Macbride, M., *With Napoleon at Waterloo, and Other Unpublished Documents of the Waterloo and Peninsular Campaigns* (London: Francis Griffiths, 1911).

Rocca, A. J. M. de, *Memoirs of the War of the French in Spain* (London: John Murray, 1815).

Schaumann, A. L. F., *On the Road with Wellington: The Diary of a War Commissary* (repr. London: Greenhill, 1999).

Stanhope, P. H, 5th Earl, *Notes of Conversations with the Duke of Wellington, 1831–1851* (London: John Murray, 1888).

Stothert, W., *A Narrative of the Principal Events of the Campaigns of 1809, 1810 & 1811 in Spain and Portugal* (repr. Cambridge: Ken Trotman, 1997).

Surtees, W., *Twenty Five-Years in the Rifle Brigade* ([1833]; repr. London: Muller, 1973).

Tomkinson, Lieutenant Colonel C., *Diary of a Cavalry Officer in the Peninsular and Waterloo Campaigns, 1809–1815* (repr. London: Frederick Muller, 1971).

Secondary Sources

Atkinson, C. T., *The South Wales Borderers 24th Foot, 1689–1937* (Cambridge: University Press, 1937).

Beamish, Major N. L., *History of the King's German Legion*, 2 vols (London: Boone, 1832–7).

Bourrienne, M. de, *Memoirs of Napoleon Bonaparte* (London: Hutchinson, undated).

Colin, Commandant J., *The Transformations of War* (London: Hugh Rees, 1912).

Coustumier, J. le, *Le maréchal Victor* (Paris: Nouveau monde, 2004).

Dalbiac, Colonel P. H., *History of the 45th 1st Nottinghamshire Regiment (Sherwood Foresters)* (London: Swan Sonnenschein, 1902).

Davis, Colonel J., *The History of the Queen's Royal Regiment* (London: Eyre and Spottiswoode, 1902).

Everard, Major H., *History of Thomas Farrington's Regiment: The 29th (Worcestershire) Foot, 1694 to 1891* (Worcester: Littlebury, 1891).

Fletcher, I., *Voices from the Peninsula: Eyewitness Accounts by Soldiers of Wellington's Army, 1808–1814* (London: Greenhill, 2001).

Fortescue, J. W., *A History of the British Army*, 2nd edn, 13 vols (London: Macmillan, 1935).

Gates, D., *The Spanish Ulcer: A History of the Peninsular War* (London: Guild, 1986).

Glover, M., *Wellington as a Military Commander* (London: Penguin, 1968).

Gurney, Lieutenant Colonel R., *History of the Northamptonshire Regiment, 1742–1934* (Aldershot: Gale and Polden, 1935).

Haythornthwaite, P., *Uniforms of the Peninsular War, 1807–14* (Poole: Blandford, 1978).

Headley, J. T., *Napoleon and His Marshals*, 4th edn, 2 vols (New York: Baker and Scriber, 1846).

Historical Records of the Queen's Own Cameron Highlanders, 2 vols (Edinburgh and London: William Blackwood, 1909).

Johnson, D., *Napoleon's Cavalry and Its Leaders* (London: Batsford, 1978).

Johnson, D., *The French Cavalry, 1792–1815* (London: Belmont, 1989).

Knight, C. R. B., *Historical Record of the Buffs (East Kent Regiment) 3rd Foot, 1704–1814* (London: Medici Society, 1935).

Leslie, Major J. H., *The Services of the Royal Regiment of Artillery in the Peninsular War* (repr. Cambridge: Ken Trotman, 2003).

Macbride, M., *With Napoleon at Waterloo, and Other Unpublished Documents of the Waterloo and Peninsular Campaigns* (London: Francis Griffiths, 1911).

Maxwell, Sir Herbert, *The Life of Wellington*, 3rd edn, 2 vols (London: Sampson Low, 1900).

Muir, R., *Tactics and the Experience of Battle in the Age of Napoleon* (London: Yale University Press, 1998).

Nafziger, G., *Imperial Bayonets: Tactics of the Napoleonic Battery, Battalion and Brigade as Found in Contemporary Regulations* (London: Greenhill, 1996).

Napier, Colonel W. F. P., *History of the War in the Peninsula and in the South of France from the Year 1807 to the Year 1814*, 6 vols, Chandos Classics (London: Warne, 1890).

Nosworthy, B., *Battle Tactics of Napoleon and his Enemies* (London: Constable, 1995).

Oman, Sir Charles, *A History of the Peninsular War*, 7 vols (Oxford: Clarendon, 1902–30).

Oman, Sir Charles, *Wellington's Army, 1809–1814* (London: Edward Arnold, 1912).

Pearse, Colonel H. W., *History of the 31st Foot (Huntingdonshire Regiment) and the 70th Foot (Surrey Regiment): Subsequently the 1st and 2nd Battalions the East Surrey Regiment*, 2 vols (London: Spottiswoode, Ballantyne, 1916).

Petre, F. L., *The Royal Berkshire Regiment 49th/66th Foot* (Reading: Barracks, 1925).

Rigaud, Major General G., *Celer et Audaux: A Sketch of the Services of the Fifth Battalion Sixtieth Regiment (Rifles) during the Twenty Years of Their Existence* (repr. Cambridge: Ken Trotman, 2002).

Rogers, Colonel H. C. B., *Wellington's Army* (London: Ian Allan, 1979).

Rogers, Colonel H. C. B., *Napoleon's Army* (New York: Hippocrene, 1982).

Ross, M., *The Reluctant King: Joseph Bonaparte, King of the Two Sicilies and Spain* (London: Sidgwick and Jackson, 1976).

'The Spanish at Talavera', *The Napoleon Series*, http://www.napoleon-series.org/military/battles/c_spanishattalavera.html

Wylly, Colonel H. C., *History of the 1st and 2nd Battalions the Sherwood Foresters, 45th/95th Foot, 1740–1914*, 2 vols (Frome: for the Regiment, 1929).

Index